# THE
# EVERYTHING®
## WILLS & ESTATE PLANNING BOOK

Dear Reader,

Several years ago my husband and I decided to prepare our estate plans as a gift to our children. What a sense of accomplishment we felt when those plans were complete! My goal for you in writing this book is to help you make a similar gift to your family.

After working in private law practice, I moved into planned giving for twenty years, the last fifteen at the University of Pennsylvania, my alma mater. I worked closely with donors who wanted to make a gift to the University, but who also wanted to support their heirs. They shared with me their dreams of a legacy—for their families, for Penn, and for their community. Our goal was, through thoughtful planning, to make their dreams come true.

While in legal practice with a firm that dealt solely with domestic issues, I learned firsthand about the financial ramifications of a failure to plan, about broken families and unmet dreams. My background for writing this book includes a law degree and freelance writing. In law school I was an editor of the law review and also wrote for the legal newspaper.

My hope in writing this book is that you will be inspired to create your own legacy and will feel that same sense of accomplishment we felt upon completing our own plans.

Sincerely,

Deborah S. Layton

# Welcome to the EVERYTHING® Series!

These handy, accessible books give you all you need to tackle a difficult project, gain a new hobby, comprehend a fascinating topic, prepare for an exam, or even brush up on something you learned back in school but have since forgotten.

You can choose to read an *Everything*® book from cover to cover or just pick out the information you want from our four useful boxes: e-questions, e-facts, e-alerts, and e-ssentials.

We give you everything you need to know on the subject, but throw in a lot of fun stuff along the way, too.

We now have more than 400 *Everything*® books in print, spanning such wide-ranging categories as weddings, pregnancy, cooking, music instruction, foreign language, crafts, pets, New Age, and so much more. When you're done reading them all, you can finally say you know *Everything*®!

## QUESTION?
Answers to
common questions

## FACTS
Important snippets
of information

## ALERTS!
Urgent
warnings

ESSENTIALS
Quick
handy tips

**PUBLISHER** Karen Cooper

**DIRECTOR OF ACQUISITIONS AND INNOVATION** Paula Munier

**MANAGING EDITOR, EVERYTHING SERIES** Lisa Laing

**COPY CHIEF** Casey Ebert

**ACQUISITIONS EDITOR** Lisa Laing

**SENIOR DEVELOPMENT EDITOR** Brett Palana-Shanahan

**EDITORIAL ASSISTANT** Hillary Thompson

Visit the entire Everything® series at *www.everything.com*

# THE
# EVERYTHING®
# WILLS & ESTATE
# PLANNING
# BOOK

**2ND EDITION**

Professional advice to safeguard your assets
and provide security for your family

Deborah S. Layton

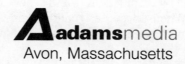

Avon, Massachusetts

*To my husband, Richard Layton, and to Marcia Layton Turner
and Charles Turner, Jonathan and Abigail Layton,
and our grandchildren.*

An Everything® Series Book.
Everything® and everything.com® are registered trademarks of F+W Media, Inc.

Published by Adams Media, a division of F+W Media, Inc.
57 Littlefield Street, Avon, MA 02322 U.S.A.
*www.adamsmedia.com*

ISBN 10: 1-59869-831-1
ISBN 13: 978-1-59869-831-2

Printed in the United States of America.

J  I  H  G  F  E  D  C  B  A

**Library of Congress Cataloging-in-Publication Data**
is available from the publisher.

*This book is available at quantity discounts for bulk purchases.
For information, please call 1-800-289-0963.*

# Contents

**Top Ten Reasons for Creating a Will and a Sound Estate Plan** / x

**Introduction** / xi

**1**

**Everyone Needs a Plan** / 1

Why You Should Plan **2** • Protecting Your Family **5** • Protecting Your Assets from Creditors **9** • Avoiding or Reducing Probate Costs **9** • Reducing Taxes **10** • Leaving Your Legacy **11**

**2**

**Preplan Prerequisites** / 12

Know What Is Available **13** • Start with a Will **13** • Consider the Advantages of a Trust **15** • Appreciate the Convenience of Joint Property **16** • Understanding Contractual Arrangements **17** • Make Your Wish List **18** • Shop for a Lawyer **21**

**3**

**The Five Steps of Creating a Plan** / 27

Step One: Learn the Rules **28** • Step Two: Organize Your Assets **29** • Step Three: Decide Who, What, and When **33** • Step Four: Choose Your Planning Tools **34** • Step Five: Implement Your Plan **36**

**4**

**Understanding the Probate Process** / 37

Why an Estate Needs to Be Probated **38** • Property That Is Not Subject to Probate **40** • The Probate Proceeding **42** • Probate Takes Time **44** • Probate Usually Requires a Lawyer **45** • The Cost of Probate **46** • Meeting with a Lawyer **47**

**5**

**How to Avoid Probate** / 48

Reasons for Avoiding the Probate Process **49** • Titling Property to Avoid Probate **50** • Place Property in Trust **52** • Make Good Use of Life Insurance **55** • Consider Creating Retirement Accounts **57** • Annuities May Be an Option **57**

**6**

**The Parts of a Will / 59**
An Overview **60** • Declarations **61** • Payment of Debts **62** • Specific Devises **64** • Memorandum for Tangible Property **65** • Residuary Devise **69** • Taxes **70** • The Powers of Your Executor **71** • Self-Proving Signature to Your Will **72**

**7**

**Decisions to Include Within the Will / 74**
Who Will Serve as Your Executor? **75** • Who Should Receive Your Property? **78** • How Should Your Property Be Distributed? **80** • Do You Want Your Property Sold? **83** • What Is Best for Your Minor Child? **83**

**8**

**Drafting Your Will / 87**
Filling in a Form Will **88** • Handwritten (or Holographic) Wills **89** • Using Computer Software **90** • Hiring a Lawyer to Prepare the Will **90** • Sample Will **91**

**9**

**Changing Your Will / 99**
Ways to Change Your Will **100** • Make a New Document **100** • Strike a Provision **102** • Make Written Changes **103** • Add an Amendment **104** • Destroy the Document **106** • Where Should You Keep Your Original Will? **106** • A Lawyer Isn't Required **108**

**10**

**Owning Property in Joint Name / 109**
The Joint-Property Estate Plan **110** • Advantages and Disadvantages **110** • Property Owned Jointly with Your Spouse **112** • Taxes and Cost Basis **113** • Joint Property with Someone Else **115** • Gift Tax Consequences **118**

**11**

**A Trust May Be Right for Your Plan / 119**
What Is a Trust? **120** • The Creator **120** • The Trustee **121** • The Beneficiaries **123** • Powers of Appointment **123** • Reasons for Creating a Trust **125** • Advantages of a Trust **126** • Disadvantages of a Trust **127**

## 12 Decisions to Include Within a Trust / 131

Choosing Your Trust Beneficiaries **132** • When Your Property Is Distributed **133** • Triggering Events **134** • Restrictions and Penalties **135** • How Your Property Should Be Distributed **136** • The Power to Sell Your Property **140**

## 13 Choosing a Trustee / 142

Sequence of Trustees **143** • Duties of the Trustee **144** • Important Considerations **147** • The Trustee and Your Property **149** • If Your Family Doesn't Agree **150** • Financial Guardian for Your Minor Child **151**

## 14 Creating a Trust / 152

Identify the Parties and Describe the Property **153** • Assigning the Power to Control the Trust Property **155** • Timing and Distribution of Assets **156** • Assigning a Trustee **161** • Miscellaneous Trust Provisions **163**

## 15 The Lowdown on Life Insurance / 166

Three Parties to a Policy **167** • Types of Life Insurance **167** • Choice of Beneficiary Is Contractual **169** • Life Insurance and the Probate Process **169** • Tax Consequences **171** • If Your Estate Exceeds the Exclusion **172** • A Simpler Solution for Life Insurance **173**

## 16 Reviewing Retirement Accounts and Annuities / 174

Retirement Accounts, Annuities, and the Probate Process **175** • Naming Your Beneficiary **176** • Penalty for Early Withdrawal from Tax-Deferred Accounts **178** • Income Tax Consequences **179** • Estate Tax Consequences **183** • Planning Ahead **184**

## 17 Death and Taxes / 185

What Is the Federal Estate Tax? **186** • Property That Is Subject to Federal Estate Taxes **188** • Taxable Gifts **192** • Gifts That Are Not Taxable **193** • Deductions Against Your Taxable Base **193** • Should You Leave All of Your Property to Your Spouse? **196** • Figuring Your Federal Estate Taxes **197**

**18**

**How to Reduce Taxes / 198**
Credit Shelter Trusts (or Bypass Trusts) **199** • Make Gifts of Your Assets **203** • More Sophisticated Methods for Reducing Taxes **204**

**19**

**Charitable Gifts Can Reduce Taxes / 208**
Gifts During Lifetime **209** • Planned Gifts During Lifetime **211** • Charitable Gifts from Your Will or Trust **215** • Advantages and Disadvantages of Charitable Gifts **217**

**20**

**Powers of Attorney / 219**
Types of Power of Attorney **220** • Reasons for Having a Power of Attorney **222** • Sample Durable Power of Attorney **223** • Decisions to Make **230** • Naming More than One Person **231** • Creating a Power of Attorney **232** • Reasons for Having a Medical Power of Attorney **233**

**21**

**Guidance for Your Family / 235**
What Instructions to Provide Your Family **236** • Where to Keep Your Documents **236** • Safe-Deposit Boxes **237** • Funeral or Cremation Instructions **240** • Prepayment Plans **242** • Organ Donations **243** • Keeping Your Plans Up-to-Date **243** • Estate Planning Checklist **244**

**Appendix A: Glossary / 246**

**Appendix B: Resources / 251**

**Appendix C: Asset Inventory Worksheet / 253**

**Appendix D: Sample Trust / 261**

**Appendix E: Sample Advance Health Care Directive / 271**

**Index / 279**

# **A**cknowledgments

I would like to thank Marcia Layton Turner and Jonathan Layton, Esq., for their assistance in bringing this book to completion. Thanks also to Gary Bryde, Esq., and Diane Clarke Streett, Esq., Register of Wills for New Castle County, Delaware, for their research assistance and for updated information about current estate planning practices and probate rules.

I would like to acknowledge the many donors to the University of Pennsylvania for sharing their hopes of a long-term legacy and for their philanthropic spirit. Their generosity and commitment to Penn, to education, and to future students are an inspiration. And special thanks to my editor, Lisa Laing, and agent, Robert G. Diforio, for helping make this book a reality.

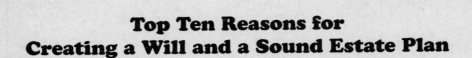

# Top Ten Reasons for Creating a Will and a Sound Estate Plan

1. A sound estate plan can save your family thousands of dollars in taxes and legal fees.

2. If you don't have a plan, the government will decide who will receive your property.

3. If you don't have a plan, your spouse or partner may not receive the property you intended to provide.

4. Most people can avoid or reduce estate taxes with the right plan.

5. Naming a legal guardian in your will is the way to choose who will raise your minor children if you are gone.

6. Creating a durable power of attorney ensures that someone can pay your bills and sign legal documents if you become disabled.

7. Having a medical directive will provide guidance about your health care wishes in the event you become incapacitated.

8. You can avoid the unexpected results of owning property in joint name when you understand the rules.

9. You can make gifts to your favorite charity to reduce estate taxes but still provide for your family.

10. A good estate plan can preserve your assets for your children's use and prevent them from wasting those assets.

# Introduction

▶ SOMEONE ONCE SAID that people spend more time watching TV or shopping for a car than they spend planning their estate. Don't let that be true of you. Your heirs deserve more consideration than a TV program or a car, and a good estate plan is one of the best gifts you can provide for your family.

Sadly, a recent survey conducted for Martindale-Hubbell® reports that 55 percent of all adult Americans don't have a will. According to the same survey, there are several reasons most people don't plan. Nearly one in four (24 percent) thought they didn't have enough assets to warrant writing a will. Ten percent said it's because they don't want to think about dying or becoming incapacitated. A third group of adults said they don't have a plan because they don't know who to talk to.

Another reason not mentioned in the survey is that many people don't want to spend the money to have a will or trust prepared. There is a misconception that it costs too much to have documents prepared, and that estate planning is only for the very rich. Others are simply procrastinators, even though they know they should plan ahead.

The goal of *The Everything® Wills & Estate Planning Book* is to encourage you to be in the group of those who *do plan*. This book will help you preserve the assets you've worked so hard to accumulate over your lifetime. It is a how-to guide for ways to distribute your assets and to minimize income and estate taxes in the process. You will find there are many different options to consider when you begin planning how you want to leave your estate.

Once you understand the process, you can create documents yourself or have a lawyer help you in a cost-efficient manner. The fact is, it is not expensive to create an estate plan, but it can be very expensive to die without a plan. By becoming knowledgeable about the process, you can save your family considerable time and money.

As you read through this book, you will discover that planning your estate is not as overwhelming a task as you may have thought. The *Everything® Wills & Estate Planning Book* carefully guides you through the decisions you need to make before you have documents prepared. It discusses several methods that are available and gives you suggestions as to which planning documents might be best for your family.

The book teaches you the rules on each topic and will assist you in making the necessary decisions for your family in a cost-efficient manner. It will point out issues to consider, goals you might like to reach, and people and institutions you may want to support.

Another aspect of planning to include is the effect your health might have on your estate plan. With lengthening life expectancies and the uncertainties about the safety of Social Security and many corporate pension plans, it is crucial for you to make plans for your own care and possible health needs during a longer life expectancy than your parents or grandparents experienced.

According to the survey mentioned earlier, 41 percent of adults now have living wills in place, a 10 percent increase over a prior survey. The increase in living wills indicates that more adults are thinking about their own health care and how their families should deal with an illness or incapacity.

Once you begin planning for your financial future and for your heirs, you will discover that planning will provide a great sense of relief and accomplishment. Use the suggestions in this book to create a plan that works best for you and your family. Planning ahead will provide peace of mind and reassurance that you've done all you can to protect your family. Let's begin.

## CHAPTER 1

# Everyone Needs a Plan

There are many reasons, both emotional and financial, for having a sound estate plan. It really doesn't matter how old you are; your family and loved ones will suffer when you leave them. While you cannot undo the loss they will feel, if you plan ahead, you can spare them a great deal of additional grief and expense.

## Why You Should Plan

Nearly everyone owns something at death—a car, computer, jewelry, clothing, furnishings. These belongings are your "estate," and they need to be directed somewhere at your death. If you haven't decided ahead of time where those things go, your family has to dig through your home and files to find the information they need after you are gone—further reminding them of their loss. There are many things that need to be done that you may not think about until you have experienced the loss of a loved one.

## Planning in Your Twenties

You may think you don't need to plan because, after all, you're only twenty years old. The chance that something will happen to you is very slim but, if it does, your family will have a lot to do. Accidents can and do happen at all ages. Everyone at any age should have certain legal documents in place.

If you already have a living will or medical directive, check the laws of your state to be certain your living will complies with that state's requirements. If you move, you may find your living will is not recognized in your new state.

The most important of these are a medical designate or agent and a living will. If you are injured, a medical designate is the person who will make medical decisions on your behalf. A living will is a legal document that expresses your wishes regarding whether or not you want your life artificially prolonged in the event that you are permanently incapacitated with no chance of recovery. This may seem morbid, but if you have strong feelings either for or against life support, you should specify your personal wishes in a document. You've undoubtedly read stories about injured people who did not have written instructions and the disastrous—and expensive—situation that resulted for their families. Appendix E has a sample advance health care directive (also called a living will) to give you an idea of the issues you need to consider.

You should also consider preparing a will at this age. You may not have a lot of belongings, but it will be much easier for your family if you have a document stating how you want your property to be distributed.

The amount of planning you need to do for your property will depend on how much property you have. Chapter 2 includes steps to take to help you determine whether you need something more than a will.

## Just Married

If you are newly married, you should consider creating a will promptly to protect your spouse. If you do not have a will naming your spouse as your beneficiary, the intestacy laws of your state may direct assets to other family members such as parents or siblings. "Intestacy" means dying without a will. Although you may think your spouse will automatically inherit everything you have, that is not necessarily the case. Your spouse will receive a portion of your estate and, if you have children from a prior marriage, they will also inherit a portion. If there are no children, your parents or siblings may receive a portion of your estate, probably not at all what you anticipated or wanted.

## Congratulations! You Just Had a Baby

One of the most important decisions you will ever make (besides whether or not to have a baby) is who will take care of your baby if you are gone. If something happens to you, your spouse will become the legal guardian of your child. If something happens to both of you, someone will have to be given the responsibility of raising your child. Wouldn't you like to be the one to decide just who that someone will be?

The only document that allows you to name a guardian for your baby, if both you and your spouse die, is your will or, in at least one state, a written declaration. Most young parents don't—or don't want to—think about this possibility. However, it is a very important matter concerning the well-being of your child, so it's best to be prepared, just in case.

## Supporting and Educating Your Young Children

After you have started a family, you need to protect, support, and educate them. Just as with an infant, you need to be sure you have sufficient insurance or other assets to take care of them if you die before they are on their own.

If you have school-age children, they will need not only a guardian, but also funds for such things as clothing, music or sports equipment, books, field trips, and the like. You might want to consider a fund such as a 529 plan for your children's education costs. There are many different plans available today, and you should check to see what your state offers. Two possible sites to assist you are: *www.collegeanswer.com/paying/content/529_plan_statebystate.jsp* or *www.savingforcollege.com*.

## The Children Have Left the Nest

When the children have all gone to college or have moved out of the house, parents' lives change dramatically. The daily planning associated with teenagers has ended and perhaps been replaced with long-distance telephone bills.

**FACT**

One of the reasons people don't prepare when they are in their later years is because they don't want to make an appointment with a professional to talk about their deaths. Some individuals think talking about death will cause it to happen sooner than if they pretend it won't happen!

When your children leave home, it is an excellent time to consider your own future. You will probably think more about retirement. This is the perfect time to take a serious look at your estate plan. You are at a point in your life when you have likely accumulated a lot of things and have not had time to evaluate what would happen to these things if you were gone. And, more important, you've probably not had the time until now to assess whether you are making the best use of your property and investments. Creating an estate plan will help you do just that.

## Entering Retirement

Retirement is the time when most people take a close look at their estate plan. If you have decided to retire, you probably took the time to gather most of the information you needed to evaluate your estate plan. That involved calculating how much money you have, and whether you will have enough money coming in to retire from your job. This is an excellent time to complete the planning process. After all, you've already gotten started; why not just finish the job?

## After Retirement

Every person during his lifetime has known someone who has died. The stories about the cost, delay, and turmoil are probably the general rule and not the exception. It doesn't have to be like this. Many times people think they are prepared but, sometimes, when it is too late, the family discovers that the plan was not as complete as everyone thought. Put your mind at rest and do what you can now to ensure a well-organized and comprehensive plan.

Spending time and funds now to set up your plan can save your family considerable stress, time, and money later. Having no plan may cost your family more than paying a lawyer today. It's worth the effort to put your plan in place.

Another reason people avoid planning is because it is frustrating and expensive to try to figure out what needs to be done. Others may be concerned that their families may fight over their estate once they're gone. This book will help address these concerns.

## Protecting Your Family

The most important reason for you to plan, regardless of where you are in the cycle of life, is to protect your family. The issues that face you at different points of your life change. For instance, as you mature, there are usually more family members who depend on you. The modern family is more complicated than it was in the old days when Mom stayed home and raised the children, Dad went to work and, after the children left home, Mom and Dad started planning for retirement. This picture has changed dramatically.

## Your Spouse

When you think about your spouse, you should consider whether there is anyone who might create difficulties for her or take advantage of her when you pass on. For example, when you are newly married, if something happens to you, it is not uncommon for your relatives to be resentful about what your new bride or groom owns and where the property came from. These disagreements can be about small items that relatives feel belong to them, or about major financial issues. You need to protect your spouse by at least having a will that defines the property that belongs to your spouse and those items that belong to your relatives.

Oftentimes, people create a plan that leaves all of their property to their spouses, believing that the surviving spouse will take care of the children. Though this may sound reasonable, it may not be the best plan. Your children may put pressure on your spouse and cause tension among family members. The spouse may not act as you thought she would, or your spouse may not be capable of handling finances or family disputes.

If you have been married for a long period of time, it could be your own children who disagree with your spouse's plans. When this happens, it is usually because your spouse has a soft spot in his heart for one or more of your children. If you have more than one child, you know that your children have different needs. You and your spouse may sometimes argue about what your children should or should not have. These emotional pulls will continue, and often heighten, after you are gone.

You may want to put a plan in place that will help your spouse say no to your relatives and your own children. The more complex your property holdings, the more important it is for you to plan ahead for these contingencies.

## Remarriage

If this is a second marriage for you, there are bombshells you might not have expected. There may be children from your former marriage or children from your spouse's former marriage who can complicate matters. Conflicting interests may emerge after you are gone. Perhaps you avoid putting a plan in place because it is difficult for you to address these competing needs. But just imagine how difficult it will be for your spouse to make important decisions after you are gone if you have left no guidance.

If you are concerned about who would manage your property and money for your children if something happened to you, you should consider creating a revocable trust. A revocable trust allows you to name a trustee who will manage your property according to the instructions in your trust. See Chapters 11 through 14 for details about trusts.

It is best if you and your spouse can develop a plan together, but if you do put a plan in place without discussing it during your lifetime, at least everyone will learn what you wanted after you are gone. When you are involved in a second marriage, it is imperative that you complete a plan to protect everyone involved—your spouse and your other family members and loved ones.

## Your Children

If both you and your spouse pass on and do not leave a plan, your property will be distributable to your children, but not necessarily distributed in the way that you would wish. This could also create tension among siblings.

When you think about what would happen to your property if both you and your spouse were gone (or, if you are not now married but have children), you should think about when your children should receive your property after your death. You should consider the age of your children, their maturity, and whether inheriting all or a share of your property would promote responsibility in them.

If your children are minors and you do not have a specific plan in place, the person who becomes the legal guardian of your children will have control of their money and property. You should think about whether that guardian will make the best financial choices on behalf of your children. If your children are in their twenties or thirties, you should consider whether they will pursue their education if they receive an inheritance (if that is important to you) and whether they will make the best choices. You are going to learn that there are ways you can help preserve your assets for your children's use and prevent them from wasting those assets, but it takes some thought and planning.

**FACT**

Leaving funds to a grandchild could cause your estate to owe generation-skipping tax. The calculation of this tax is complex and generally affects gifts to a person two generations younger than you. It is another tax you need to be aware of if you are making gifts to your grandchildren in excess of your annual exclusion. (See Chapter 17 for more about the annual exclusion.)

## *Your Grandchildren*

When you evaluate your property and the needs of your children and your grandchildren, you may want to create a plan that leaves some money or property for the benefit of your grandchildren. Sometimes when you leave a small inheritance for a grandchild, it can have a dramatic impact on her or his future. For instance, you can encourage your grandchild to attend college by setting up a fund that can be spent only for educational purposes. Many states have started prepaid college funds. Some of these state funds require that the child attend a college located in the state where the fund was created. Other states allow the fund to be used in some manner, typically at a discount, in another state. Most funds even allow you to name someone who can use the benefit if the child does not use the funds to attend college. If such funds interest you, check on the availability of a college fund in your state and the limitations that fund may have.

If you want to provide maximum flexibility, you can establish a trust for your grandchildren from which funds are disbursed only for educational purposes. For instance, if one grandchild does not attend college, the funds can then be spent on another grandchild who does want to attend.

**ALERT!**

It can be very difficult for your family and loved ones to keep your hard-earned assets if you do not have a plan. You can substantially reduce the costs and save taxes if you are organized and understand what happens to your assets after you are gone.

## Protecting Your Assets from Creditors

Protecting yourself from creditors while you are alive is quite different from protecting your family from creditors after you are gone. In most states, if you own or control property, your creditors can access your property to pay outstanding bills. Of course, there are exceptions to this rule in every state. Some states protect your home from creditors while others protect certain types of investments. Almost all states protect your retirement plan.

As you will learn in later chapters, after you are gone, it is a different game. You can create trusts that will give your family the benefit of the income from your property and even distributions of the property itself, and the trusts will keep creditors from touching that property. If asset protection is important to you, read the chapters in this book that discuss trusts so you will have an understanding of them. Then you should organize the information concerning your assets and make an appointment with an asset protection lawyer who can answer specific questions regarding your state's laws.

## Avoiding or Reducing Probate Costs

Most people don't understand that, even if you have a will, your family most likely will need to go through the probate process to distribute the property you owned. However, having a will reduces the cost of probate because it provides instructions about how your property should be distributed. If you don't have a will, your state law will govern who gets your property.

There are certain things you can do to save taxes and avoid the cost and delay of probate, but you must plan for it. The key is to understand the options, and then you will be in a position to make the right choices for your family. Chapters 4 and 5 will delve deeper into the probate process but, for now, keep in mind that this is one way in which your careful planning and preparation will come into play.

## *Reducing Taxes*

Believe it or not, to protect your family and loved ones, you will need to concern yourself with the issue of taxes after your death. Primarily, you will want to focus on income taxes and estate taxes, but there are also gift and generation-skipping taxes if you leave a bequest to your grandchildren.

Avoiding probate does not mean you won't owe income, gift, generation-skipping, state, or estate taxes. You might owe any or all of those taxes depending on your plan and the size of your estate.

The rules about income taxes on property that is received by someone when you die are very tricky. One small mistake can cost your family thousands of dollars, and perhaps hundreds of thousands. The rules about what property is subject to income tax and how you can reduce or eliminate that tax by owning your property in a different way are complicated but rewarding. Don't panic; you will learn these income tax rules and get tips on how you might create a plan to minimize the income tax consequences to your family and in many cases even eliminate income taxes on inherited property.

The laws about taxes that are owed on your estate are complex. But like most topics that are complex, if the presentation is broken down into bite-sized pieces and you are given examples about how each piece works, you can understand estate taxes and create a plan to minimize those taxes or avoid them altogether.

**FACT**

If you hire a lawyer to draft documents to eliminate or reduce the federal estate taxes, you may pay what you consider to be substantial lawyer's fees in the process. But when you are organized and understand the tax rules yourself, you can reduce the time and expense of a lawyer. You will more than likely reduce expenses for your family, and you will be reassured that your plan is properly executed.

When you understand how you need to prepare—the decisions you need to make and the possible solutions—it reduces the cost of having to get something fixed. Each chapter in this book is designed to teach you rules that would cost $250 to $300, or more, per hour to learn from a lawyer. Even if or when you hire a lawyer to prepare your documents, being educated will save an enormous amount of time and money.

## Leaving Your Legacy

A well-designed plan can make your dreams live on even after your death. If you don't have a plan, your family might not know what your dream was. Or even if the dream was known, it may not be realized because a big chunk of your money and property is being spent on legal fees and taxes that could have been saved if you had understood the rules and had a plan in place.

Wills, trusts, probate, annuities, and retirement plans are all tools you can use to leave your own legacy—for your family, friends, and possibly your community. You will soon learn what tools you have to work with and how to use them to their maximum effect. While some of these tools are designed to help after you are gone, some of them will help you accumulate or retain more while you are living. Learn the rules, and let your dreams live on!

# CHAPTER 2

# Preplan Prerequisites

Becoming familiar with the rules and what strategies are available to you during the preplanning stages will save you and your loved ones a substantial sum of money. More important, you will be able to rest assured that you have found a plan that both carries out your wishes and protects your loved ones after your death.

## Know What Is Available

Before you can create a plan that will provide for your family and loved ones, you need to know what types of documents and legal arrangements are available to you. Some documents are easier to create now, but are more expensive for your family and loved ones after you are gone. Other documents are more challenging to create now, but will save your family and loved ones a substantial amount of money as well as hassle.

There are four ways you can pass property to your loved ones: a will, a trust, joint property, and certain types of contracts. Each of these documents or legal arrangements has advantages and disadvantages.

## Start with a Will

A will is the easiest and cheapest estate planning document to prepare. Most people can create their own will without hiring a lawyer. After you are gone, your will must be probated. Probate is a process whereby your loved ones must petition the local probate court, open a probate file, administer the property pursuant to your state's probate code, and then distribute the property.

By becoming familiar with estate planning, you can reduce the need for a lawyer by doing most of the work yourself. The average attorney charges $250 to $300 per hour. If you save your lawyer ten hours of time, you have saved $2,500 to $3,000!

Because of the complexity of the probate process, it is almost impossible for a family to probate a will without hiring a lawyer. Each state has its own detailed court rules and forms required to effectively probate a will and close an estate.

## The Document for Young Families

A will may be the document of choice for a young family for several reasons. The first reason is that, in some states, a will is the only document that allows you to name a guardian for your minor children. It is not necessary to name a guardian if there is a natural parent living. However, if both natural parents are gone, a will gives you the opportunity to choose the person or persons you would like to raise your children.

**ALERT!**

Most states require a will to name a guardian, but at least one state allows a written declaration designating your preferred guardian. If you do not wish to complete a will but are concerned about having a guardian for your minor children, check the laws of your state to see whether a written declaration is allowed or whether you must have a will.

If you do not have a will, and both natural parents are gone, the probate court will conduct hearings to determine who should serve as the legal guardian of your minor children. A person who petitions the court to serve as legal guardian may not be the person you would have chosen had you prepared for this eventuality in advance. If this thought scares you, keep in mind that it is very difficult for someone to contest your choice of a guardian when you name that person in your will.

The second reason a young person or family might choose to have a will rather than other legal arrangements is because a will is easy and inexpensive to prepare. A young person is less likely to die than is someone older. Even so, in the unlikely event of a premature death, it is important that your instructions be contained in a legally binding document. Every state has a law that directs how your property will pass if you die without making a will, and this distribution may not fit with your intentions.

## Uncomplicated Affairs

If you are older, you may choose to have a will because your affairs are not complex, but you want to make sure that your property passes to the loved ones of your choice. Although there may be some costs in distributing your assets when you are gone, a will is an excellent estate planning document.

**FACT**

A disadvantage to using a will is that there are additional costs and delays associated with going through probate. However, if you have a will, at least you have left instructions about how you want your property distributed, and the probate court will make sure those instructions are carried out.

# Consider the Advantages of a Trust

Why would you have a trust instead of or in addition to a will? As with a will, property in a trust will be distributed according to the instructions you place in the document. But the added bonus is that your loved ones will not have to use the probate process, saving them considerable time and expense. You may also choose to have both a will and a trust to handle different aspects of your estate.

## Establish a Management Plan

You may decide to use a trust because you don't want your property distributed immediately when you are gone. Creating a trust allows you to establish a management plan for your family. Assets in a trust are distributed according to a schedule that you specify.

There are many reasons why you might not want your property distributed right away. You may be concerned that your spouse is not capable of managing the property or, if both you and your spouse are gone, your children may be too young to receive your property. You may not want the legal guardian of your children to have control of your property. Or perhaps you are worried that your children's creditors or spouses will try to lay claim to your property when you are gone. A trust allows you to protect against all of these risks. In a later chapter you will learn how to create a trust and will find that the document is easy to modify when necessary.

### Choose the Trustee

Many people think you have to involve a bank in order to have a trust. This is not true. You can serve as trustee while you are living but name a family member or other loved one to serve as trustee after you are gone. A bank needn't be involved unless, of course, you want one to be.

You can place instructions in the trust document that will guide your trustee on how to manage your property. The instructions can be very flexible, granting a trustee the power to distribute property when the trustee feels it is appropriate, or the trust document can set out very specific instructions that must be followed.

**FACT**

If your estate is subject to federal estate taxes, you will probably want to consider using a trust. A trust may well reduce the taxes owed by your estate. Trusts are extremely flexible legal documents. There are a few more steps involved to create the trust, but the savings may be considerable when your estate is being closed. Chapters 11 through 14 will cover trusts in more detail.

## Appreciate the Convenience of Joint Property

Owning your property in joint name with another person is also a simple estate plan. The primary advantage to owning property in joint name is that title passes automatically to the surviving joint tenant when you die. This means your joint tenant doesn't have to hire a lawyer to probate your property after your death. This method of passing property is especially useful for unmarried partners, who do not have the benefits a married couple enjoys.

Many parents put a child's name on property. For example, they may add a child's name to a bank account. This is often done for convenience, to allow that child to assist with bill paying and banking. However, let's say the parent has a will that says, "Divide all of my property equally among my children." The parent thinks the will controls and overrides joint property rules. That is not true! The joint property, in this case a bank account, belongs only to the child whose name is on the account. You might believe or hope that the child named on the account would divide the property with his siblings, but that is not always the case. You need to be careful in creating a joint tenancy.

It is important for you to understand that your will has absolutely no effect on who receives property that is held in joint name with you and someone else. The property automatically passes to the joint tenant. A major disadvantage to owning property in joint name can be liability for increased income taxes and possibly estate taxes that could have been avoided through careful estate planning.

## *Understanding Contractual Arrangements*

Many people think that all their assets will be divided in equal shares among their children if they have a will or a trust that says, "I hereby leave all of my property in equal shares to my children." Unfortunately, that may not be what will happen. A will or a trust has no effect on how certain types of property are distributed. There are several types of property that pass according to the terms of the contract and are not affected by your will.

- Life insurance
- Annuities
- IRAs and retirement accounts
- Certain business contracts
- Pay-on-death contracts

Life insurance and annuities are paid to the person you named as a beneficiary when you purchased them. Both of these types of property are paid according to the terms of the contract. Sometimes people have the same misunderstanding about life insurance and annuities as they do about joint property. People tend to think that a will or a trust controls all of their property. You will find as you proceed through the process of planning that you need to evaluate how each piece of property, including life insurance and annuities, will be paid when you are gone.

**ALERT!**

> You may want to consider a "pay-on-death" arrangement for a bank account or your stocks. In these arrangements, the proceeds are transferred immediately to the person named in the document. The person named on the account has no right, however, to the asset until your death.

IRAs (Individual Retirement Arrangements) and other retirement accounts also are paid to the person you named as a beneficiary. Your will or trust will have no effect on who receives those benefits. Also, more complex business contracts for partnerships and corporations often have buy-out provisions that will control and cause the partnership or corporate stock to be excluded from the probate process.

## Make Your Wish List

Before you can create your plan, you need to know what you're working with. Buy a three-ring binder or notebook, a set of divider tabs, a package of three-hole-punch paper, a pencil, a pencil sharpener, and an eraser. These are the supplies you will need to create your plan. A three-ring binder or notebook is important because you will likely add or remove sheets of paper quite often. Your plan will be divided into categories and organized in a way that will help you make the best decisions.

### Who You Wish to Include in Your Plan

The first tab of your notebook will be used to define who will be part of your plan. On one sheet of paper, list everyone you want included—your spouse or partner, children, grandchildren, parents, siblings, friends, and perhaps a charity or your community. Then, make a separate sheet of paper for each person or entity to whom you plan to leave property. Write down all of the basic information about each person on the separate pieces of paper, including the person's full legal name, relationship to you, birth date, Social Security number, address, telephone number, and e-mail address.

Who you include in your plan may change as you continue through the planning process. Circumstances also may change for your loved ones. You may find yourself using that eraser to eliminate a name from the master list, or adding a sheet of paper for someone you forgot.

**FACT**

Making decisions about your property is like playing a game. Each piece of paper that describes your property can be moved around as if the property were on a game board. The important part of the game is to match your property to the right person at your death.

The reason you want to use a separate piece of paper for each person or entity is because you are going to create a miniplan for each, allowing you to make notes or record any special needs. You will also have to decide what happens to that person's share if she dies before you do. Should her share go to her children, your siblings, or another person? Create a flow chart for each person's share.

## What Are Your Assets?

The next tabs in your notebook should be used to summarize and describe your property. Make a separate tab for each category of property you own, such as:

- Real estate
- Stocks
- Bonds
- Mutual funds
- Life insurance
- Retirement accounts and annuities
- Bank accounts
- Business ownership or share

Each piece of property gets its own sheet of paper. List the value of the property, the amount of debt against the property, what you paid for the property, and the cost of any improvements you have made. This core information is important to help you make decisions about the property. You don't need to have your property appraised. A fair estimate of the value of the property is typically sufficient to begin your plan.

Once you have all the information down, you will learn to analyze it in various ways. This will not only help you decide how you are going to distribute your property, but it will also help you make critical decisions about the income tax results and the estate and gift tax consequences of your choices.

## Where, When, and Why

Now you can think about where, when, and why. The decisions you make about one or more pieces of your property may change when you start thinking about the needs of your loved ones, the practical ramifications of what your loved ones would do with your property, and the tax consequences associated with your choices.

For fun, keep track of the number of hours you spend getting organized and making basic family decisions. Then figure out how much it would have cost if you had paid a lawyer to gather the information about your family and your assets. Multiply the number of hours by $250 to $300 per hour and be pleased about the money you saved!

For example, assume you own a vacation cottage. You recorded the value of the cottage, what you paid for it, and the cost of any improvements made, and you placed this information in your notebook. Now, on the same piece of paper, list the annual operating costs, such as utilities, taxes, and normal upkeep of the cottage.

When you start asking yourself who should receive your cottage and why, your initial decision about the cottage might change. Let's say you started the planning process thinking you would divide all of your property equally among your children. But when you focus on the information you have about the cottage, you realize how difficult it would be for your children to own the property together. You should think about who is going to pay the bills, who will maintain the cottage, and whether one child will use the cottage more than another. Your children may fight over whether or not the cottage should be sold. Maybe your children are too young to maintain the cottage. Perhaps one child is better equipped to own the cottage. You are now beginning to analyze not only who and what, but where, when, and why as well.

When you take all of the sheets of paper representing the property you own and lay them out on the table, it may make more sense to leave your personal residence to one child, your cottage to another, and to divide the investments among the remaining children. Your children's needs and what they are capable of managing often differs quite a bit among them. It could be a mistake to leave equal percentages to all your children.

The biggest misconception about wills is that most people think that if you have a will, there will be no probate. This is not true. In order to avoid probate, you need to have documents in place other than a will, such as a trust or jointly owned property.

The process of organizing your property piece by piece helps to crystallize the decisions you make for your family. As you think through your choices, you may find yourself changing your mind about who should receive each piece of property or when the property should be distributed. Remember, those pieces of paper can come in and out of the three-ring binder. Also, as you learn the rules about what legal arrangements you can use, you may change your mind about who, what, where, when, and why.

## *Shop for a Lawyer*

People price-shop for almost everything they buy. Yet most people don't price-shop for a lawyer. This is because most don't know how—where to look and what to ask. If this describes you, read on.

The best way to find a lawyer is a referral from a satisfied client. Ask your friends, neighbors, and work colleagues if they have had any planning done. Ask who they used, how much it cost, and whether they were satisfied with the results. If you don't find a lawyer this way, contact your local or state bar association. Many of the state bar associations have a referral service or a directory that will help you find a lawyer in your area who does estate planning.

> Some attorneys prepare an estate planning package such as a will, trust (if needed), durable power of attorney, medical directive and HIPAA (Health Insurance Portability and Accountability Act) document for a flat fee. You may want to compare the cost of a package fee with a lawyer's hourly rate.

When you find a lawyer, it is important to understand what she will do for you. A lawyer does different things for you when helping you plan than she does after you are gone.

## Planning

During the estate planning process, your lawyer spends a relatively small amount of time drafting documents for you. Most of your lawyer's time is spent learning about your family and your property and informing you of your options. Your lawyer does five things for you:

1. Learns about your property
2. Learns about your family
3. Learns what you want to do with your property
4. Explains the law
5. Drafts documents to implement your plan

If you are organized and have played the who, what, where, when, and why game, you have done most of the lawyer's job. Then, when you learn the rules about the various legal documents you can use, you have done another part of your lawyer's job. Imagine how much money you will save by doing these things in advance! You can then make an appointment with your lawyer. The only job that will be left is to have your lawyer prepare the documents in accordance with your well-thought-out plan and the laws of your state.

## Post-Death Tasks

The functions a lawyer will perform for your loved ones after you are gone depend on what type of documents you had in place. If you had a will, the lawyer will start a probate proceeding in your county probate court. If you didn't have a will, or any other estate planning document, the steps the lawyer needs to take are almost the same. The difference is that your state's laws will determine who takes your property. The particulars regarding the probate process are covered in Chapter 4.

**FACT**

The lawyer will typically arrange to close credit cards, terminate Social Security, secure final wages, and pay final expenses. Your executor or family member can handle many of these tasks with some guidance from the lawyer. This will save your estate money.

If you have used a trust, a lawyer might be necessary to explain the trustee's duties to the person you appoint. But, frankly, if you are organized and understand your documents, you will be able to explain the duties to your trustee while you are living, preparing your trustee to serve as your successor trustee after you are gone.

If your estate is subject to federal estate taxes, you will need to hire either a lawyer or an accountant to prepare the federal estate tax return. It is nearly impossible for a person to prepare the federal tax return without professional help. A federal estate tax return is more than fifty pages long and has terms and phrases that even many lawyers don't understand.

You will need to hire a lawyer or an accountant who prepares federal estate tax returns on a regular basis. He will also need to file the final income tax returns.

## Questions You Should Ask

When you contact the lawyer's office, find out if the initial consultation or meeting is free—this is a common practice. Ask the lawyer how long he plans for the first meeting and what information you should bring. If the lawyer tells you that you have a half-hour appointment and you don't need to bring anything to the meeting, you can be sure you won't get much information free: You are being invited to be sold on the lawyer's services.

Sometimes law firms include separate charges for filing costs, photocopies, telephone charges, or research time. Be sure to inquire about each of these. It isn't a pleasant surprise to get a bill for several hundred dollars for miscellaneous charges you expected to be included in the hourly fee. Ask what will be covered by the hourly fee.

Ask the lawyer to send information about the firm in advance of your appointment. Having information on the firm readily available is often a sign of a well-organized professional. The information does not have to be glossy and expensive, but it should be informative. Find out if there is a website describing the firm. A nicely presented website indicates that the lawyer is on top of technology. This can be important because a technologically sophisticated office typically saves you money. Ask the lawyer how many areas of law she covers. If the answer is all areas of the law, this is probably not the lawyer you want to draft your plan. It is impossible to be an expert in every area of law.

## Let the Interrogation Begin!

Ask the lawyer a few basic planning questions and be prepared with the answers yourself, in order to better evaluate him. For instance, you might ask, "What is the main disadvantage to owning property in joint name?" The answer is that when you own property in joint name, there can be negative income tax consequences for the surviving joint tenant. Or you could ask, "If property is placed in a revocable trust, does the trust protect the property from creditors?" The answer is no. As long as you hold a power to revoke the trust, creditors can reach the assets held in trust.

If the lawyer does not know the answers or tells you that he has to get back with you, this is not the lawyer you want. If the lawyer is offended that you are asking questions, then you'll likely want to look elsewhere.

## Should You Ask How Much?

Yes. You should definitely ask how much it will cost. The answer to this question is often, "Well, it depends." Don't let it rest at that. Follow up with more specific questions. Find out if the lawyer bills by the hour, by the project, or by the nature of the documents prepared. If the lawyer charges by the hour, find out what the hourly fee is.

**QUESTION?**

**Should you ask for a confirmation?**
Yes. The lawyer should put her estimate in writing and confirm the services that will be provided. Also, ask the lawyer to confirm, in writing, the maximum amount you can expect to be billed.

It is also important to ask if other people in the office will work on your file. Different lawyers in a firm typically have different billing rates. Find out whether the bills will list who worked on your file and how much each person billed per hour. You should also ask whether a paralegal will work on your file. If so, how much will you be billed per hour for the paralegal's work? Then ask how many hours the lawyer thinks each person will spend on your job. Don't feel as though you are being intrusive or demanding. This is your money, and you have a right to know where it goes.

It is extremely important to ask the lawyer what the fees will be after your death to "settle" the estate or plan. It is quite common to be charged a reasonable amount—$500 to $1,500—for preparing the will or trust, only to find that when you die, the lawyer charges a percentage of the estate to "settle the estate" after death. It's not unusual for a lawyer to charge 1 to 1½ percent of the fair market value of the assets to settle the estate, and another flat fee or additional percentage of the fair market value of the assets to prepare the federal estate tax return, if one is required. There may be a separate fee for handling probate assets and nonprobate assets. Add up the value of your assets and compute the cost!

It is possible to find a lawyer who charges a flat fee to prepare your documents but will charge an hourly fee to settle the estate after you are gone. This is typically more cost-efficient.

## Paying in Advance

Many lawyers ask for what is called a *retainer*. This is an amount of money the lawyer requests be placed on deposit before he starts the job. You should not have to pay for all of the services in advance, only a portion of the estimated cost. It is common to pay a retainer in advance, but it is also possible to find a lawyer who will not bill until the job is done. This really depends on the billing practice of the lawyer or law firm. It does not mean the lawyer is bad or evil merely because he requests money in advance.

# CHAPTER 3

# The Five Steps of Creating a Plan

Sometimes you don't start a project such as estate planning because it seems overwhelming. It is easier to approach any challenge if you have step-by-step instructions. Creating a plan for your family and loved ones is a five-step process that will make planning less intimidating.

## Step One: Learn the Rules

Learning the rules can be fun if you have the right attitude. However, most don't view this as fun; rather, they see it as a chore to do when they are ready to die. But what these people don't realize is that they are actually doing estate planning every day.

You make decisions all the time about where you are going to work, how much money you make, how you spend your money, and how your money makes you and your family happy. As you make your daily decisions, you are probably thinking about what your children are going to do when they grow up.

Do you have a special-needs child? Have you considered whether someone would be able to take care of that child properly at home, or would the child need to be in an institution? The loss of a parent or parents could be disastrous for any child, but you need to think especially carefully about the best plan for a special-needs child. There are also rules about eligibility for institutions relating to income. Consider a "special-needs trust" if you have a child in this situation.

You may be considering how you are going to save money to help your children with college or assist them with their career choices. At the same time, you are planning for your own retirement. When you make everyday decisions for yourself and your family, you are engaged in the process of estate planning.

## Several Options Available

When you learn the rules about probate, wills, trusts, joint property, and taxes, you are working on a plan that will come into being at your death. While you are doing your everyday planning, start thinking about how you would want your property managed for the benefit of your family when you are gone. You may decide that when something happens to you, it would be best to have your property distributed as soon as possible to your spouse or partner. If this is your plan, you may choose a simple will or you may decide that owning property jointly is the best plan for you.

If you have young children, you may think about who would manage your property and money for your children if something happened to you and your spouse. As you've learned, you can name a guardian for your minor children, but you may decide that the person you've chosen to raise your children isn't the best person to oversee their financial property. In this case, you could name one person to take physical care of your children and a different person to manage your children's money and property.

Perhaps during the planning process you discover that your family would need more money than you initially anticipated if something happened to you. This may lead you to investigate life insurance, or obtain more insurance, to provide for their security. As you can see, one thing often leads to another. It helps to know the rules and be aware of all the options available to you.

## Estate Planning Can Be Like a Jigsaw Puzzle

Planning can be compared to completing a picture puzzle. Every piece of property you own and who is to receive it are pieces of that puzzle. Does a will fit in the overall picture? Where does insurance or your retirement plan go? Are any pieces missing from your plan?

Estate planning is a dynamic process. It can be exciting to learn the rules and to keep your plan current and ready. It's important to learn about all the options available to you before setting forth with one specific legal document or estate plan. In the following chapters, you will learn everything you need to know about your options. It's a good idea to keep a pencil handy. You may want to jot down notes on each option, naming the advantages and disadvantages, and whether that option fits into your picture puzzle.

# Step Two: Organize Your Assets

It is important to keep the information about your property and the debts you owe current. If you are organized, you will be able to have a plan in place that is ready for your family immediately following your death. You may be able to save money now as well as save time and money for your family in the future. In addition, you will relieve the family from having to make decisions after your death.

## Organizational System

Chapter 2 recommended that you develop a system to organize the information about your property. In your three-ring binder or notebook, you should have a separate piece of paper for each asset you own, whether real estate or personal property such as an automobile. Each property should include information such as the value of the property, what you paid for it, the cost of any improvements you made, the debt against the property, and how it is owned.

You should think about each asset you own from two perspectives: whether you are currently making the best choices about that asset, and what would happen to that asset if you were gone.

When you organize the information and keep it up-to-date, it will help you make the best choices while you are alive. It will also allow you to evaluate all of your property together and to have a plan in place for your family to follow. It's best to mark your calendar for an annual review of your notebook contents and your overall plan.

## Evaluating the Information Gathered

Evaluating the information about each piece of property you own can reap tremendous benefits for you now as well as after you are gone. For example, assume that you have a piece of paper that describes your car. If you think about the costs associated with your car, you might take the time to evaluate whether you are paying too much for insurance. Shop around! You might save money by keeping track of when your car has been serviced—tires, oil change, brakes, and so on. And, of course, you can plan for what you want to happen to your car if you are gone.

You might discover that you owe more on your car than the car is currently worth. Or, if you lease your car, you may discover that your family would owe money on the lease if something happened to you. These discoveries might lead you to make choices now about your property as well as what will happen to your property upon your death.

If you are concerned that your heirs will not be able to make the mortgage payments after your death, you may want to consider mortgage insurance. It is not inexpensive, but it may allow your heirs to keep the home rather than having to sell. Or you can increase your life insurance coverage, which might be cheaper, depending on your age and insurability.

Let's say you have a sheet of paper that describes your home. One of the pieces of information about your home would be how much you owe and the interest rate you are paying on any loans against it. When you are organizing your notebook for your estate plan, you should evaluate the interest rate you are currently paying. If there are interest rates available that are less than when you financed your home, you may find you can save money now by refinancing your home. And, of course, while you are evaluating all of the current costs associated with your home, you can decide who you want to receive your home upon your death and whether that person could afford to maintain it.

If you have life insurance, describe the attributes of the life insurance on a piece of paper. You may discover that there are new life insurance products available that will pay a larger death benefit for lower annual premiums. This can help you now with current cash flow. And you can also evaluate who will receive the life insurance benefits when you are gone. You may discover that your life insurance will cause your estate to owe federal estate taxes. You will learn a way to make changes to your plan to avoid any estate taxes on your life insurance. See Chapter 15 on Life Insurance and Chapter 18 on Taxes.

## *Planning Inventory*

You may not be the notebook type of person. Or you may feel that you do not need to organize your assets this way to create a plan that meets your needs. Another way to get organized is to complete a planning inventory. A planning inventory is a form that gathers the information you need to evaluate the property you own, assesses whether your estate would be subject to federal estate taxes, and prepares you to create the documents you need. A sample inventory is included in Appendix C. The inventory guides you through the steps to gather the information you need to plan, and it also brings all of the information together in one place for your family to access easily when you are gone. It is worth your time now to review the details requested by the inventory and to gather that information.

When something happens to you, your family is full of grief. In addition to their grief, having to go through all of your papers trying to gather the needed information is a painful burden. You can avoid this additional crisis for your family by being prepared. If you do not organize the information about your property by either filling out an inventory or preparing a three-ring binder or notebook, your family may not know what you owned or what you wanted done with that property.

It is not enough to complete the inventory or notebook. You must be sure your family knows where you keep the notebook, keys, statements, health care preferences, and other details about your plan.

Sometimes even when a person chooses to organize the information in a three-ring notebook, she also likes to complete the inventory, because the inventory summarizes the information in the notebook.

# *Step Three: Decide Who, What, and When*

An old journalism adage applies here: You get the right story when you tell who, what, where, when, and why. Your family is a story. It is a story that changes all the time. Who are your loved ones? What are your goals for them? Where are your loved ones living? When would you want your loved ones to receive your property, and why? Get ready to tell your story.

Think about your notebook. If you haven't already, take out a separate piece of paper and write down the name of every person you would include in your plan. Then begin to ask yourself what that person is currently doing. Which piece of property or properties would you like that person to have? Put the piece of paper that describes that property under the piece of paper describing the person to whom you would leave that property. Develop little stacks of paper under each person's name. Then when you look at the stacks, you can ask the next question: when would you like that person to receive the property? You might find yourself beginning to think about things such as these:

- Would that person be able to take care of the property if something happened to you tomorrow?
- Would it promote maturity in that person if he received the property tomorrow?
- Would it be better if that person received the property later in life?
- If something happens to you, should the property be sold?
- How much income tax or estate tax would it cost if you leave that piece of property to the named person?
- Is your plan fair?

When you think about your property and the persons who would enjoy your property if something were to happen to you, you may discover that the goals you have now for your loved ones and family are very different from the goals you had ten years ago.

You need to look at your plan to see if it meets your family's needs today and re-evaluate it at least annually or when any major changes occur in your life or theirs. The answers to the questions who, what, and when will change over time. Most people do not keep their plans current because they don't understand the planning tools that are available or how they work.

They don't know how to change their plan to meet the changing needs of their family. Last, but not least, they don't want to spend a lot of money keeping their plan current every year.

The beauty of learning the rules is that it allows you to do most of the work. Many times you can make the necessary changes yourself, without the help of a lawyer. But even if you do need the help of a lawyer, when you understand the planning tools available and how they work, it will be much easier for you to have your plan tweaked.

Your plans and goals change over time, so don't prepare a will or trust and hide it safely away to be forgotten. Be sure to keep your plan current with the changing needs of your family. And since you don't know when something might happen to you, it's best to try to keep up with changing times.

## Step Four: Choose Your Planning Tools

There are many helpful planning tools available. When you understand your options and how the planning tools work, you can become an involved player in your plan rather than a passive observer. It is always scary to have someone tell you what you need to do without explaining why you should do that particular thing. In the same way, it can be disturbing when you don't understand the planning tools or what the consequences will be if you don't plan. When something scares you, it's natural to try to avoid it. Yet think of the relief and self-confidence you gain when you tackle and conquer the task you thought might be difficult.

**FACT**

Every person should have a written plan such as a will or trust. Even if all of your property is in joint name with your spouse or partner, you should have a document that will direct how your property passes in the unlikely event that both of you die in a common accident.

You simply need to figure out how the planning tools can work for you. Once you do, you don't have to be nervous about planning for your family.

You can make decisions that may help you save money now and provide for the security of your loved ones later.

## Planning Tools Available

There are numerous planning tools available. You will soon learn the rules regarding:

- Wills
- Trusts
- Joint property
- Contractual agreements
- Retirement plans
- Annuities
- Life insurance
- Taxes

## One Tool Affects Another

You will probably have or need more than one planning tool. When you create anything, there are typically parts that are combined to make a whole, finished product. When you make a decision about one planning tool, it may change what you do with another planning tool. For instance, let's say you have an IRA, and you learn how the IRA is taxed when you die. You aren't happy with this outcome, so you conduct more research. What you find allows you to change some of your IRA elections to reduce the tax impact.

Or perhaps you already have a will in place, but you learn that it has no impact on how or to whom your insurance, annuities, IRA, and joint property are paid and distributed. You might have thought that if you put instructions in your will about how these items were to be distributed, your will would control them. As you now know, this isn't true, so you will probably want to re-evaluate your plan to make it coincide with your wishes.

Most families have different types of property and so need multiple planning tools to accomplish their goals. When you understand what each of the planning tools can do for you, you will be in a position to work on your own picture puzzle, participate in the selection of pieces of the puzzle, and create a plan that you can maintain and change as the needs of your family change.

## *Step Five: Implement Your Plan*

A plan is no good unless you take the steps that are necessary to implement it. Many people sit around and think about plans, but don't do anything to set them in motion. This failure to implement a plan is even more common with estate planning. The reason is that most plans you make result in something you look forward to. Let's face it; it's unlikely that there are people out there who jump out of bed in the morning and say, "I can't wait to do my estate planning today, because I'm really looking forward to passing on!" But when you think about estate planning as part of your everyday life and consider the benefits you can enjoy today by creating and implementing a plan, you may have a little more motivation to get started.

A good estate plan is not set in motion in one hour. It's probably not accomplished in one day or even one week. In order to implement a plan, you need to be organized, understand your options and planning tools, and think about how your property should be distributed or managed if you are gone. This all takes time and effort.

If you follow the steps recommended in this book, you will be well prepared to implement your plan. Implementing your plan is not about having a lawyer draft documents. It is about knowing your story—who, what, where, when, and why. When you understand your story, you can take steps to determine which planning tools meet your needs. Then, you can either prepare the necessary documents yourself, or you can make an appointment with a lawyer who will be able to draft the documents for you. And remember, your plan will probably change regularly as your needs and the needs of your family change.

## CHAPTER 4

# Understanding the
# Probate Process

If you stopped several people on the street and asked, "What is probate?" the majority of people would respond, "Probate is what happens when a person dies." You are going to learn in this chapter that this is not an entirely accurate statement.

## Why an Estate Needs to Be Probated

You may think that probate happens automatically. However, there is no arm of government that starts the probate process when you die. The probate process begins when someone, usually your chosen executor or a close family member, files the necessary papers with the probate court in the county where you die. The best way to understand probate is to learn why an estate needs to be probated. There are several reasons:

- You owned property in your individual name.
- You had unpaid bills and debts that are not paid by your survivors.
- There is a dispute about how your property will be distributed.
- You died with a minor child or children and there is no surviving natural parent.
- Your individually owned assets exceed your state's minimum threshold.

The primary purpose of probate is to distribute your assets in accordance with the law and to pay your outstanding bills. It may be the best route for you to take, even with some expense.

## Property Owned in Your Individual Name

If you own property that was titled in your individual name, such as real estate, stocks, bonds, cars, boats, and so on, and you die, there needs to be someone who can sign your name after you are gone to transfer the title from your name to someone else's. If you had a checking account, a savings account, or some other financial account in your individual name, there must be someone who can sign your checks or withdraw money after you are gone. The only person who is legally authorized to sign for you is your executor. In some states the executor is called a personal representative. An executor is the person you name in your will to carry out the instructions contained in the will. If you do not have a will, the probate court will name an executor.

## The Creditors

The second reason an estate might need to be probated is to pay your bills and debts after you are gone. The persons or entities to whom you owe money, such as credit card companies or the bank for the mortgage on your house or the debt on your car, are called *creditors*. If your creditors are not paid after you die, they are entitled to file papers with the probate court to open a proceeding if your survivors have not already done so.

**FACT**

The probate process allows a set time period, usually three or four months, for creditors to file a claim. If they do not file a claim during the period allowed, the debt may not be collectible from the estate.

When probate is opened, an announcement in a newspaper is required to let creditors know the time for filing a claim against an estate has started. If your loved ones have already opened a probate proceeding, the unpaid creditors will file a claim seeking an order to be paid. If all of your bills and debts are paid after you are gone, there will be no creditors who can open a probate proceeding.

## Disagreements about Distribution

The third reason your estate might be probated is because your heirs and loved ones disagree on how to distribute your property after you are gone. If your family disagrees, one or more members of your family are entitled to file a petition with the probate court to resolve the dispute.

## Naming a Legal Guardian

Another reason there might need to be a probate proceeding is if upon your death you leave a minor child or children and there is no surviving natural parent. If this occurs, there must be a probate proceeding to name a legal guardian for your minor child or children. If you have a will or document that names a legal guardian, the court will enter an order naming that person as legal guardian unless there is an objection to the person named.

Relatives of the minor child or children, stepparents, foster parents, even a governmental agency, may object to the person selected by the court and may petition to be named as legal guardian. In some states, minor children over the age of fourteen, or a state-specified age, may object as well. If you haven't given written instructions, the court will hear testimony about the person or persons best suited to serve as the legal guardian. It does not matter whether you do or do not have a will; there will always be a probate proceeding when you die if you leave a minor child or children and there is no surviving parent.

**ALERT!**

When there is a dispute about how to divide your property after your death, those persons who disagree need to hire a lawyer to represent their interests in the probate court proceeding. At $250 to $300 per hour, imagine how expensive this can be! There also will be court fees that must be paid, either by those filing the suit or by the estate.

When families object to your plan for distribution of your property, the probate court judge will typically order your property sold and the proceeds from the sale of your property distributed to your family.

### Assets Less than State's Threshold

Most states have a "small estate" exemption for assets below a certain figure. If your individually owned property is less than, for example, $50,000, you would not need to go through probate. Your executor would sign a statement that says your estate is below the minimum, and your estate would then be distributed without the probate court's involvement. State minimums vary, so your heirs should be alerted to check on your state's threshold.

## Property That Is Not Subject to Probate

Property that is titled in your individual name must be probated when you are gone because you are not available to sign your name to transfer the title to your family. The easiest way to understand this concept is to learn what property is not subject to probate.

The following property is not subject to probate:

- Property you owned in joint name with another person or persons
- Life insurance proceeds, as long as the estate is not named beneficiary
- IRAs, as long as the estate is not named beneficiary
- Other retirement plans, as long as the estate is not named beneficiary
- Annuities, as long as the estate is not named beneficiary
- Assets held in trust, as long as the estate is not named beneficiary of the trust
- Accounts that pay on death to a named beneficiary

These properties are not subject to probate even if you have a will because they either pass automatically to a surviving joint tenant or the property is distributed according to a beneficiary election you made while you were alive.

It is a good idea to have every company with whom you have insurance, retirement accounts, or annuities send you a confirmation of your beneficiary election to be certain they are directed as you wish. These choices could have been made many years ago and may have been forgotten or are no longer applicable.

To sum up: if all your property is owned in joint name with at least one surviving joint tenant; your property is held in trust; or you have life insurance, retirement accounts, or annuities, there is no property that is subject to probate. If your creditors are paid and you have no minor children, there will be no probate.

# The Probate Proceeding

There is a formal process that must be followed in each state to probate an estate. Contrary to popular belief, if a person dies with a will and the estate exceeds the minimum threshold, probate is still necessary. These are the typical steps in a probate proceeding:

1. A petition is filed with your probate court to start the probate process.
2. The probate court issues an order naming an executor.
3. A notice of death is published in the local newspaper.
4. Bills and debts must be paid.
5. Accountings and inventories must be filed with the probate court.
6. Your property must be valued.
7. Your property is distributed.
8. Papers are filed to close the estate, and probate fees are paid.

## Who Files the Petition?

If you have a will, it almost always names an executor. However, the person named in the will does not become the executor automatically. This person must petition the probate court seeking appointment as executor. The probate court judge will review your will and the petition to determine if the will has been signed with the proper formalities. It will then determine whether the person seeking appointment as executor is qualified to serve. If so, the judge will enter an order appointing the person as executor. This opens the probate process. It is the order appointing the person as executor that gives her the legal authority to sign documents for you after your death.

If there is no will, or the person named in your will is not available, the probate court will determine who should serve as executor or personal representative to handle your estate. Each state has laws that establish the priority of who should be named as executor in such cases.

Typically, the surviving spouse is given first priority, and then the children. When there is no surviving spouse, it is not uncommon for the surviving children to disagree about who should serve. When this happens, the probate court will schedule a hearing and hear testimony about who is best qualified to serve. That's when things really start getting expensive. Imagine that there are two surviving children, each one expecting to serve as executor. If they can't agree on who will serve, each will file a petition seeking appointment. Both children will need a lawyer, and the estate could be charged with some of the court fees.

**FACT**

Some states allow the judge to review the petition and enter an order without a hearing. Other states require the judge to take testimony from the persons who witnessed your will.

## After the Executor Is Appointed

After the executor is appointed, the estate places a notice in your local newspaper providing the name of the person who died, the name of the executor, and an address where the executor can be contacted. Usually the estate posts the address of the lawyer who is representing the estate as the contact. Most state laws require that once the notice is published in the local newspaper, the estate must wait three to six months before distributing the assets. This waiting period gives all of the creditors who have not been paid an opportunity to submit their bills to the estate and also allows anyone who thinks they have an interest in your property an opportunity to file a claim. The probate proceeding for your estate could possibly be closed within six months as long as no one:

- Contests the validity of your will
- Argues that you were not competent to make a will
- Objects to the appointment of the executor
- Files a claim against the estate
- Disagrees about the valuation of the property
- Contests how your property will be distributed

If you think your family might dispute some aspects of your will or trust, consider making a video of yourself in which you explain what you want and why. Such a tool would be invaluable to your executor if family members threaten to sue.

## *Probate Takes Time*

The length of time it takes to probate an estate depends on the amount of time it takes your family to gather the necessary information, the number of months your state requires the estate to wait after posting the legal notice in the local newspaper, and whether or not anyone files a contest or a claim.

The only task that needs to be done quickly after you are gone, if you had a will, is the filing of the original within a certain period of time with the probate court in the county where you died. The time period for filing typically ranges from ten to thirty days after the date of death. Any member of your family can file the will with the local probate court. Once this is done, your family has time to shop for a lawyer.

There may be a rush to open probate if there are no funds that can be accessed to pay bills because all of the accounts were in your individual name. Then your family will need to have an executor appointed as quickly as possible in order for the executor to access your money.

### *No Less than Six Months*

If everything goes perfectly, the probate process will take at least six months. Your family will typically spend the first week handling the burial or cremation arrangements. Then your family will make an appointment with a lawyer. The lawyer will get enough information to prepare the petition to start the probate process, if someone in the family has not already filed, and will provide your family with a list of needed information.

In some states the cost of probate is not high, but the process does take time to complete. You may decide that you prefer having an independent entity—the probate court—overseeing the transfer of your estate, even if there is some expense involved.

It usually takes the probate court judge one week to review the petition and sign an order appointing the executor. The executor might be appointed within one week if you live in a state that allows the judge to issue an order without a hearing. If a hearing is required, it might be several more weeks before the judge signs an order appointing the executor. If someone contests the appointment of the executor, further hearings will be needed to determine who will serve as the permanent executor. Most states then require at least a three-month waiting period after the legal posting is made in the local newspaper. Some states require a six-month waiting period.

The lawyer must file all state and federal tax returns, including a final income tax return. However, the information may not be available to file the final income tax return until after January 31 of the year following the death, when tax forms are mailed by employers and corporations. Last, the lawyer must prepare final inventories and accountings to close the estate.

## Probate Protections

The probate process has been around for a long time. It requires a lot of formalities, but the benefits are that probate ensures that your property is properly distributed after you are gone.

The probate system also protects unpaid creditors. These protections cause some cost and delay. You are going to learn, however, that there are steps you can take and documents you can prepare either to avoid the probate process or at least reduce the costs and delays of probate.

## Probate Usually Requires a Lawyer

If your family needs to probate your estate, they will likely need to hire a lawyer. It is very difficult to file the necessary papers with the probate court without the assistance of a legal professional. Your family can get the paperwork they need directly from the probate court in the county where you died. However, the employees who work at the probate court are not allowed to give legal advice. Therefore, they usually may not tell you what forms you need, and they can't help you fill out the forms even if you know what forms to ask for.

The time your lawyer needs to spend preparing the paperwork to probate your estate will be substantially reduced if you do your homework while you are alive, and your family understands the probate process. If you prepared a notebook containing all of the information about your family and your assets, and it contains a copy of your will, as well as a copy of all of the paperwork recommended in Chapter 2, you will have saved the lawyer hours of work and considerably reduced expenses for your family.

**ALERT!**

It is almost impossible for your family to work its way through the probate process without hiring a lawyer. However, when your family is prepared, the cost of the probate process will be reduced dramatically.

If you stay organized and you keep your plan updated, you will be able to be more specific about how your property should be distributed. Keeping the plan current reduces the possibility that someone will contest your choice of an executor or will disagree about what you want done with your property. It will also keep the information current about the bills you owe. If your creditors are paid, they can't file a claim against your estate, which would cause more expense and delay for your family.

## The Cost of Probate

Most lawyers charge a minimum fee, plus a percentage of the total value of the property, to probate an estate. A typical fee is a flat amount for the first $100,000 of property plus a percentage of the value of the assets above $100,000. For example, if the value of the property you own when you die equals $400,000, a typical fee would be $4,500—a flat fee of $1,500 plus 1 percent times $300,000. Some states simply say that the fee to probate an estate must be "reasonable."

It is possible to find a lawyer who will charge by the hour. If your loved ones are prepared and understand the basic steps of the probate process, it is typically cheaper to hire a lawyer who charges by the hour. If you hire a lawyer to prepare your will, you should ask the lawyer how much she bills to probate the estate when you are gone. If you are not satisfied with the answer, you may want to have a different lawyer prepare your will or to hire someone else to handle probate for you.

# Meeting with a Lawyer

When your family meets with a lawyer following your death, they should bring the information contained in your notebook. If you did not prepare a notebook, your family should gather the following information:

- The legal name, address, Social Security number, and birth date of every person named in the will
- If there is no will, the legal names, addresses, Social Security numbers, and birth dates of the spouse and children. If there is no spouse or children, provide the names, addresses, Social Security numbers, and birth dates of the parents and brothers and sisters
- A copy of the death certificate
- Driver's license or ID of the person who died
- All of the credit cards in the sole name of the person who died
- Health insurance information
- A copy of the title for everything the person owned in his or her individual name, such as any real estate, cars, boats, or motorcycles
- A copy of the most recent statement for all bank accounts and brokerage accounts
- A list of all of the retirement accounts
- All life insurance policies or annuities
- A list of all debts
- Business interests and records of ownership

Once they have gathered this information, your family is ready to shop for a lawyer to probate your estate. Price-shopping is very important, but you also want to be certain that the lawyer is experienced in handling estates. Lawyers spend a lot of time explaining the rules about the probate process, and you want one who can help your family gather the information needed to probate your estate.

If the lawyer knows that your family is prepared and has a good idea of what needs to be done, she may give your family a better price. Time is money. If you have prepared your heirs through your notebook, an inventory, or other plan summary, you may have saved them thousands of dollars in legal fees.

# CHAPTER 5

# How to Avoid Probate

If you did not own any property in your individual name, your bills are paid, no one objects to how your property is distributed, and there are no minor children without a surviving parent, your loved ones can avoid the probate process. It takes some planning while you are alive, but it is not difficult to save your family this hassle.

5

# *Reasons for Avoiding the Probate Process*

The simplest reason to avoid the probate process is to save your loved ones the cost and delay in distributing your property. The probate process exists to protect your assets when you are gone and to be sure they are distributed in accordance with your directions. Imagine, for example, what might happen if anyone could sign your name to transfer title of your property. When you own property that is in your own name when you die, the probate process requires that an executor be appointed who, under the supervision of the probate court, can transfer your property according to the terms contained in your will or according to the laws established in your state if you do not have a will.

**FACT**

If you own property in joint name with someone else when you die, your loved ones will not need an executor to sign because the title will pass automatically to the surviving joint tenant.

While these probate protections work for your best interests, they do cost time and money. You can avoid these costs and delays by structuring the ownership of your property in a way that will avoid the probate process. When you avoid the probate process by managing how your assets are owned, you may also reduce the possibility of conflict among your loved ones when you are gone.

If there are no minor children involved, you can avoid the probate process for your loved ones through the use of one or more of the following plans:

- Joint property
- Trusts
- Life insurance
- Retirement plans
- Annuities
- Pay-on-death accounts

The choices you make will depend on the type of plan you want to craft for your family. Planning for your loved ones while you are living is like completing that picture puzzle mentioned in Chapter 3, and it can be fun when you know the rules. There are several pieces you have to work with, but you win only when you figure out how the pieces fit together to create the perfect whole.

By organizing your assets and liabilities and developing a plan for your loved ones, you can easily avoid the probate process. You may find that the process of developing a plan allows you to analyze the property you own. Working on a plan helps you make decisions about your property that will let you enjoy the benefits while you are alive.

## Titling Property to Avoid Probate

There are a number of ways you can own your property that will avoid the probate process when you are gone:

- Your property can be owned in joint name with another person.
- Your property can be owned in trust.
- Your property can pass by contract and not by your will.

### Joint Tenancy

The easiest way to avoid the probate process is to own property in joint name with another person. This is technically known as holding property in joint tenancy. If your property is owned in joint tenancy with another person, title to the property passes automatically to the surviving joint tenant and probate is avoided. It is very common for a husband and wife to own property in joint name. When the first spouse dies, the property belongs to the surviving spouse because the surviving spouse was a joint tenant.

There are two factors you should consider prior to placing all of your property in joint name with your spouse. First, you and your spouse *could* die in a common accident. If this were to happen, the property would need to be probated because there would be no surviving owner. Second, there can be negative income tax consequences to owning your property in joint name with your spouse. See Chapter 10 for details on the tax consequences of owning property jointly.

**FACT**

It is not very common for a husband and wife to die in the same accident. Therefore, owning all of your property in joint name with your spouse is a "cheap" estate plan. Title will pass automatically to the surviving spouse, and there will be no need for him to probate the estate.

## Multiple Joint Tenants

You can have a will as a backup to provide instructions on how to distribute your property if you and your spouse die in a common accident. Another way to protect against that risk is to add other joint tenants to your property. There is no limit to the number of persons who can own a piece of property as joint tenants. If you add your children as joint tenants, and you and your spouse die, your property will automatically be owned by your children.

This may sound like a good idea, but there are practical reasons why you and your spouse might not want to do this. When you add someone as a joint tenant to most types of property, you are making a gift of a portion of the property to that joint tenant. For example, assume you have two children, and you and your spouse decide to add both as joint tenants on the deed to your home. When you do this, you are making a gift to the children. Depending on the value of the property, this may generate a gift tax to you and your spouse for the value of the property transferred to the children. It also means your children do not get the advantage of a step-up in basis upon your death. See Chapter 10 for an explanation of cost basis and a step-up in basis.

If you and your spouse decide to sell the property after you have added your two children as joint tenants, half of the sale proceeds must be paid to the children, since they own half of your property. You also can't change your mind. You have given half of the property to your children. If you want the property back, the children don't have to give it to you.

## Unexpected Results

There are several other things you should consider before you add other people as joint tenants to your property. Joint tenancy can have unexpected results. For example, if you add your two children as joint tenants to your property and one of them dies in a common accident with you, the property will belong to your one surviving child. The child who died with you may be survived by her own children. If you had wanted those grandchildren to share the property, it will not happen.

**ALERT!**

> Owning property in joint name with another person or a number of persons is a simple way for the surviving joint tenant or tenants to avoid the probate process. But beware; joint ownership may not accomplish the family objectives.

When you own property in joint name with someone other than your spouse, the income tax consequences may or may not be negative, depending on your circumstances. There are also estate and gift tax consequences to owning property in joint name. While these rules are carefully covered later, you need to be aware of the possibilities now before you jump into a joint tenancy. Be sure to thoroughly research all options and consequences before making any final decisions.

## Place Property in Trust

If you create a trust for your family, the property owned by the trust will avoid the probate process. Frankly, many of the disadvantages of owning property in joint name are avoided when the property is owned by a trust. If you understand the history of trusts, it will help you understand how a property held in trust will avoid the probate process.

## History of Trusts

The basics of trust law have remained unchanged for centuries. Trusts evolved from early English law. In England, no one could own property except for the king. The workers became very dissatisfied with doing all of the work and not owning the land. As the discontent mounted, the king granted the workers use of the land, though the legal title remained with him. Eventually the workers were allowed to hand down the use of the property to their heirs. It became the law in England that the king held legal title of the property for the benefit of the workers, who held equitable title. The separation of legal title from equitable title is the foundation of our trust law.

**QUESTION?**

**What are the tax results if you own property in joint name with your spouse at the time of your death?**

When you die, your property will be appraised. The appraisal will be divided in half, 50 percent to your estate and 50 percent to your spouse. Because your spouse is considered owner of one-half, that portion will not receive the step-up in cost basis. If he decides to sell the property, a portion of the sales price may include capital gains tax on his 50 percent portion. Your estate's 50 percent portion will be valued as of your date of death; this is called a step-up in basis. Again, see the details on cost basis in Chapter 10 for a better understanding of this result.

A trust is a way for you to name someone who will hold legal title to your property for the benefit of your loved ones. The person who holds the title is known as the trustee, and your loved ones, who will enjoy the use of the property, are known as your beneficiaries.

When you create a trust, you decide what rights your beneficiaries will have. You are known as the *settlor* or *grantor* of the trust. In that capacity you will name a trustee. The trustee is like the king. The trustee holds legal title to the property for the benefit of the beneficiaries. The beneficiaries are like the workers. They hold equitable title to the property and enjoy the benefits you gave them in the trust document you created.

## As Trustee, You Make All the Decisions

When you die, the trust document you created names a person or an entity to serve as trustee when you are gone. This is technically known as a *successor trustee*. Also, as creator, or settlor, of the trust, you name the persons who will enjoy the benefits of the property when you are gone. These are known as *successor beneficiaries*. The trust document you create will provide the successor trustee very detailed instructions on what to do with the property. Those instructions govern who will enjoy your property, when they will enjoy the property, and how they will enjoy the property.

The beauty of a trust is that while you are living you are the creator of the trust and define all of the rights. You can also serve as trustee of the trust, which means you hold legal title. You can also be the beneficiary of the trust while you are living. You truly enjoy all of the benefits of property ownership.

This is why property that is held in trust avoids the probate process. You own the property while you are living, but you own it in your legal capacity as a trustee. When you die, whoever you named as successor trustee automatically becomes the legal owner of the property. The rules about trusts are covered in detail in Chapters 11 through 14. But, for now, just understand why property held in trust avoids the probate process.

The value of receiving a step-up basis in property means that heirs receive property valued as of the date of your death. This step-up basis may reduce or eliminate capital gains tax due if your property has increased in value over the years, and your heirs decide to sell the property.

Don't forget, if you have designated a beneficiary of assets such as IRAs, retirement funds, life insurance, annuities, or pay-on-death accounts, those funds do not go through probate and cannot be changed by a direction in your will. The beneficiary designation form is a contract between you and the issuing company, and that form controls who will receive the funds from those accounts.

**FACT**

> There are certain types of property that are not subject to probate because the property is governed by a contractual agreement you entered into while you were living. This type of property will be distributed according to the terms of the contract, and will not be affected by whether or not you have a will.

## Make Good Use of Life Insurance

When you apply for life insurance, the application asks you who will receive the life insurance benefits when you die. You can name one or more persons as the beneficiary or a secondary beneficiary in the event of the death of your first beneficiary. When you name more than one person to receive the policy benefit, you also decide what percentage of the proceeds each person will receive.

Your will has absolutely no effect on who will receive the proceeds from your life insurance policies. As a matter of fact, your will could specifically say, "I leave all of my life insurance to my children, in equal shares," but this clause would be disregarded completely, and the policy proceeds would be paid to the person or persons you named when you bought the life insurance.

### Payable to the Estate

However, there are two ways that your will can affect how your life insurance proceeds will be paid. The first is if you named your estate as the beneficiary when you bought the life insurance policy. Then the life insurance proceeds will be paid to your estate and distributed according to the terms of your will. You might have named your estate as beneficiary of your life insurance policy if you couldn't decide on a person.

Sometimes when a young person is starting a new job and his employer pays for a life insurance policy as part of the employee benefit package, the new employee does not know who she wants to name as beneficiary. In that case, it is typical just to check the box "payable to my estate." Young people who have no one they wish to provide for could name their alma mater or other charity as beneficiary to avoid directing property to their estate.

## When the Beneficiary Is No Longer Living

The second way your will could affect how your life insurance proceeds are paid is if the person or persons you name to receive the life insurance proceeds are not alive. Then, the insurance company will pay the policy proceeds to your estate. Your will may not reference the insurance because it was supposed to be paid directly to the person or persons named in the policy. But most wills have a clause that says, "Distribute any remaining property I own to X," and the insurance proceeds would be distributed accordingly. This same circumstance could arise if you are divorced and your ex-spouse is named as beneficiary. Some policies assume the divorced party is deceased and cannot be a beneficiary.

It is not a good idea to name your estate as beneficiary of your life insurance policy because the life insurance proceeds will then need to be probated before they can be distributed.

Life insurance proceeds avoid the probate process. But before you close the book on what you need to know about life insurance, you should read Chapter 15 to make sure your family does not pay unnecessary estate taxes.

## Consider Creating Retirement Accounts

IRAs, Roth IRAs, and employer-provided retirement accounts are like life insurance. The retirement benefits are paid to the beneficiary or beneficiaries you named when you opened the retirement account or completed the paperwork with your employer.

As you now realize, it is irrelevant if your will names someone else as beneficiary. The only way your retirement benefits will be governed by your will is if you named the estate as the beneficiary of your retirement benefits or the person or persons you named are not alive. Then your retirement benefits will be paid to your estate and will need to be probated.

It is very important to double-check your documents to see who is named as beneficiary of your life insurance policies and your retirement accounts. The beneficiary or beneficiaries you named initially may not be who you want today to receive the benefits at your death.

Although life insurance proceeds and retirement accounts are alike because the proceeds avoid the probate process, the income tax consequences of each are completely different. The rules regarding the federal estate taxes associated with retirement accounts and the income tax consequences to your beneficiaries are covered in Chapter 16.

## Annuities May Be an Option

Annuities are like life insurance and retirement accounts. For some persons, an annuity is an option that could work as part of the estate planning puzzle. Annuities are not for everyone, however. As with life insurance, there are many different plans on the market. Some are set up for immediate payments and some for payments to start sometime in the future. It is also possible to have a guaranteed payment period but, because you don't know when you will die, it's hard to say whether your family will reap any benefit from an annuity plan.

Because life insurance, retirement accounts, and annuities are paid to the person or persons you name as beneficiaries, it is important that you obtain a copy of your beneficiary election forms if you have any of these investments. You would be surprised how many times the beneficiary elections are not what you thought they were. This could be because you forgot who you named, or the information was improperly recorded by the company.

# CHAPTER 6

# The Parts of a Will

A will is the legal document that provides instructions on how property that is titled in your name will be distributed when you are gone. Each part of your will serves a different purpose. Once you understand the parts, you can make the decisions needed to begin a draft of your will.

## An Overview

A will is a document that is presented to the probate court after you are gone. The probate court judge needs to be able to read that document and determine that it is in fact your will and that you signed that will. The judge then issues a court order to distribute your property following your instructions. This all sounds very simple. However, you are not available to testify that the will is in fact yours. The judge has to make sure that no one changed your will without your permission. The judge also needs to determine by reading the will who you wanted to receive your property and what you wanted each person to have. All of these decisions are made without the testimony of the one and only person who really knew what he or she wanted: you! Therefore, your will must speak for itself.

The words in a will are confusing because the law on wills came from our English heritage. Unlike most areas of law where more modern terms have been incorporated into the law, much of the terminology associated with wills has not changed for centuries.

## A Will Is Divided into Parts

The more specific you are about what you want, the easier it will be for the probate court judge to make the right decisions about your property. Each part of your will is designed to help the probate court judge interpret your intentions. A will has parts, often referred to as the *articles*. Each article is designed to accomplish a purpose.

## Don't Be Intimidated by Fancy Words

Words are intimidating when you don't understand what they mean. For instance, let's say you take your car to a mechanic. The mechanic starts talking about the lifters, pistons, plugs, serpentine belt, and catalytic converter, and you become nervous because you have no idea what he is talking about. When your will includes phrases like "descendants by right of representation" or "property passing per stirpes," that same sense of unease fills your mind. Don't be intimidated! By the time you finish reading this chapter, you will understand those fancy words.

Because the words in a will have a particular meaning to the court, it is important for you to learn those terms and use them correctly, especially if you are thinking of preparing your own will.

# Declarations

The first part, or Article I, of your will identifies you and your heirs. This part is referred to as the declaration section. An heir is any person who would receive your property if you died without a will. If you think about a ladder, it will help you understand the heirs you should list in this first part. If you have living heirs at the first step of the ladder, you don't need to go to the second step. If you have no heirs at the first or second step, you need to list your heirs at the third step.

## The Ladder of Heirs

The first step, or level, of heirs is your spouse and your children. If you have no spouse, the only heirs at this first step are your children. If one or more of your children have died and are survived by one or more of their own children, the children of the child who is gone are included as heirs on the first step of the ladder. If any of these persons are living, you can stop here. Most people identify or declare the names of their spouse and children.

If there is no one living at the first step, you must go to the second step, which includes your mother and father. If your mother is gone, your father is your only heir, and vice versa. If your mother and/or father are living, you can stop. If your mother and father are gone, go to the next step.

The third step is your siblings or their children. If one of your siblings is gone, the child or children of the deceased sibling will become heirs and should be listed. If you have no spouse, children, grandchildren, parents, brothers, sisters, or children of siblings, you need help from a lawyer to define your heirs. It may seem silly to spend so much time teaching you about your heirs, but the probate court judge wants to be sure that you knew who your heirs were. Then, if you decide not to leave any property to an heir, later in your will you can explain why you have excluded that heir.

**FACT**

Remember, the probate court judge's job is to issue an order to distribute your property to the persons you name in your will. If you don't identify your heirs in the declaration portion of your will, you run the risk that an excluded heir will contest your will, alleging that you forgot him.

Also, if you die without a will, the court will distribute your property in accordance with your state's intestacy laws, which usually follow this same order in the ladder of heirs.

### Defining Children

The next part of the declaration section of your will defines the words *child, children,* and *descendants.* The most important thing for you to understand is that the word *child* (or children) will not include stepchildren or foster children. If you want to make a distribution to a stepchild or a foster child, you can do so in Articles III or IV, but you will need to be very specific. As you read on about how to distribute your property, you will learn about the significance of the word *descendant.*

## Payment of Debts

The next part of your will, Article II, directs that all of your debts, obligations, and taxes be paid. Any person or entity to which you owed money when you died is called a creditor. You've learned that when you die, one of the first jobs of the executor is to hire a lawyer to file the necessary papers with the probate court. The lawyer will also tell the executor what she needs to do to administer your estate. One of the jobs of your executor is to pay the debts and obligations you owed when you died.

If your executor does not pay the creditors, an unpaid creditor is allowed to file a claim against your estate demanding payment. If there are not enough assets to pay all of your debts and obligations, there is a process to determine which debts will be paid in full, which debts will be either partially paid or not paid, and in which order.

## Secured Debt

There are certain types of debts that are secured. When a debt is secured by property you own while you are living, that piece of property can be sold to pay the debt. The best example of this type of secured debt is the debt you owe on your home.

When you borrowed money to buy your home, you signed two types of legal papers. The first was a promissory note. The promissory note made you and whoever else signed the promissory note personally liable for the debt. The second type of paper you signed gave the lender, typically your bank, a security interest in your house known as a mortgage. If you don't make your payments, the lender has two choices. The lender can sue you and whoever else signed on the promissory note, or the lender can take the house back and sell your home under the terms of the mortgage.

## Lenders Have Rights When You Die

When you die, if you owed money on a promissory note, secured by a mortgage on your home, the lender typically has the right to demand that the debt be paid in full. Anytime you own property secured by a mortgage, that property can be sold to pay the debt. Lenders typically don't exercise this right as long as someone continues to make the monthly payments.

Article II of your will may include a passage such as the following:

*If any property owned by me jointly, or individually, passing under this will or otherwise, shall be encumbered by a mortgage, pledge, security interest, loan, lien, or unpaid taxes, the indebtedness secured by such encumbrance shall not be charged to or paid by my estate but such property shall pass subject to all encumbrances existing at my death.*

This language is merely telling your executor that if there is a secured loan against a particular piece of property you owned, the executor is to distribute that property without paying off the loan against the property.

Please understand that these instructions are not binding on the lender. The lender will have the right to be paid in full before the property is distributed to your heirs, if the lender chooses to exercise its rights under the loan documents. A lender may choose to exercise its right to demand that the property be sold if your estate has more debts than it has assets, and the lender is not comfortable that the other person who signed the note, if there is one, is capable of making the payments.

## Specific Devises

Devise is the term that is used in a will to describe the fact that you are leaving property to someone. The person to whom you devise property is called a devisee. When you make a specific devise, you are describing a piece of property and giving specific instructions to give that property to a named person.

### Specific Devise of Tangible Personal Property

Tangible personal property is any property other than real estate that you can feel or touch. Tangible property does not include bank accounts, shares of stock, certificates of deposit, bonds, partnership interests, or any other financial interests. These items are known as intangible personal property.

Even if your will states that the decision of the executor shall be final and binding, someone could file a contest with the probate court, alleging that the executor is breaching his or her duty. It will be tough for that person to win, but it is expensive for your estate to spend money on a lawyer to defend the contest.

Most wills include a separate article telling the executor what to do with your tangible personal property. For example, let's say a will specifies that all of the tangible personal property is to be left to the spouse and, if the spouse is not living, to the children.

The will also states that if the children cannot agree on how to divide the tangible personal property within six months, the executor shall decide how to divide the tangible personal property, and that the decision of the executor is final and binding.

## *Memorandum for Tangible Property*

Some states allow you to list tangible property and the beneficiary of that property on a page separate from your will, frequently called a "memorandum." The will and memorandum should cross-reference each other (some states require the cross-reference), but this method is an easier way to direct tangible property. A will memorandum can be as simple as that shown below.

This _____ day of _____, 20__, pursuant to Article _____ of my Last Will and Testament dated _____, which provides that I may effectively dispose of my tangible property in accordance with the most recently dated memorandum which I have signed and left with my personal papers, I have executed this Memorandum.

I bequeath absolutely the below-listed items of my tangible personal property as follows:

1. _____ to _____

2. _____ to _____

3. _____ to _____

4. _____ to _____

5. _____ to _____

6. _____ to _____

Signature_____
      *Testator or Testatrix*

The benefit of a memorandum is that you can change your mind every day, if you wish, without having to rewrite your will or a codicil. Just remember to sign and date the latest memorandum and destroy all previous ones.

## Avoiding Conflict

If you think your children or heirs are going to fight about what each one receives, you can specifically describe each piece of tangible personal property and who should receive that property. Even in families in which heirs care deeply about one another, disagreements can arise about jewelry, crystal, china, furniture, cars, boats, and collectibles. It takes time and thought on your part to include specifics in your will or memorandum, but it can avoid hard feelings after you are gone.

Or you might consider putting a clause in your will that says, "If my children cannot agree on how to distribute the rest of my tangible personal property within six months after my death, I hereby instruct the executor to sell the disputed items and divide the proceeds equally among my children." Such a clause might encourage them to cooperate!

## Who Pays Expenses

You should include instructions about who pays the expenses incurred in storing, packing, or moving the tangible personal property. A will may state that these expenses are not to be charged against the devisee who receives the tangible personal property. In plain English, this means that if there are expenses in storing, packing, or moving any tangible personal property, those expenses are to be paid from other assets or property in your estate, and are not charged to the one who receives the property. If this is not your intention, you should instruct your executor that any expenses for storing, packing, or moving will be charged against the devisee who receives the property. For example, if one child lives 3,000 miles away, it may not be fair that the other heirs must bear the expense of packing and moving the property!

## *Specific Devises of Other Property*

There is no magic number of how many articles there will be in your will. If you want to make specific devises of any other property, you should have another article titled "Specific Devises of Other Property." You should number each paragraph. In each paragraph you should describe in detail each piece of property and who is going to receive that property. For instance:

1. I leave the property located at 7301 Chase Drive, Sarasota, Florida, to my daughter June.
2. I leave my brokerage account held at X Company to my son Scott.
3. I leave the balance of my savings account held at X Bank to my daughter Rebecca.

There are two points you should consider regarding specific devises. First, if you don't own the described property when you die, the devise is ignored, and the devisee does not get other property unless it is already specified. Second, you should specify what happens to the property if the devisee you name is not living. For example, if you leave to your daughter June the property at 7301 Chase Drive, that provision should continue and state that if June is not living, the property shall pass to her children, or to her brother or sister, or according to the residuary clause of your will. These are choices you need to make when you include specific devises in your will.

When you leave a specific devise of property to a named individual in your will, make sure that the property you are attempting to leave to the named person is actually titled in your individual name. The property could be very clearly described but, if the property is owned jointly with someone else, the will has no effect.

## *Per Stirpes*

There are two legal terms you should understand. The first is *per stirpes,* and the second is *per capita.* Let's first take a look at per stirpes. Whenever you leave property to a person per stirpes, this has a very definite legal effect. It means that if the named person is dead, the property passes to the lineal descendants, by representation. The best way to understand this concept is with a diagram.

Per stirpes means that if Child 1 is deceased, Child 1's share will be divided equally between GC1 and GC2. In other words, Child 1's ⅓ share will be divided equally between GC1 and GC2, who will each receive ⅙ of the property. If you would rather have Child 1's property distributed to your other two children, Child 2 and Child 3, you don't want to use the term *per stirpes.*

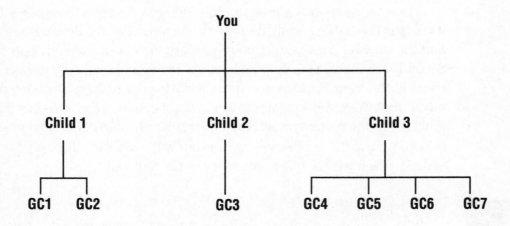

Assume that all three of your children are gone. If you have left the property per stirpes, Child 1's children will each receive ⅙ (½ × ⅓); Child 2's child will receive ⅓ because Child 2 had only one child; and Child 3's children will each take ¹⁄₁₂ of the property (¼ × ⅓). This may not be what you intended. If your children are all gone, you might want each of the seven grandchildren to take equal shares and, in that case, you shouldn't use the term *per stirpes.*

## Per Capita

Another option is to use the term *per capita*. If you leave the property to a group per capita, and a member of the group is gone, the property goes in equal shares to the remaining persons in the group.

For instance, if you leave your property per capita to your three children and one child dies, then the property will pass to your two living children, and not to the children of your deceased child.

# Residuary Devise

This is the clause that distributes the rest of your property. This may also be the clause that will distribute specifically devised property if the person to whom you specifically devised property is not living, and you put in a provision that reads, "If this person is not living, the property shall be distributed according to the terms of my residuary clause." You can direct your executor to distribute the residue of your property to one or more persons. If you include very few specific devises in your will, most of your property will pass according to the instructions contained in the residuary clause.

## Testamentary Trusts

You have the option of creating a complete trust in the residuary clause of your will. Your residuary clause will then read, "I leave the rest and remainder of my property to John Doe, Trustee. John Doe shall administer the trust as follows." The trust you create inside of your will is called a *testamentary trust*.

The testamentary trust is identical in every single way to a revocable trust that you might have created while you were living, with two very important distinctions. First, the trust is not created until after you are gone. The trust is created after you are dead and is funded by the residuary clause of your will. Second, the trust document will not include provisions about how to administer the trust property while you are living, because the trust won't be created until after you are gone.

## Advantages and Disadvantages

You might create a testamentary trust in your will because you don't want to go through the trouble of transferring all of your property into your name as trustee while you are living as you must do when creating a revocable trust. But you still want the benefits of creating a trust plan for your family that will govern after you are gone.

It is very important for you to understand that if you create a testamentary trust, your property must be probated. Once the testamentary trust is created in your will, it will be governed by the same rules as a revocable trust, except that a testamentary trust remains under the annual supervision of the probate court, because that is where the trust was created.

## Taxes

Your will instructs your executor to pay all taxes that are owing—local, state, and federal taxes. The most common taxes owing when a person dies are income taxes or estate and gift taxes. Chapter 17 covers your federal gift and estate tax exposure. (This book does not cover state gift or estate taxes, as each state has different rules governing these taxes. You should check with your state's taxing agency to learn what might be due at your death.)

**QUESTION?**

**Will my heirs have to pay any taxes on their inheritance?**
It will depend on the asset being given to your heirs and what your will says. If your will directs heirs to pay a proportional share of taxes, their share of taxes will be paid before distribution. The executor is responsible for seeing that the estate taxes are paid before any distribution is made.

Your executor will be responsible for filing your final federal and state income tax returns. Most of the rules about how to compute the final income tax returns are the same whether you are living or it is your final return.

If your estate is required to file a federal estate tax return, there are elections to take certain deductions on the federal estate tax return versus your final income tax return. You should ask the accountant or lawyer who prepares the federal tax return about these elections.

If you leave a deferred account such as an IRA to your heir, she will have to pay income taxes on receipt of the funds. She will not owe estate taxes, however, on the value of the IRA, as taxes on that asset were paid by the executor prior to closing the estate.

If you choose to use a will as your planning document, the probate court will not allow your executor to close your estate until he has verified that all tax returns have been filed. In most cases, this means that your estate cannot be closed until after January 31 following the year of your death. This is because payers are not required to send tax statements (W-2s, 1099s, K-1s, other tax forms) that you need to complete the return until January 31. Also, the federal estate tax return, if one needs to be filed, is due no later than nine months after the date of your death. Preparing this return may delay final distributions and the closing of your estate.

## The Powers of Your Executor

Your will names the executor who will be in charge of administering your estate. Your executor is legally responsible for doing everything necessary to probate your estate. Chapter 7 covers who should serve as your executor, the duties of the executor, and considerations in choosing an executor. The only document that allows you to appoint an executor is your will.

If there are certain assets or property you definitely don't want sold or encumbered, you can place a limited restriction on your executor in relation to that piece of property.

Your will also defines the powers of your executor. You typically want to give your executor all of the powers to deal with your property that you would have had if you were still alive. You can't anticipate how long it will take to probate your estate. It is difficult to complete the probate process more quickly than six months and, because your executor can't close the estate until all claims have been resolved and all tax returns have been filed, it is quite common for an estate to be open for at least one year.

If you restrict the powers your executor has to buy, sell, mortgage, lend, or deal with the estate property, it may hurt your heirs. For example, if you placed a restriction on the executor that she cannot sell your property and your estate holds a particular stock, your executor will not be able to sell the stock even if its value begins to decline.

## Self-Proving Signature to Your Will

Almost all states require that you sign your will in your own handwriting in the presence of two witnesses and a notary. Some states require that the witnesses be over the age of majority, and some states permit a beneficiary to be a witness, although it will eliminate potential questioning if you have independent signers.

### Physical Presence Is Mandatory

Although signing your name seems easy enough, there are a couple of things that could create problems. As you know, you must sign in the presence of two witnesses. This can be tricky. You should make sure that you sign the document in the physical presence of the two witnesses who sign in your presence and in the presence of each other. In some states, a will can be found invalid if it is established that the witnesses signed in your presence, but signed at different times. For example, let's say you sign your will in the presence of Witness Number One. Two hours later, Witness Number Two stops by to sign his name. Because these witnesses did not witness your will in the presence of each other, the will may be invalidated. If you sign your will in the presence of two witnesses, and then the witnesses go to the room next door and sign your will, the witnesses did not sign in your presence, and again, the will might be invalidated.

It is strongly recommended that, in addition to the two witnesses, you include a notary, also present with each of you, who can attest she saw you and the two witnesses sign in the presence of each other. If a notary also signs your will at the same time, the will is called a "self-proving will." (Some states require an Affidavit of Execution, which means the same thing.) Having a self-proving will or Affidavit of Execution means that the probate court will not need to call the witnesses to testify that they actually signed your will; the notary has already attested to everyone's signature and the court can accept the signatures without further action.

## *Your Legal Signature*

It is best to sign your legal name. If the way you normally sign documents is different from your legal name, the probate court judge will usually require testimony from someone who can prove that the way you signed your will is the way you normally sign legal documents. Although there have been cases in which a person signed his will with an *X*, and the will was valid because the person always signed his name with an *X*, this is not the time for you to be tricky or unusual.

# CHAPTER 7

# Decisions to Include Within the Will

The more decisions you make about your assets while you are living, the easier it will be for your loved ones when you are gone. There are several issues that need to be addressed and several choices to be made. Once you have made it through the decision-making process, however, drafting the will is not difficult.

## Who Will Serve as Your Executor?

The first decision you need to make is who will serve as your executor. Your executor is the person or entity that is in charge of probating your estate after you are gone. You should make this decision in the same way you might decide whether or not you want to become chairperson of a committee. For instance, if you were asked to be chairperson of your homeowner's association, you would probably ask questions such as, "What do I have to do?" "How much time do you think it will take?" "Will I have help from the neighbors?" "Do you think I'm the best-qualified person to serve?" Interestingly enough, these are the same kinds of questions you need to ask regarding who should serve as your executor. When you learn the duties of the executor, you will be prepared to choose the right person or entity to serve.

If you are concerned that your executor might tamper with your will, that person is not a good choice to handle your estate. You want someone you can depend on to carry out your wishes just as you would have.

Your executor needs to be a person or an entity that you trust to handle the job. The duties of your executor will depend on several factors:

- The instructions you put in your will
- The nature and extent of your property
- The special needs of your loved ones
- The possibility that someone will contest your will

Pretend you are writing a job description. The more detailed and specific you are about what you want the executor to do, the easier it will be for him to do the job. There are certain duties all executors must perform:

- Locate your will
- Probate your estate
- Decide how and when your property will be distributed

## Locating Your Will

The first job for your executor is to locate your original will. You can make this job very easy by simply telling her where to find it. However, this requires a great deal of trust. If you are worried that your executor might try to change your will without your permission, you obviously don't want her to have access to the original document.

**FACT**

You can also put your original will in a safe-deposit box. If you do this, your executor either needs to have access to the safe-deposit box or be able to contact the person who does have access after your death. See Chapter 21 for a further discussion of safe-deposit boxes.

You can protect against this possibility by filing your original will with your local probate court for safekeeping. After you are gone, your loved ones can present the probate court with proof of your death, and the original document will already be on file with the court.

Or, the lawyer who drafts your will can keep the original will for safekeeping. The important thing is for the executor to know where to find it.

## Probate Your Estate—Hiring a Lawyer

The executor's next job is to probate your estate. It is almost impossible to probate an estate without the assistance of a lawyer. Many executors think they have to hire the lawyer who drafted the will, no matter how much the lawyer charges. This is not true. Your executor is free to ask the lawyer to hand over the original will, if he is holding it, and then shop around and hire a lawyer who will do the best job for the best price.

It is important for your executor to know how the lawyer bills, and how much the lawyer estimates the job will cost. Here is another opportunity for you to lighten the burden. When you are thinking about hiring a lawyer to draft your will, ask not only how much he will charge to draft the will, but also how much it will cost to probate your estate after you are gone. You can then make a recommendation to the executor about using the same lawyer or seeking someone else.

## How and When Your Property Will Be Distributed

The lawyer will prepare the necessary paperwork for the court to probate your estate. Your executor is the one who must decide how and when to distribute your property unless, of course, you make those decisions and include the instructions in your will.

> If you think the lawyer is charging too much to prepare your will or will charge too much to probate your estate when you are gone, don't be afraid to shop elsewhere!

The number of decisions your executor needs to make will vary, depending on how specific you were when you created your will. The executor has no choice but to follow the instructions you left. If you give the executor very general instructions, such as "Divide all of my property equally among my children," the executor is left with the responsibility to decide exactly what each child receives. On the other hand, if you are very specific in your will—for example, "My son should receive my fifty shares of XYZ stock, and my daughter shall receive my ABC mutual fund"—the executor must distribute the XYZ stock to your son and the ABC mutual fund to your daughter. You have made the decisions about what each child should receive rather than shifting the responsibility to your executor.

## Considerations in Choosing an Executor

Choosing who should serve as executor is dependent on how specific your will is. If you make most of the decisions while you are living and your will is very specific about what each person is to receive, it is less important who you name as executor. But if your will is very general, the job requires more discretion by the executor. The person you choose to serve must make all of the decisions about what property each person named in your will is to receive. It is much more likely that your loved ones will disagree and perhaps contest the decisions of your executor when you are less specific.

More than one person can serve as your executor. When you name two people to act as executors, both executors must agree on all decisions and sign all of the paperwork. Naming multiple executors to provide a check and balance on the decision-making process makes sense. However, when you name more than two co-executors, making decisions and executing the necessary paperwork often becomes difficult.

If any of your loved ones have special needs, this may affect your choice of executor. For instance, you may choose one of your children to serve as your executor because you know that child will make the best decisions for the child who has special needs.

You also can name a professional executor. Banks and trust companies are available to serve as an executor of your will. The fee professional executors charge varies, but it is typically a flat fee, possibly $5,000, and a percentage of the value of your probate property. The company may also charge an additional fee for handling nonprobate property. As you can see, it is very expensive to use a financial institution as your executor. That is one reason most people who choose a will as their estate planning document do not name a professional executor.

## Who Should Receive Your Property?

A typical response to this question would be, "I want my spouse to have all of my property when I die and, if my spouse is gone, I want my property divided equally among my children." There are several reasons why this may not be the best plan:

- If your estate is subject to federal estate taxes, you probably don't want to leave all of your property outright to your spouse. Federal estate taxes and how to reduce those taxes are covered in Chapters 17 and 18.
- If this is a second marriage, you may not want to leave all of your property to your spouse.
- If one of your children is not living, you need to decide whether her share will go to her siblings or to her children.
- You may be concerned about your property going to your child and then becoming part of a divorce proceeding if your child later divorces.

**FACT**

The percentage for a bank to serve as executor may start as high as 5 percent of the first $100,000 and then decline with an increase in the estate value, e.g., 4 percent on the next $100,000, down to 1.5 percent on a balance above $1 million or $2 million. Be sure to check out the fee schedule ahead of time, and keep in mind that the fees could go up further by the time of your death.

If this is a second marriage, you may want to make sure your current spouse has enough income and property for life, but want your children from a former marriage to receive your property when your spouse dies. If this is your objective, a will is not the best estate planning document for you.

**ALERT!**

You need to decide how your property will be distributed if the person to whom you leave the property is not living at the time of your death. Be sure to name a second beneficiary of your property or add the property to your residuary estate.

If you want to protect against the possibility that your child will divorce after you are gone and that your child's spouse will take your child's inheritance, you should consider using either a revocable or testamentary trust as your estate planning document, not just a will.

**FACT**

The divorce laws in most states provide that inherited property is not marital property, but there are a lot of exceptions to this rule. Establishing trusts for your children will protect the inherited property from ex-spouses.

Who you leave your property to is obviously your decision. Take some time and view it from all angles. You need to be assured that your goals will be met and your wishes granted. The best way to do this is to be very specific.

## How Should Your Property Be Distributed?

There are several ways you can distribute property in your will:

1. You can draft a will that leaves specific pieces of property to each person.
2. You can draft a will that provides for a fractional division of your property.
3. You can draft a will that has a mix of specific instructions and a fractional division of the remainder of your property.
4. You can specify that the property be sold and the proceeds divided among your heirs.
5. You can direct all or some of your property to a testamentary trust for later action.

There are advantages and disadvantages to each method that you should consider in making a decision.

### Specific Instructions

When you want to leave specific property to named individuals, you will need to make even more decisions before you draft your will. However, you will have almost eliminated the possibility that your loved ones will disagree, and you will have made the job of the executor much easier.

For example, if your will reads, "I leave my property located at 7711 Clinton Drive to my son" and "I leave my property located at 437 Mountain Drive to my daughter," it doesn't matter if the properties are equal in value when you die; the executor must distribute the Clinton Drive property to your son and the Mountain Drive property to your daughter. Putting instructions in your will directing the executor to distribute specific property to each child eliminates the possibility that the children will contest the choice the executor makes about what property to distribute, because they really have no say. Your will has told the executor what he must do.

If you dispose of property that has been specifically directed to someone, you need to review your will and determine whether you want to re-adjust the share of your estate to be received by each person.

If your intentions are to treat your children equally, you will have to go through your inventory of property carefully, determining the value of each piece of property, subtracting the debt owing against each piece of property, and equalizing the end result by deciding which pieces of property to distribute to each child. You may think these are difficult decisions, but if you don't decide what each child is to receive while you are living, the executor must do so after you are gone.

The danger with specific instructions is that if the property is already gone at the time of your death, no other property can be substituted for the property that no longer exists. For example, if your will leaves the property located at 7711 Clinton Drive to your son, and you sell the property before you die and buy a different piece of property with the proceeds, your son will not receive the newly acquired property unless it is specified.

## General Instructions

General instructions in a will are much more common than specific instructions. You use general instructions when you want to identify who will receive your property and instruct the executor to make a fractional division of your property. For example, your will might read, "I leave 50 percent of my property to be divided equally between my children and 50 percent to be divided equally among my grandchildren." You have given the executor clear instructions on who should receive your property, but you have provided no guidance on what property each person will receive.

General instructions in your will regarding distribution of your property provide your executor with the least amount of guidance. They require her to make the decisions you could have made while you were living. By not being specific, you make the job of executor more difficult.

If your executor has been given general instructions on how to distribute your property, and if the persons you name to receive your property cannot agree on what they should receive, any one of the persons can petition the probate court to present arguments about why he thinks the proposed distribution is not fair. It is very expensive when your heirs argue over what they are going to receive from your estate. Ultimately the probate court judge might order your executor to sell your property and distribute the cash proceeds rather than the property itself.

## A Combination of Instructions

It is much more typical to use a mix of instructions in your will. For example:

*I leave my diamond wedding ring to my daughter.*
*I leave my watch to my son.*
*I leave my car to my son.*

*I leave my boat to my daughter.*
*I direct that the rest of my property be divided equally between my two children.*

The executor must distribute the ring, the watch, the car, and the boat as instructed. These are specific instructions. The executor is then left with the difficult task of deciding how to divide and distribute the rest of your property.

## Do You Want Your Property Sold?

Once you analyze each piece of property you own, you must evaluate the cost of maintaining that property. You need to consider whether it would be practical for your family to own the property jointly after you are gone. You may be surprised to find you would like to instruct the executor to sell that particular piece of property. The proceeds will then be distributed as you instruct.

Even if you have given your executor full discretion as to the sale of your property, she has a duty to make prudent financial choices about your property during the course of administering your estate. Your executor may decide that it will cost too much money to maintain the property during the estate administration, and that the property should be sold. Or your executor may feel that the property might go down in value and, therefore, decide it is best to sell the property and distribute the cash proceeds before the decline in value.

Of course, if you don't want a particular property sold, you can also stipulate this in your will. Sometimes it is difficult to decide between sentiment and practicality. However, if you don't make these tough decisions yourself, someone else will have to.

## What Is Best for Your Minor Child?

It is very important, if you have a minor child, to have a will. Your will is the usual document that allows you to name a legal guardian for your minor child if you die. If you don't have a document that names a legal guardian, and there is no surviving parent, the probate court will need to conduct a hearing and take testimony from persons interested in serving as legal guardian of the child. When this happens, a person you might not have chosen to raise your child could be appointed guardian by the probate court.

## The Surviving Parent

If a minor child has a surviving parent, the surviving parent becomes the legal guardian of the child as a matter of law. If you name someone other than the surviving parent as guardian in your will, the attempted appointment will be disregarded. This doesn't prevent an interested person from petitioning the probate court to have the surviving natural parent declared unfit but, if this happens, it is a separate proceeding that has nothing to do with your will.

## Contesting Your Choice of Guardian

Anyone can contest your choice of legal guardian. The duty of the probate court is to determine what is in the best interest of the minor child. When the will is admitted to probate, various hearings might be scheduled. When there is no surviving parent, the probate court will provide your family with a notice of a hearing to determine the legal guardianship of your minor child. If no one objects at the hearing, the person you name in your will is appointed. But if someone objects, she will bring witnesses and any documentation she may have to prove to the court that the person you named as legal guardian is not in the best interest of the minor child.

**ALERT!**

There is a very strong presumption that the person you name in your will to be the guardian for your child is the person who should be appointed. But the court's primary duty is to ensure the safety and well-being of the minor child. If the person contesting proves that the person you name is not fit, a different guardian will be appointed.

When you have a will naming a guardian for your minor child, it is very unlikely that a different guardian will be appointed. On the other hand, if you did not make a will to name a legal guardian, the probate court judge must listen to all of the evidence and make an independent determination as to what is in the best interest of your child.

Parents typically have strong preferences about who should raise their children if something happens to them. But the only way to make sure the right person serves is to create a will or written declaration naming a guardian.

## How Do You Choose a Guardian?

The answer to this question depends on your family values. You may choose a legal guardian who is most financially able to support the child. Or you may feel it is more important to name a person who will provide for your child's emotional support. Typically, the preferred legal guardian is one whose goals, philosophies, and child-rearing values are most similar to those of the natural parents. Ideally, you should discuss these issues with the person you are considering naming.

Sometimes one or more family members expect to be named as legal guardian of your minor child. If you think a family member would be tremendously hurt if he thought you would choose someone else, you need to decide whether to discuss your plans ahead of time with that family member or let the court deal with it after you are gone.

There is no legal obligation for you to discuss your choice of guardian or get the approval of the person you have named in your will. However, after you are gone, the legal guardian named must agree to serve. If the person you name is not willing to accept the appointment, the probate court will seek applications from those who do want to serve as legal guardian. Then the probate court will conduct a hearing to make an independent determination about who should be appointed.

## The Child's Property

Unless you create a different legal arrangement, the person who is appointed legal guardian of your minor child will also control your child's property. This means that if your will leaves property to your children, the legal guardian will have control over the funds and property. The legal guardian is supposed to use the property for the benefit of your child, but it is very difficult for a minor child to protect her property.

When you evaluate all of the property your child would receive from you if you and your spouse died, you may decide that you don't want the guardian to have control of it. If this is your decision, you need to create a trust for your child's property, and name someone to serve as trustee.

It is possible to create a trust for your minor child in your will. This is called a testamentary trust. It would contain specific instructions about who should serve as trustee for the benefit of the property of your minor child. The trust would also contain instructions on how your property should be managed and distributed. This trust would come into existence only when you died. If you want to create a trust for your child's property, you should read Chapters 11 through 14.

# CHAPTER 8

# Drafting Your Will

You have multiple options about how to draft your will. You can buy forms from your local office supply store, download forms from the Internet, or purchase inexpensive software packages that will create a will for you. Or, you can hire a lawyer to prepare a will and other estate planning documents.

## Filling in a Form Will

Some office supply stores still carry paper will forms you can buy. These forms allow you to fill in the blanks to create your will. However, it is difficult for such a form to meet everyone's needs. A will that might meet the goals and objectives for one family often is different from a will that meets the needs of another family, even when the two families seem similar. Frankly, it is hard even to find an office supply store that still sells paper forms. Instead, most now sell computer software packages that generate wills, as well as other common estate planning documents.

You may not be comfortable with computers and prefer the old-fashioned method. If you can't locate a paper form, you can use the information you learned in Chapters 6 and 7 and the sample will found in this chapter to help you draft your own will.

**ALERT!**

You need to be careful when you use any self-help methods of creating a will. The words in a will have very specific meanings and can have surprising results if you don't understand the definitions and the rules.

Generally speaking, it is better in the long run to have a lawyer prepare your will to be sure it is valid in your state. Then, you won't need to wonder if you've made a mistake or left out something important. And your heirs and the court won't have to deal with wondering what you meant.

## Internet Forms

There are hundreds of websites where you can find a form will. Some of the websites allow you to download the document free of charge, while others charge a fee for the download. Some documents are in PDF format and cannot be changed, and others are downloaded into a word-processing format. There are also websites that have interactive forms, allowing you to create a will online and download the finished document. Most of the interactive websites charge a fee, sometimes very little, as noted in Appendix B.

The American Bar Association has recommended that state bar associations begin providing self-help legal information on the state bar association websites. The sentiment seems to be that if a state bar association is providing information on its website, it will be accurate and reliable. Visit *www.bestcase.com/statebar.htm* to find the bar association in your state.

## Books

There are several books that contain legal forms in text or on CDs and some that are now devoted to will forms. Take time to visit your local library or law school to see whether one of the will samples works for you. You may be surprised by the many varieties of forms a will can take!

The rules you must follow to create a valid will can vary slightly from state to state. If you draft your own will, even with the best form available, it's a good idea to have a lawyer who is licensed in your state review the form you've prepared. He can make sure it is valid and that the will has been signed following the proper formalities.

Many brokerage firms, financial planners, and bank trust departments offer brochures and information about investments and estate planning. If you don't want to get on someone's mailing list by requesting their materials, check your library or bookstore for publications that teach you about wills and estate planning. Some of these books cover topics in such complicated terms that it is difficult to get what is often referred to as "meat and potatoes advice." But there are more on the market today that offer understandable suggestions.

## Handwritten (or Holographic) Wills

You need to be very careful with handwritten wills. A handwritten or holographic will typically refers to a will that you write in your own handwriting and did not sign in the presence of two witnesses and a notary.

Unless it is an emergency situation that prevents you from obtaining a will form or visiting a lawyer, it isn't a good idea to write your will in your own handwriting. Even if you sign the document in the presence of two witnesses and a notary, you could make a mistake, accidentally omit something important, or use words that may be confusing to the probate court.

**QUESTION?**

**If I write my will in my own handwriting, will it be valid?**
If you write out your will, date the document, and sign your name in the presence of two witnesses and a notary, you have a valid will in most states. You'll need to check with the register of wills in your state or county to see whether a holographic (handwritten) will is acceptable.

## Using Computer Software

There are numerous computer software programs that allow you to create your own will. Some of the programs have wills you can print and then fill in the blanks. Most of the programs guide you through a questionnaire regarding who you would like to serve as your executor and how you would like your property distributed. When you complete the questionnaire, the computer program generates a will for you.

Wills generated by computer software can be very good. The programs ask you very straightforward questions, then take your answers and convert your instructions into a will. When you use any computer program to create your will, however, it is very important that you understand the questions the program is asking. The computer program cannot read your mind. It can only generate a will in response to your answers. Again, check with an attorney in your state to be certain the will meets your state's requirements.

## Hiring a Lawyer to Prepare the Will

A lawyer understands the legal significance of the technical words and can make sure you sign your will with the proper formalities. He knows to ask about your assets, the persons or institutions you wish to support, and any specific directives you might want to include that you hadn't thought of. A lawyer can also advise you about any unusual laws that might exist in your state about inheriting property and advise you regarding any exposure your estate might have to federal or state estate taxes. He can also provide guidance on powers of attorney, medical directives and other estate planning issues.

## Sample Will

When a lawyer completes your will, it will look similar to the sample will contained in this section. The information specific to the hypothetical client, Jane, is in bold.

LAST WILL AND TESTAMENT
OF
JANE A. DOE

I, **JANE A. DOE**, a resident of **Sarasota County, Florida**, do make, publish, and declare this to be my Last Will and Testament, hereby revoking all former wills and codicils.

I.
DECLARATIONS

My husband is **JOHN ALEXANDER DOE**. I have **two (2) children, JACK JOSEPH DOE and JAMIE ANN DOE.** Except as otherwise qualified, the words "child" or "children" when used in this Will with reference to me shall mean all my above-named children. The words "child" or "children" when used in this Will with reference to any person other than me **shall mean all natural and adopted children** including natural children born after the death of their parent **but excluding stepchildren and foster children.** The word "descendants" when used in this Will shall mean all of the person's lineal descendants of all generations, except those who are descendants of a living descendant, with the relationship of parent and child at each generation being determined under governing law. To be a child or descendant by virtue of adoption, the person must be adopted while a minor.

## II.
## PAYMENT OF DEBTS

I direct payment of all debts enforceable against me during my lifetime which are presented in a timely manner during the administration of my estate, the expenses of my last illness and funeral, burial, cemetery marker, cremation, or other disposition of my body, and the expenses of administration of my estate, provided that if any property (including life insurance) owned by me jointly, or individually, passing under this Will or otherwise, shall be encumbered by a mortgage, pledge, security interest, loan, lien, or unpaid taxes, the indebtedness secured by such encumbrance shall not be charged to or paid by my estate but such property shall pass subject to all encumbrances existing at my death.

## III.
## SPECIFIC DEVISES OF TANGIBLE PERSONAL PROPERTY

(1) I devise **to my husband**, if he survives me, all my clothing, jewelry, watches, household goods, personal effects, motor vehicles, household furniture and fixtures, dishes, china, silver, athletic and sporting equipment, books, collections, yard and maintenance equipment, tools, works of art, antiques, and all other tangible personal property (excluding therefrom tangible personal property owned by me and used in connection with any business I may own) not heretofore specifically devised or otherwise effectually disposed of, such items hereinafter referred to collectively as my "personal property." Further, I may leave a list or other document directing certain items of my personal property to particular children or other persons. If I do this, I request that my bequests be honored.

(2) If **my husband** fails to survive me, I devise my personal property and the tangible personal property of a similar nature received by me from **my husband** at his death, **to my surviving children** (or all to one if only one survives), **to be divided by them as they agree, or if they fail to agree within six (6) months after my death, in equal shares, the assets constituting such**

equal shares to be determined by my Executor, whose decision shall be final and binding on all interested parties.

(3) **If my husband and children all fail to survive me,** these specific devises shall lapse and become part of the residue of my estate.

(4) All expenses incurred in the safeguarding and delivery of tangible personal property, including, without limitation, storage, packing, shipping, and insurance expenses, shall be treated as an expense of the administration of my estate and shall not be charged against the devisee who receives such tangible personal property.

(5) I devise all of my insurance policies that provide indemnity for the loss of any of my personal or real property by fire, windstorm, or other similar casualty (including any claim for the loss of any such property that I might have at the time of my death against any insurance company) to those persons or entities who shall become the owners of such properties by reason of my death, whether such ownership be acquired under the provisions of this Will or otherwise.

## IV.
## RESIDUARY DEVISE

All the rest and residue of my estate, wherever situated, including lapsed devises, but expressly excluding any property over which I may have power of appointment at my death, **I devise to my husband, JOHN ALEXANDER DOE. In the event he predeceases me, my residuary estate shall be distributed to my children, JACK JOSEPH DOE and JAMIE ANN DOE, in equal shares, per stirpes.**

**If my husband and all my children and their descendants all fail to survive me, I devise said residue to the SOUTHEASTERN DOG RESCUE, INC., 1234 Puppy Lane, Anytown, FL 12345, (555) 555-5555.**

## V.
## TAXES

All inheritance, estate, succession, transfer, and other estate taxes, both federal and state, including any interest or penalties thereon, charged against my estate or any person or entity, which become payable by reason of my death, whether in respect to property passing under this Will or otherwise, except any taxes imposed on any generation-skipping transfer under Chapter 13 of the United States Internal Revenue Code of 1954, as amended, or any corresponding provision of any future United States law, and except taxes attributable to any taxable power of appointment I have, shall be paid out of the residue of my probate estate without apportionment and no part thereof shall be charged back or imposed on any such person or entity. My Executor shall have the power to select tax years and make all other decisions and elections permitted under any applicable income, estate, or inheritance tax law, including the imposition of a lien on estate assets to secure tax payments, without regard to the effect thereof, if any, on any devisee of my estate, and, if any such decision or election shall be made, to apportion, or refrain from apportioning, the consequences thereof among the devisees of my estate, all in such manner as my Executor shall deem appropriate. If my Executor in good faith decides that there is uncertainty as to the inclusion of particular property in my gross estate for federal estate tax purposes, then such property may, in the discretion of my Executor, be excluded from my gross estate in my federal estate tax return. The decision of my Executor as to the date that should be selected for the valuation of property in my gross estate for federal estate tax purposes shall be conclusive on all concerned.

## VI.
### SURVIVORSHIP

Any devisee of this Will who dies within sixty (60) days after my death shall be deemed to have failed to survive me and this Will shall be interpreted and my estate administered as though I had survived such devisee.

## VII.
### NO CONTRACT

This Will is being executed on even date with a Will of my husband, but in no event shall said Wills be considered joint and/or mutual. It is my express intent that the survivor of myself and my husband shall in no way be restricted thereby in the use, management, enjoyment, or disposition of our estates or his separate estate by subsequent gift, will, or sale.

## VIII.
## ADMINISTRATIVE POWERS OF EXECUTOR

I give to my Executor, in addition to and not in limitation of all common law and statutory powers, the following powers: to retain any estate asset at any time received, for such period as my Executor shall deem advisable; to invest or reinvest in any property, real or personal; to sell, exchange, lease, give options upon, partition, or otherwise dispose of any property, real or personal, in my estate, at public or private sale, without regard to the necessity of such sale for the purpose of paying debts, taxes, or legacies, for cash or other consideration or on credit and upon such terms and conditions as my Executor deems advisable; to adjust, compromise, and settle all matters of business and claims in favor of or against my estate; to insure, repair, maintain, and preserve property; to retain and continue any business or business interest in which I am engaged or which I own; to give proxies and hold or register securities in the name of a nominee, a securities depositor, or in any other form convenient for my estate; to exercise any stock option or any other kind of option; to join in mergers, reorganizations, joint creditors actions, or other similar arrangements; to allocate and apportion receipts and disbursements to income or principal reasonably and in accordance with sound estate accounting principles; to sue for tax refunds; to borrow in the name of my estate, including the right to borrow from a corporate Executor or any affiliate, and in connection therewith, to mortgage, pledge, or encumber estate assets, provided my Executor shall not be personally liable and that any such loan shall be payable out of estate assets only; to join in the filing of joint income or gift tax returns with my husband; to petition for the appointment of or actually appoint an ancillary estate fiduciary and to pay the expenses of ancillary administration; to distribute my estate in cash or in kind, or partly in cash and partly in kind, as my Executor deems advisable, and to satisfy a specific dollar amount devise in kind, in the discretion of my Executor, and, for purposes of distribution, to value assets reasonably and in good faith as of the date of distribution, provided that my Executor shall not be required to distribute a proportionate amount of each asset to each devisee but may instead make nonpro rata distributions, and provided further, that in making distributions, my Executor may, but shall not be required to, take account of the income tax basis in relation to market value of assets distributed; to distribute assets directly to the devisee, to a legally appointed Guardian or Conservator or, whereby permitted by law, to a custodian under any Uniform Gifts to Minors Act, including a custodian selected by my Executor; and to do any and all things necessary or proper to complete the administration of my estate, all as fully as I could do if living. All such powers may be exercised without application to any court and shall be exercisable by any alternate, survivor, or successor Executor(s).

## IX.
## EXECUTOR

**I appoint JOHN ALEXANDER DOE as Executor. In the event JOHN ALEXANDER DOE cannot serve, I appoint my daughter, JAMIE ANN DOE, as Executor. If JAMIE ANN DOE cannot serve, I appoint JACK JOSEPH DOE as Executor. I direct that no bond be required of any executor named in this Will.**

IN WITNESS WHEREOF, I have set my hand and seal to this, my Last Will and Testament, consisting of this and the preceding **(insert number of pages)** typewritten pages, and the witness provisions hereinafter, and for the purpose of identification I have signed this and the preceding pages, all in the presence of the persons witnessing it at my request at Sarasota County, Florida, on this _____ day of June, 20____.

_____
**JANE A. DOE**

On this ___ day of June, 20____, **JANE A. DOE** declared to us, the undersigned, that the foregoing instrument consisting of these witness provisions and the foregoing **(insert number of pages)**, was her Last Will and Testament and she requested us to act as witnesses to the same and to her signature thereon. She thereupon signed said Will in our presence, we being present at the same time. We now, at her request, in her presence, and in the presence of each other, do hereunto subscribe our names as witnesses. We, and each of us, declare that we believe this Testatrix to be of sound mind and memory.

WITNESSES:

_____

Witness Number One

_____

Witness Number Two

AFFIDAVIT OF EXECUTION

STATE OF FLORIDA
COUNTY OF SARASOTA

We, **JANE A. DOE, [Insert Name Witness 1], and [Insert Name Witness 2],** the Testatrix and the witnesses, respectively, whose names are signed to the attached or foregoing instrument, having been sworn, declared to the undersigned officer that the Testatrix, in the presence of witnesses, signed the instrument as the Testatrix's Last Will, that the Testatrix signed, and that each of the witnesses, in the presence of the Testatrix and in the presence of each other, signed the Will as a witness.

_____

**JANE A. DOE**

WITNESSES:

_____

Witness Number One

_____

Witness Number Two

Subscribed and sworn to before me by **JANE A. DOE**, the Testatrix who is personally known to me or who has produced _____ as identification, and by **[Insert Name Witness 1]**, a witness who is personally known to me or who has produced _____ as identification, and by **[Insert Name Witness 2]**, a witness who is personally known to me or who has produced _____ as identification, on this ___ day of June, 20____.

_____
Signature of Notary Public
Sarasota County, Florida
My Commission Expires:

Some states require that your will have an Affidavit of Execution like the one found in the sample document. The Affidavit, which is the same as the self-proving will mentioned earlier, must be signed in the presence of the same two witnesses and a notary. It's a good idea to make sure your will would meet the requirement of any state where you might live or have property.

# CHAPTER 9

# Changing Your Will

There are very few things in your life that stay the same forever. Your life changes, as do the lives of your loved ones. You need to know how to change your will to accommodate those changing needs. It is not difficult to change your will; you just need to know the rules.

## Ways to Change Your Will

Although it is not hard to change your will, it is important to follow the proper formalities and to check your state law about its requirements. If you don't make the changes correctly, you may actually make your entire will invalid. The formalities you need to follow may not make sense to you, but they exist to make sure that someone does not change your will without your permission.

There are two primary ways to change your will:

1. You can make and sign a new document.
2. You can amend your will by a codicil.

Changing your will requires following the same rules as for your original will. Although this process may seem cumbersome, it is for your protection and to be certain the will is valid.

When you make a new will, make sure that you sign it in the presence of two witnesses and a notary. You need to sign the new will with the same formalities you followed when you signed your original will.

## Make a New Document

The best way to change your will is to make a new one. In the old days, making a new will meant typing a new document. Today almost everyone has access to a word processor. Making the changes you want is as easy as pushing the delete button and inserting the changes. When you make a new will, it gives you a chance to review all of the provisions of the old will. By the time you alter your will, you may own different property, there may have been a birth or a death in your family, and it's likely that the needs of your loved ones have changed.

### Repeating the Process

When you change your will, you should again ask yourself who, what, where, when, and why. Who is receiving your property, what are they receiving, where are they going to take possession of the property, when do you want them to have the property, and why?

When you make a new will, it is highly recommended that in addition to stating all prior wills are revoked, you destroy the old will and all copies. This is not the time to keep your old papers to memorialize what you wanted several years ago. You don't want multiple wills presented to the probate court after you are gone.

When you follow this process regarding each piece of property you own, it is much more likely that your instructions will be clear, minimizing the possibility that someone will contest your will. Think of the process as a game—the players and the property are constantly changing.

## The Former Will

When you revoke your old will by making a new one, you need to be very careful that your new will specifically states that you are making a new will and that it completely revokes all prior wills.

There is a very good reason why you need to be very specific when you make a new will: if the new will does not say that all old wills are revoked, and an old will is found, both documents could be admitted to probate. Then, your property will be distributed according to the provisions of both documents.

For example, assume you sign your first will and leave $50,000 to your friend Jane. Three years later, you sign will number two. You intended the second will to revoke the first one, but it does not specifically state that the first will is revoked. The second will leaves $100,000 to Jane. If the second will does not revoke the first will, Jane might receive both the $50,000 distribution from the first will and $100,000 from the second. This may not be what you intended, but you are not alive to tell the probate court what you did intend.

## Strike a Provision

In some states it may be possible to change your will by striking one or more provisions. If a person contests your will, seeking a distribution of the property, your executor must prove that you struck the provision with the intent to revoke that provision. There needs to be proof because the court wants to be satisfied that you were the person who struck the provision and that you intended to revoke the provision.

Not all states permit striking or writing on a will. Check your state laws before taking this route to changing your will.

To prove your intent, you should sign any changes you make and have the changes witnessed and notarized just as you did with your original will.

### Family Fights Get Expensive

To show how important proof is, let's say your daughter finds your original will in your desk drawer. She discovers that you left your business to her brother and the rest of your property to her and your son equally. She takes out a pen and strikes the provision leaving the business to her brother. She then puts the will back in the desk drawer.

After you are gone, your daughter argues that you wanted all of your property divided equally between her and her brother. Your son, on the other hand, will need to introduce evidence to the probate court that you did not strike the provision regarding the business, and that he is entitled to the business and that the rest of your property should be divided between him and his sister. Your daughter will hire a lawyer to argue her position, your son will need to hire a lawyer to prove that you did not strike the provision, and the executor must hire a lawyer to represent the estate's interest. It gets very expensive when your family fights over what you intended.

**FACT**

If you did not sign or initial the change in the presence of two witnesses and a notary, the lawyer for the estate must prove that it is your initial or signature, and that it is evidence that you intended to make the change.

## Proving Your Intent

If you change your document by striking a provision and someone contests, there will be a hearing before the probate court judge to prove your intent. The lawyer for the estate might try to prove your intent by calling witnesses who were with you and saw you strike the provision. But if the witness has an interest in your property, the probate court judge might not believe him. Or perhaps you signed your name or initialed the document when you struck the provision.

If your will was in a secure place, such as your safe-deposit box, proof may be available that you were the only one with access to the will and, therefore, the change had to be made by you. Because of the need to prove your intent after you're gone, and because state laws vary, striking a provision is not the best way to change your will.

## Make Written Changes

It used to be very common for a person to try to change her will by making written changes to the existing document to save the hassle of retyping. Let's say you do one of the following:

- Insert a handwritten change within the will.
- Write on the back of the will, "I hereby revoke this will."
- Write on the last page of the will, "I hereby revoke this will."

If you did not sign your name to the written change in the presence of two witnesses and a notary, the attempt to change or revoke your will may not be accepted by the court. You could argue that the need to have two witnesses and a notary for a change is unnecessary. However, the rules are designed to protect against someone making a change without your permission. In the end, if you didn't follow the proper procedure, it won't matter whether the whole world knew that you wanted to make the change or revoke the document. You will not be available to tell the probate court what you wanted.

In prior years it was acceptable to strike out a provision or to insert changes into an existing will as long as you initialed it. Today, however, some states may not accept a will with any markings or writing on it.

Striking or writing in changes on a will is a risky method of making revisions, even with witnesses and a notary, and you could be invalidating your whole will.

Modern technology makes it easy to make changes on a word processor, and a new will can be printed out with minimum fuss. You can even keep your will on your home computer instead of relying on the lawyer's office to make the changes for you.

## Add an Amendment

You can also make a change by adding an amendment to your will. This is called a codicil. If you choose to change your will with a codicil, you should:

- Make your changes on a separate piece of paper.
- State that you are changing your will.
- Identify the date of the original will you are changing.
- Write down the changes you want, noting the article(s) in the original will.
- Sign the amendment in the presence of two witnesses and a notary.

When you change your will with a codicil, you need to make sure that the changes you are making are clear and that they do not conflict with any of the provisions in your original will. For example, assume you want to change your executor. Your codicil would look like the example below.

John Doe and the two witnesses should sign their names to the codicil in the presence of two witnesses and a notary. The notary will then sign the codicil and stamp it with her notary stamp. Since you need to sign your name to any changes you make to your will in the presence of two witnesses and a notary, you might just as well make a new will!

### CODICIL TO WILL

I, John Doe, on this 10th day of May, 2003, hereby execute this Codicil to my will dated February 1, 1997. I hereby revoke the portion of Article X that named Bill Smith as my Executor. I hereby name David Jones to serve as Executor.

Witnesses:

_____          _____

Anna Miller                                                          John Doe


_____

Betty White
County of Sarasota
State of Florida


On this 10th day of May 2003 personally appeared John Doe. John Doe executed a Codicil to his will, originally executed on the 1st day of February 1997. John Doe executed his Codicil in the presence of the two witnesses, Anna Miller and Betty White. Anna Miller and Betty White are over the age of 21 and believe John Doe is of sound mind.

_____

Notary,
Sarasota County, Florida
My commission expires on _____

## *Destroy the Document*

You can revoke your will by the physical act of burning, tearing, or obliterating it. When you revoke your will by physical act, the executor bears the burden of proving that the physical act was done with the intent to revoke your will. This is not a foolproof way to revoke your will, unless you destroy the original and all copies.

The more complicated the changes you want to make, the harder it is to change your will with a codicil. If you have many changes or your changes are confusing, you run the risk that a loved one will not understand what you wanted and will contest your will.

If you destroy only your original will and someone happens to find a copy of it, he can try to introduce the copy to the probate court. However, the person introducing the copy has the burden of proving that you did not destroy the document with the intent to revoke. Although this can be difficult for someone to prove, whenever someone contests anything about your will, the person contesting must hire a lawyer to present his case, and your executor has to hire a lawyer to represent the estate.

## *Where Should You Keep Your Original Will?*

Whoever has control of the original will can affect whether or not a change you made will be accepted as valid. Your original is likely in one of the following places:

- In your possession, typically in your home
- In a safe-deposit box
- With your lawyer
- On file with the probate court

## In Your Possession

When your original will is in your possession, it is less likely a question will arise as to whether any changes were made. The more people who have physical access to your will, however, the greater the chance someone can alter the will without your permission.

Perhaps you are thinking about making a change. For example, assume you take your will out of your desk, and you make some notes on the document or put a line through several provisions. You aren't certain you are ready to make the change, so you put your will back into the desk drawer. You die. When the document is admitted to probate, there will probably be a debate about whether you struck certain provisions with the intent to revoke them or were merely thinking about making changes.

Unless you have interviewed and documented how the lawyer is going to charge to probate your estate when you are gone, you need to remind your family that they don't have to hire that lawyer to probate your estate merely because she has possession of the original will.

## In a Safe-Deposit Box

The significance of having your will in your safe-deposit box depends on who had access to the box while you were alive. If someone has access to your safe-deposit box, she could remove your will and make changes without your permission. Even if you were the only one with access to the box, you might bring your will home, where someone could alter it. The fact that the will was kept in the safe-deposit box may or may not help your executor prove that a change was made to your will.

## With Your Lawyer

When your lawyer keeps the original will, the chance that changes were made without your permission is minimal. No self-respecting lawyer would allow you to make a change to your will without having you sign a document that makes the changes in the presence of two witnesses and a notary. If you leave your original will with your lawyer, you need to make sure your loved ones know how to contact him.

### On File with the Probate Court

If you put your original will on deposit with the probate court in the county where you are living, you are the only person who has access to the will. When you want to make changes, you can do so and then return the new, changed will to the probate court. Having the document on deposit with the probate court minimizes the chance that someone other than you will alter your will. If you remove your will from the probate court to make changes, you need to be sure to make the desired changes with the necessary formalities.

It is not difficult to change your will, but it is important that you make the changes correctly. Otherwise, the probate court will invalidate your will or a portion of your will, and your intentions will be defeated. The best way to change your will is to make a new one.

## A Lawyer Isn't Required

When you understand the rules about how to change your will, you do not have to have a lawyer. You just need to be careful that you are making the changes correctly and that the formalities to make the changes valid have been met. Even if you follow the rules, it is possible that someone will challenge your will and allege that you were not the one who made the change. Remember, when you are gone, you are not available to tell the probate court what you wanted.

While not necessary, sometimes enlisting the help of a lawyer is in your best interest. If you have your lawyer change your will, she will talk to you about your changes and have you sign your will or codicil in the presence of two witnesses and a notary. The lawyer and her staff will be available to testify, if needed. This assures that the changes you want will be found valid after you are gone.

# CHAPTER 10

# Owning Property in Joint Name

Owning property in joint name is the simplest way for you to leave property to your loved ones. But it is important to understand that simple is not always the best. There are advantages and disadvantages you should consider before you decide that joint ownership is the estate plan for you.

## The Joint-Property Estate Plan

How many times have you heard the statement, "I don't need an estate plan; we own all of our property in joint name"? Joint property is a simple estate plan, but you need to weigh the advantages and disadvantages. As long as all of the joint tenants do not die in a common accident, joint property will pass automatically to the surviving joint tenant(s) when you die, avoiding probate.

You could set up a joint checking account with each of your children, in equal amounts, as a way to leave cash to each one at your death. You should have a very good reason for setting up a joint banking account with just one child—a reason other family members will understand.

For some people, owning property in joint name is their entire plan. For others, owning property in joint name is part of the estate plan. Get out those sheets of paper that describe each piece of property you own, and prepare to calculate the consequences of owning property in joint name. When you know the rules, you will be able to decide whether joint property is the best plan for you.

## Advantages and Disadvantages

The primary advantage of owning property in joint name with another person is that when you are gone, your property passes automatically to the surviving joint tenant. If you own property with one joint tenant, the surviving joint tenant will inherit 100 percent of the property upon your death. If you own property with more than one joint tenant, the property will pass in equal shares to the surviving joint tenants.

### Unexpected Consequences

Owning property in joint name is a simple way to have title to your property pass when you are gone, but there can be unexpected consequences when you die. There are several reasons that you may not want to place all of your property in joint name with another person or persons.

When you place most types of property in joint name with another person, you have made an irrevocable decision. If you change your mind about owning your property with the person you added as a joint tenant, you can't get the property back without the permission of your new joint tenant.

Also, with most types of property, when you add a person as a joint tenant (other than a spouse), you have made a taxable gift to that person. You will need to read Chapter 17 to learn the rules about gift taxes.

## Bank Accounts

When you add a person's name to your bank account, you usually are creating a joint tenancy. But, in the case of bank accounts, there is an exception to the rule that the joint tenancy is an irrevocable decision and a taxable gift to the other person. You need to ask your financial institution to outline the rights created when you add a name to your bank account. These rights can vary among financial institutions.

**ALERT!**

Beware! Any joint tenant can withdraw all of the funds from the account. Even though the decision to add a person's name to your bank account is not irrevocable, you might wake up one morning and find all of your money gone.

You have not made an irrevocable decision when you open a joint bank account because you are not treated as having made a gift until the person whose name you added withdraws money that he did not deposit.

## Your Will Doesn't Affect Joint Property

This is probably one of the most misunderstood concepts in estate planning. Your will has absolutely no effect on joint property. As a matter of fact, your will could say, "I leave the funds in XYZ Bank in equal shares to my children," but such a clause would be ignored if the bank account is in joint name. If you have four children but you have put one child's name on your bank account, the entire balance will belong to the child named on the account and will not pass in equal shares to all of your children. Remember, one reason you put your property in joint name was so that title would pass automatically to the joint tenant when you die.

Imagine the shock and disappointment of your children who are not joint tenants on your property. The other children will wonder whether you loved the child you included as a joint tenant more than you loved them. You may have put one child's name on an account as a matter of convenience. But after you are gone, your children have no way of knowing what you really intended.

## Property Owned Jointly with Your Spouse

Joint ownership of property between spouses makes a lot of sense. But, like most things, you need to consider whether any of the disadvantages of owning property in joint name with your spouse apply to you. The main advantage to owning property in joint name with your spouse is simplicity. When the first spouse dies, the surviving spouse owns the property and doesn't need to probate the property to obtain title.

There are differences among states about how property passes when a joint tenant dies. Most problems that arise after a person dies relate to confusion about how the property was actually titled. You should confirm with a lawyer in your state exactly how your property should be titled in order for it to be treated as joint property with survivorship rights.

There are three potential disadvantages to owning property in joint name with your spouse. First, your surviving spouse may lose an income tax advantage she might have had if the property had not been owned jointly. Second, if the property owned by both spouses is subject to federal estate taxes, it can cost a family a considerable amount of money. Third, joint ownership does not allow the spouse who died first to have any control over what the surviving spouse does with the property.

## Taxes and Cost Basis

There are special income tax rules that apply to property owned jointly by spouses. To understand a potential disadvantage to joint ownership, you need to learn the rules about cost basis. Cost basis is the amount you subtract from the sale price of the property to compute your gain or loss when you sell a piece of property. When you die, most of the property you own on the date of your death will get a step-up in cost basis equal to the fair market value of the property at that time.

**FACT**

Cost basis is usually your purchase price plus expenditures such as improvements on real property or other allowable expenses. You should check the IRS rules about which expenses may be added to your cost. You should also keep track of those costs for reference if you were to sell.

For example, assume you bought one share of ABC stock for $10; $10 is your cost basis. Now assume that when you die, the stock is worth $90 a share. You owned the stock in your individual name and not in joint tenancy with your spouse, and you leave the stock to your spouse in your will. Your spouse will get a new cost basis in the stock equal to $90. If your spouse sells the stock later for $95, your spouse's gain on the sale will be $5 ($95 sale price minus $90 cost basis). If you had sold the stock while you were alive for $95, you would have had an $85 gain ($95 sale price minus your cost basis of $10).

The tax rules are different, however, if you own property in joint name with your spouse. As you know, when you own property in joint name with your spouse, the spouse owns the property automatically. But your surviving spouse receives only a 50 percent increase in cost basis plus half of the original basis.

Let us return to the earlier example. You paid $10 for the one share of stock in ABC Company and put the stock in joint name with your spouse. When you die, the stock is worth $90. Your spouse has a cost basis of 50 percent of the fair market value of the stock when you died, or $45, plus she gets to add half of what you paid for the stock, or $5. Your surviving spouse's cost basis is $45 plus $5. Now when she sells the share of ABC Company stock for $95, she has a $45 gain ($95 sale price minus $50 cost basis). Compare this to the $5 gain she would have had if you had left the share to your spouse in your will. This is a very important consequence to owning property in joint name with your spouse, since the gain may be subject to income taxes.

**FACT**

When spouses own property in joint name, they make a trade. They exchange the advantage of a full step-up in cost basis for the simplicity associated with the fact that joint property passes automatically to the surviving joint spouse.

## Property May Go Down in Value

If the property you own has gone down in value, and you leave the property to your surviving spouse, she will take the lower value as her cost basis. For example, assume you bought one share of DEF stock for $100. The stock is worth $20 when you die. If the stock was in joint name with your spouse, her new cost basis would be $60—half of what you paid ($50), plus half of the value of the stock when you died, or $10 ($50 + $10 = $60). If the stock of DEF had been in your individual name, your spouse would have a cost basis equal to the value of the stock on the date of your death: $20.

In this case, joint ownership with your spouse gives you a better cost basis. You would like the cost basis to be as high as possible. If your spouse sells the one share of DEF stock that had been owned in joint name for $20, he will have a loss on his return of $40 (sale price of $20 minus cost basis of $60 equals $40 loss). If you had owned the stock in your individual name and left the stock to your spouse, she would not have any gain or loss if she sold the stock for $20 (sale price of $20 minus cost basis of $20 equals no gain or loss).

**ALERT!**

If you think the income tax cost-basis rules could be a disadvantage for you, you need to read Chapter 17 about federal estate taxes. In certain circumstances, owning all of your property in joint name with your spouse could cause your family to owe federal estate taxes. Chapter 18 teaches you how this result could be avoided.

When you summarize information about each piece of property you own on a separate piece of paper for your notebook, you should compute the cost basis for each. Calculate the cost basis your spouse would receive if you owned your property in joint name and compare it with the cost basis he would receive if your property was owned in your individual name. This may help you plan.

## Loss of Control

When you own all of your property in joint name with your spouse, you have no control over what your spouse does with your property when you are gone. Many people say this doesn't matter, because they are confident that their spouse is capable of managing the property. But the world is a more complicated place than it was in days gone by.

There are ways you can leave property to your spouse and not have to worry about whether your spouse will be sued and lose the property, or whether someone will try to take advantage of him when you are gone. Before you make the decision to own your property in joint name, you should read Chapters 11 through 14 and consider the advantages of creating a trust for your spouse.

# Joint Property with Someone Else

The basic rule that the property passes automatically to the surviving joint tenant is the same whether your joint tenant is your spouse or someone else.

However, the income tax cost-basis rules are different, as noted in the previous section. For persons who are not your spouse, the surviving joint tenant gets an increase in cost basis equal to the percentage of contribution to the acquisition cost of the property made by the person who just died.

You need to analyze the cost basis of the property that will be acquired by your surviving joint tenants. The cost basis rules for spouses who are joint tenants are different from those for all other joint tenants. You should also calculate the federal estate tax exposure that may be created for your surviving joint tenants.

For example, assume you and your brother purchase a piece of property and put the title in your joint names. Assume the property cost $100,000. You contributed $40,000, which equals 40 percent of the purchase price. Your brother contributed $60,000 to the purchase price. When you die, the property is worth $200,000. Your brother keeps his original cost basis of $60,000, the amount he paid for the property, plus he will increase his cost basis by $80,000. The increase in your brother's cost basis is the percentage of the purchase price you contributed, 40 percent, times the value of the property when you die (40% × $200,000 = $80,000). Your brother's new cost basis is $60,000 + $80,000 = $140,000. If your brother sells the property for $210,000 after you are gone, your brother will have a $70,000 gain ($210,000 selling price minus his cost basis of $140,000).

This rule can work very nicely when parents place property in joint name with their children and pay for the entire purchase price. For example, assume you place the same property worth $100,000 in joint name with your daughter. You pay the entire purchase price of $100,000. When you die, the property is worth $200,000. Your daughter will receive the property automatically because she is the surviving joint tenant. Because your daughter contributed nothing toward the purchase price of the property, she gets a 100 percent step-up in cost basis. This result occurs because the surviving joint tenant who is not a spouse increases her basis equal to the percentage contributed to the purchase of the property by the person who died. You contributed 100 percent; therefore your daughter gets 100 percent of the value of the property at the date of your death as her new cost basis. If the property is worth $200,000 when you die, her new cost basis is $200,000.

**QUESTION?**

**Is it a good plan to place property in joint name with your children?** It can be. The child will receive the property automatically as the surviving joint tenant. The child also gets a full increase in cost basis (assuming the child contributed nothing to the acquisition).

But remember, when you place property in joint name with someone other than your spouse, you are making an irrevocable gift to that individual.

## *Unmarried Partners*

Today there are many relationships in which a couple is not married. These unmarried partners do not have the gift and tax advantages that married couples enjoy. For example, married couples can make unlimited gifts to one another during their lifetimes. At death, their entire estate can be left to the surviving spouse without any tax under the unlimited marital deduction.

**ALERT!**

If you are not married to your partner, you need to be particularly careful in the way you title property, make gifts, or include that partner in your estate plan. If your estate is less than the $1 million gift exclusion or the unified credit in effect at the time of your death, you may be able to transfer your estate to your partner without tax. See Chapter 17 and the Glossary for more details about the unified credit.

Families may object to your leaving your estate to a partner instead of to them. And, if you and your partner have jointly owned property and you later separate, you will need a lawyer to help undo any planning you have put into place.

## Multiple Joint Tenants

You can have as many joint tenants as you want. Assume your spouse is gone, and you have two children. You decide to add the children as joint tenants on the deed to your home. Assume your home is worth $100,000 at the time you add your children's names to the deed. When you add the children's name to the deed, you have made an irrevocable gift of $33,333.33 to each child. When you die, your children will each own a 50 percent interest in your home. Then, if one of your children dies, the home will belong 100 percent to the surviving child.

This may or may not be what you want. Some parents would want the children of a child who dies to have the property. This would not happen if you add your children's names to the deed. The title to the home would automatically pass to the surviving child, even if the child who died had children.

## Gift Tax Consequences

There are different gift tax consequences when a person creates a joint tenancy with his spouse versus anyone else. When you create a joint tenancy with your spouse, there are no gift taxes. You can give your spouse an unlimited amount of property without gift taxes. The IRS calls this benefit the unlimited marital deduction.

When you create a joint tenancy with someone other than your spouse, you are making a gift that is subject to gift taxes. If you take a piece of property that is worth $100,000 and put the property in joint name with your son or partner, or anyone else, you have made a $50,000 gift to that person. While this book won't get into the particulars of gift taxes until Chapter 17, for now it is important to understand that when you create most joint tenancies with someone who is not your spouse, you are making an irrevocable gift that is subject to gift taxes.

## CHAPTER 11

# A Trust May Be Right for Your Plan

You don't have to be rich to enjoy the benefits of a trust. Nobody wants her family to spend money on lawyer fees that could have been avoided. When you understand the rules, you can have a trust prepared at a reasonable cost, and your family can enjoy the same benefits as rich people. This chapter will show you how.

# What Is a Trust?

A trust is a legal document that allows you to maintain 100 percent control of your property while you are living. After you pass on, your trust can either transfer your property to your loved ones immediately or stay in place and distribute your property over time.

A trust involves three parties: the creator, the trustee, and the beneficiaries. What most people don't understand about a trust is that you can be all three parties while you are living. The fact that you wear all three hats allows you to control all of the decisions and puts a plan in place to distribute your property when you are gone.

Don't get confused by the terminology. You may have heard about living trusts, family trusts, marital trusts, insurance trusts, or revocable trusts. These are all terms that describe the purpose of that particular trust. In fact, all trusts have the same basic components.

# The Creator

You are the creator of your trust. The creator of the trust is often referred to in legal terms as the grantor or the settlor of the trust. These are just different words to describe exactly the same thing. As the creator, you are going to make all the decisions about your trust. You will decide:

- What property is going to be transferred to your trust
- Who will serve as trustee while you are living
- Who will serve as trustee after you are gone
- What the trustee will do with the property while you are living
- Who will receive your property upon your death

After your trust document is complete, you will take all the property you now own in your individual name, or the property you want to be in the trust, and transfer ownership of the property into the name of the trustee. Most people name themselves as the initial trustee. It seems unnecessary, even silly, to transfer ownership of your property from your name to your name as trustee, but keep reading. You'll see what happens.

## The Trustee

When you create a trust, you need to name a trustee. The trustee will hold legal title to the property you transfer into the trust. You will usually name yourself as the initial trustee because you want to maintain control of your property. However, it is possible for you to name someone else to serve as the initial trustee if you are uncomfortable managing the property.

**FACT**

When you create your trust, you can name more than one initial trustee; they are called co-trustees. Sometimes a husband and wife will want to serve as co-trustees of each other's trust. This allows the spouses to continue to make joint decisions about the property that has been transferred to either of their trusts.

You also need to name a trustee who will become the trustee when the initial trustee is gone. This is called a *successor trustee.* You can have more than one successor trustee. Successor co-trustees are very common when parents are creating trusts and they have more than one child. Typically a parent creates his trust, names himself as initial trustee, then names his spouse to serve as successor trustee. The parent then directs the trust to his children, when both spouses are gone, to serve as successor co-trustees.

## The Trustee Takes Control

When you can no longer serve as trustee, either because you have died or because you have become incapacitated, the person or entity you name as successor trustee automatically becomes the new trustee. It is like your successor steps into your shoes. When your successor trustee begins to serve, there is no change of ownership of the trust property and, therefore, your family does not need to probate your estate. Your trust owns all of your property. The trust just happens to have a new trustee after you are gone.

## Giving Instructions

Your next job as creator of your trust is to give your trustee instructions on what to do with your property and when. The instructions you put in your trust document typically have two parts. The first part of the instructions deals with what the trustee is required to do with the trust property while you are living. The second part of the instructions deals with what the successor trustee may or must do with the trust property after you are gone.

When you name all of your children as successor co-trustees, the children will have to agree on all of the decisions about your trust property. If your children can't make decisions together while you are living, don't expect them to develop this talent after you are gone.

While you are living you can do all of the things with your property you could do before you created the trust. Your trust document will give the trustee, who is typically you, the power to:

- Change the trust document.
- Use all of the income from the property for whatever you want.
- Sell the trust property.
- Borrow against the trust property.
- Give the trust property away.

The second set of instructions you put in your trust document tells your successor trustee how and when to distribute your property. These are the hard decisions and the most important part of the trust document. Chapter 12 describes in detail the types of instructions you can include. After you read Chapter 12, you will be able to create a plan for your property to put in your trust document.

## *The Beneficiaries*

Your trust document needs to establish who will receive your property. The person or persons who receive the benefits of the trust property are called beneficiaries. While you are living, you will probably name yourself as the beneficiary of your trust.

**FACT**

If you are the beneficiary of your trust, your trust document typically instructs the trustee (you) to distribute any of the trust property to you. Notice you are both the trustee and the beneficiary. Therefore, you are deciding what trust property to distribute to yourself. This is why you have control while you are living.

Most people know who they want to provide for, but don't understand the types of limitations that can be placed in a trust document to provide for the security of the beneficiaries. When you understand the types of powers you can give a successor trustee, and how you can limit the enjoyment of the property by your beneficiaries, it may actually change your mind about who you want to include in your plan. For instance, you may feel more comfortable including persons in your plan you otherwise wouldn't have because you can create conditions about what each person must do, or not do, to receive a distribution from your trust.

## *Powers of Appointment*

While you are alive, you can change anything about your trust document, including the beneficiaries. Although you are not available to make changes after your death, you can give someone else the power to change the beneficiaries after you are gone. This is called power of appointment. There are two types of powers of appointment: limited power of appointment and general power of appointment.

## Limited Power of Appointment

A limited power of appointment is when you name someone in your trust document giving that person the power to direct the trust property among a limited number of persons. This is a very important provision you should consider putting in your trust.

> The persons you name as beneficiaries in your trust document will become irrevocable when you are gone, unless you have given someone a limited or a general power of appointment to change the beneficiaries.

For example, assume you have a spouse and four children. You want your spouse to be the primary beneficiary of your trust after you are gone, and you want any property left in the trust after your spouse is gone to be distributed to your children. However, you may be reluctant to name your four children as equal beneficiaries. In that case, you can give your spouse a limited power of appointment to change the amount of property each of your four children will receive. Your spouse could live a long time after you are gone, and she may want to reward a child who is more helpful or even eliminate a child completely as a beneficiary.

The reason this power is called a limited power of appointment is because your spouse can only change the share each of your four children will receive. Your spouse can't remarry and leave all of your property to his new spouse because the new spouse is not within the limited class you established in your trust, namely, your four children.

## General Power of Appointment

The second type of power allows the person to whom you give a general power of appointment to convey or appoint your property to anyone she chooses.

Before you give anyone, even your spouse, a general power of appointment over your trust property after you are gone, you should understand that this person could change all of your beneficiaries and give your property to someone you might not have chosen as a beneficiary.

## Reasons for Creating a Trust

There are many reasons why you might want to create a trust. A trust allows you to control your property while you are living. If property is owned by your trust, it doesn't need to be probated when you die. A trust can save taxes. And a trust allows you to create a plan for your family.

Some of the reasons for having a trust may not apply to you. For instance, there are ways you can own your property that will allow your property to pass automatically to the surviving joint tenant without probate when you are gone. When you compare the advantages and disadvantages of owning property in joint name with the advantages and disadvantages of owning property in a trust, you may decide that you don't need a trust.

You could also learn that your estate will not owe any federal estate taxes. If that is so, you do not need to create a trust to reduce your taxes, but you might have other reasons to establish a trust.

Perhaps you are not interested in a management plan for your property after you are gone. You may simply want your property distributed to specific persons and decide that, even though it will be necessary to probate your property to transfer title to your loved ones, you need only a will to carry out your goals.

Every family is different. This is why it is important to carefully consider the advantages and disadvantages of all plans to find the one that would best suit your wants and the needs of your loved ones.

# Advantages of a Trust

There are many advantages to creating a trust. For example, your family can save money on probate and taxes, and you can put a more detailed plan in place to manage your property after you are gone. One of these advantages to creating a trust may be more important to you and your family than another.

## Probate

One of the biggest advantages to creating a trust is that the property that is owned by your trust avoids the probate process after you are gone. When you create a trust, you usually name yourself as the initial trustee. You transfer the property you want owned by the trust to yourself as trustee.

When you serve as trustee while you are living, about the only thing that has changed for you by creating a trust is that your property is not owned by you as an individual, but is owned by you as trustee for your own benefit. You maintain 100 percent control of your property.

You also name a successor trustee in your trust document. The successor trustee automatically owns the property when you are gone, thus avoiding the probate process. This is a huge advantage. It can be expensive for your family to probate your estate after you are gone, depending on the fees in your state, and it does takes time to complete the process.

## Management

This is an advantage that is not available with any other type of estate planning document. Your trust document has detailed instructions on who will manage your property after you are gone or if you become incapacitated. The successor trustee you name will automatically hold the legal title to your trust property. Your trust document will provide instructions to your successor trustee on what to do with that property.

The instructions you give your successor trustee might be very simple and straightforward. For instance, the trust could say, "My successor trustee shall distribute all of the trust property to my spouse," or "My successor trustee shall, if my spouse and I are both gone, distribute my trust property in equal shares to my children." If this is your plan, the only advantage you have gained by creating a trust is that of saving your family the cost and delay associated with the probate process.

When you read Chapter 12 and discover the types of powers and discretion you can give your successor trustee, you will be surprised. You may consider creating a trust even if you thought your property and estate plan was very simple.

### Taxes

It is important that you determine whether your estate will be subject to federal estate taxes after you and your spouse are gone. Federal estate taxes are very expensive, but usually can be reduced by careful planning.

**FACT**

A trust can also be used to shelter the estate exclusion amount for estates that may owe federal estate taxes. If after you have read Chapter 18 you discover that your estate is subject to federal estate taxes, you absolutely should see a lawyer.

If you are married and you and your spouse own property in excess of the unified credit amount that can be transferred free of federal estate taxes, you can use trusts that include special tax-savings provisions to save your family federal estate taxes on that excess.

## Disadvantages of a Trust

The main disadvantage to creating a trust is that it takes you quite a bit of time to get organized and make the decisions needed. It is also more expensive to create a trust than it is to create a will. However, if you understand the rules, are organized, and have made all of the necessary decisions, the cost of creating a trust will be substantially reduced, and it will save your family money after your death.

## Time and Expense

The reason it is more expensive and time-consuming to create a trust than a will is because you need to transfer ownership of each piece of property from your own name to your name as the trustee of the trust. Earlier, it was recommended that you begin the planning process by purchasing a three-ring binder or notebook. Take a look at how many different sheets of paper you have, describing each individual piece of property. By flipping through your notebook, you can evaluate how complicated or expensive it will be to transfer ownership of your property to your trust. However, you may be pleasantly surprised to discover that you can transfer ownership of most of your property without the help of a lawyer and, possibly, without fees.

Be sure to check your state law, or the law of the state where you own property, to determine whether there is a real estate transfer fee for retitling.

On each of those separate pieces of paper, which describe every piece of property you own, you should write the following questions: "How do I transfer title to this piece of property?" "Is there a cost to do so?"

## Transferring Real Estate

If you own real estate, you need a deed to transfer the real estate from your name, or from joint name, to your name as trustee of your trust. It is highly recommended that you not try to prepare your own deed—there are too many ways you can make a mistake.

If you have a copy of your current deed, unless there is something complicated or unusual about your real estate, it should not cost a large sum to have a lawyer prepare a new deed to transfer the real estate to your name as trustee of your trust. The only change in the deed is the title.

## Transferring Bank Accounts

Most of your bank accounts can be changed into your name as trustee by completing a form with the bank. Sometimes the bank will require that you close the existing account and open a new one in your name as trustee of your trust. This may mean a visit to your bank, but it is not something you need to hire a lawyer to do. The bank may also require a copy of your trust document.

If you understand what a trust is and have made the necessary decisions, it should not take your lawyer much more time to prepare a trust document than it would take him to prepare a will. And it may save your family time, money, and hassle to have a trust in place. Remember that the fewer questions the lawyer has to ask you, the less time and expense it will take to create a will or trust.

## Transferring Stock Shares

If you own shares of stock in your individual name in certificate form, it may be almost impossible to change the name on those certificates.

If you have a brokerage account, ask if you can change the name on the account to your name as trustee of your trust. You may have to open a new brokerage account in your name as trustee. Though time-consuming, it isn't a difficult task.

Some brokerage firms will complete the paperwork to transfer the individual shares and certificates from your name to your new brokerage account free of charge.

## *Transferring Life Insurance, Annuities, and Retirement Accounts*

If you own life insurance or annuities or have retirement accounts, you are going to need to understand the rules about each of these individual investments before you decide whether you want your trust to be the beneficiary or owner of these types of assets. Each asset is covered in a later chapter.

Even though it takes time to transfer your assets to your name as trustee of your trust, imagine how expensive it would be for your survivors to transfer title after you are gone. Furthermore, if your property was in your name and you have no will or trust, your loved ones would have to pay a lawyer to obtain the approval of the probate court to make the transfers after you are gone.

# CHAPTER 12

# Decisions to Include Within a Trust

This chapter will help you understand the types of powers you can give your successor trustee and the conditions you can place on your beneficiaries. There are a lot of decisions to be made, but you will end up with a trust that accomplishes your goals and meets the needs of your loved ones.

# *Choosing Your Trust Beneficiaries*

Chapter 2 guided you through a process of deciding who should receive your property, what the person should receive, when your property should be distributed, and why. You were encouraged to develop a miniplan for each person. However, when you learn about the flexibility of trusts and the types of decisions you can make for your family, you may find yourself revising those pieces of paper.

You are going to learn about the types of powers and discretion you can give to your successor trustee. If you create a trust that is going to be in existence for many years after you are gone, it may change your decisions about how and when you want to distribute your property.

Most people know who they want to provide for in their estate plan. It is also fair to say that even when you know who you would like to include in your plan, you often have concerns about what will happen. You may have some of the following concerns:

- How should you divide your property?
- What is fair?
- Is this a second (or more) marriage for you?
- Do you want your surviving spouse to have complete control over your property after you are gone?
- What will happen if your child divorces?
- Are you concerned that your daughter- or son-in-law will take your child's inheritance?
- Do any of your beneficiaries have special needs?
- Will your beneficiaries squander their inheritance?

If any of these issues concern you, you need to continue reading to learn how you can create a trust that can relieve those concerns.

# When Your Property Is Distributed

Your trust document can instruct your successor trustee to distribute your property immediately after your death or to make delayed distributions. As you continue to read this chapter, you will probably develop both a short-term and long-term plan for your beneficiaries.

## Current Distributions

If all of your property is in your trust, you need to give your successor trustee the power to make current distributions after you are gone. Even if you don't want to do this, state law will force your successor trustee to use your trust property to pay your outstanding unpaid bills, debts, and taxes if you had the power to alter, amend, or revoke your trust document while you were living, which is common for most people if they want to maintain control of their property.

In addition to giving your successor trustee the power to pay your bills, debts, and taxes, you typically want to give her the power to make current distributions of cash or property because your beneficiaries will need money within a short period of time after you are gone. How much beneficiaries will need is different for all families.

Alternatively, you may simply want all of your property distributed as soon as possible after your death. If this is your plan, you will instruct your successor trustee to distribute your property to your named beneficiaries as soon as the trustee provides for the payment of your outstanding bills and taxes.

## Delayed Distributions

One of the primary reasons people create trusts is to delay distributions to their beneficiaries. There are some limits on how long you can delay the distributions from your trust, and all states have different laws regarding this length of time. For instance, some states won't allow you to postpone the final distribution from your trust longer than twenty-one years after a "life in being." This is the classic rule against perpetuities. In the states following the classic rule against perpetuities, if you had a great-grandchild who is living and the beneficiary of your trust, all the trust property must be distributed within twenty-one years after the death of the great-grandchild.

**FACT**

The rule against perpetuities is so complex that many states changed to a rule that says your trust property must be distributed within a specific number of years after your death. If you are looking to extend your trust for any length of time, check with your state law to see what its time limits may be.

It is very typical to delay trust distributions until a beneficiary has reached a particular age. Unless you are trying to delay distributions for multiple generations, there are very few limits on how you can structure the distributions of your trust property. Some people think that a beneficiary should not receive property until he is twenty-five years old; others feel thirty is the magic age; and still others want to make sure their beneficiaries plan for their retirement and, therefore, distributions to the beneficiaries are restricted until they reach the age of fifty-five or sixty!

## Triggering Events

You can put triggering events into your trust document. A triggering event is something that must happen before the beneficiary is entitled to receive a distribution of trust money or property. Likewise, you can put in your trust document triggering events that might cause the termination of trust distributions of money or property.

For instance, if you put in your trust document that the successor trustee must distribute one-third of the trust property to the beneficiary when the beneficiary reaches the age of twenty-five, reaching the age of twenty-five is a triggering event. It would not matter how badly your beneficiary might need the trust property when he is twenty-three years old; the successor trustee cannot distribute cash or property until the beneficiary reaches the triggering age of twenty-five.

**Is it a good idea to have restrictions in a trust?**
That depends on the type of restriction. If you want to determine when your beneficiaries receive trust distributions, restrictions and guidance are necessary. But if you include restrictions that are not specific, you have put your trustee in the position of being a watchdog.

You can be even more disciplinary about your triggering events. For example, you may stipulate that your beneficiary will receive one-third of the trust property when she graduates from college with at least a B average. If she graduates from college with a C+ average, she will not receive the distribution. Or, if your beneficiary does not graduate from college at all, she will not receive the distribution.

## *Restrictions and Penalties*

Some people want to include a triggering event that is a penalty. For instance, you could state that if your beneficiary ever smokes cigarettes, the distributions he is receiving will stop. The problem with this kind of restriction is that you are asking your trustee to monitor the behavior of a beneficiary, a virtually impossible task.

A restriction that some people put in their trust documents is to require the spouse of a beneficiary to execute a release of any interest the spouse may have in the beneficiary's trust property. This helps protect your trust assets in the event a beneficiary divorces.

You cannot put any restrictions or triggering event in your trust document that are illegal or contrary to public policy. For instance, you cannot direct your successor trustee to make a distribution if the beneficiary commits an illegal act, such as "the beneficiary receives $1,000 when she robs the local convenience store." Examples of restrictions that violate public policy are not as definitive. Public policy issues typically involve restricting your beneficiary's choice of religion, freedom to associate, right to vote, and other things of this nature.

Keep in mind that if you put restrictions in your trust document, you have more decisions to make. If a beneficiary is going to lose her trust distributions or does not qualify to receive the trust distributions because the conditions were not met, you need to include instructions in your trust document telling your successor trustee what he should do with the forfeited property, and whether there is a time limit for meeting the condition.

A public policy issue that is common is restricting a beneficiary's right to marry. Placing a restriction in the trust document such as "The beneficiary won't receive any trust distributions if she marries before she is twenty-five years old" has been deemed reasonable. However, limiting the class of persons your beneficiary can marry is typically considered a restriction that will violate public policy and will not be enforced.

## How Your Property Should Be Distributed

When you think about how your property should be distributed, it may affect what each beneficiary will receive. If you instruct your trustee to divide your property equally among your beneficiaries, such as your children, he must decide who gets what. He will consult with your beneficiaries regarding how to divide your trust property but, if your beneficiaries disagree, any of them can petition your local probate court to resolve the controversy. When the beneficiaries argue about the trust property, the probate court becomes involved, lawyers need to be hired, and things get expensive. This outcome can be avoided if you provide more specific instructions to your successor trustee.

There are three types of instructions you can give a trustee: specific instructions, general instructions, or a blend of specific and general instructions. The types of instructions you put in your trust document will depend on the nature of the management plan you are creating for your beneficiaries.

**FACT**

Most people think that if they have a trust, the property in the trust will avoid the probate process. This is true as long as there are no disagreements among the beneficiaries.

The first thing you need to understand is that your trustee has no choice but to follow the instructions you put in your trust document. Specific instructions can be a one-time instruction or continuing instructions. It depends on how long you want your trust to remain in place after you are gone.

## Specific One-Time Instructions

Specific one-time instructions are typically included in a trust document because the trust is going to terminate shortly after you are gone or there are certain immediate distributions you want your successor trustee to make. You could list all of your property and give your trustee specific instructions on how to distribute the trust property. For example, you could instruct your trustee to distribute:

- My two-carat diamond ring to my daughter
- My Rolex watch to my son
- My ABC brokerage account to my son
- My XYZ savings account to my daughter
- My 2003 Saab to my son

If you took the time to give your trustee specific instructions about each piece of property you own, the trustee would have no discretion. This is a rather unrealistic example because it would be almost impossible to create a trust document that describes every single piece of property you own. You would need to change your trust document every time you bought something! Specific instructions are also commonly included in a trust document when you want to include persons or organizations as beneficiaries who are not your family members. For example, you may instruct your successor trustee to distribute $20,000 to your friend Mary Smith and $30,000 to your religious organization.

## Continuing Specific Instructions

Continuing specific instructions are included in a trust document when you want to provide money or property to a beneficiary over a period of time, but you don't want to put the successor trustee in a position of deciding how much money or property should be distributed. The specific continuing instructions can be a stated amount of money or a percentage of the trust. For example, you can instruct your successor trustee to distribute $1,000 per month to your beneficiary until the beneficiary reaches age twenty-five. Or you can instruct your trustee to distribute 5 percent of the value of the trust to your beneficiary each year for a period of twenty years.

**FACT**

There are any number of reasons you may choose to have continuing specific distributions. For instance, perhaps you don't trust your beneficiary to make the right decisions if she receives too much property at one time. Or you may want to make sure that if your spouse dies, the remaining trust property will be distributed to your children and not other beneficiaries your spouse might choose.

## General Instructions

General instructions give the successor trustee the power to exercise his discretion in deciding the amount or timing of a distribution from your trust. While you are living and serving as the trustee, your trust document typically gives you 100 percent discretion to do anything you want with the trust property. You can create your trust document to give the successor trustee as much discretion as you had when you were alive. Most people would only consider giving this amount of discretion to a spouse who is the successor trustee, and the spouse and the natural children of both spouses are the beneficiaries.

## *Specific and General Instructions Combined*

There are instructions you can give your successor trustee that are a blend of specific instructions and general instructions. The most common example of a blended instruction is to direct your successor trustee to make any distributions to a beneficiary that he believes the beneficiary needs for a particular purpose. The purpose you define can be narrow or broad. A broad, blended instruction would be to instruct your successor trustee to distribute such amount of money or property for health, education, maintenance, or welfare. Although this instruction is broad and gives your successor trustee a great deal of discretion, he cannot make distributions that are not necessary for health, education, maintenance, or welfare. If your beneficiary wants to buy a $100,000 car, your trustee can refuse the request for funds because the car does not fall under one of the specified categories.

**ALERT!**

If you give general instructions to your spouse as your successor trustee, you may be giving your spouse so much control that you subject her estate to federal estate taxes that could have been avoided had you not given your spouse such broad discretion. See Chapters 17 and 18 for further details.

You may decide that you want to give your successor trustee general instructions, but you want to limit her discretion. You could put in your trust document that the successor trustee is to distribute $1,000 per month, plus any amount of money she feels the beneficiary needs for health or education. Now you have given your successor trustee a specific instruction as well as a general instruction. It is difficult for a beneficiary to argue that he needs money to buy a car or take a vacation when the instructions to the successor trustee are that additional money can be distributed only for health or education.

You could give your successor trustee an intentionally vague instruction. For example, "My trustee shall pay for all housing costs for the beneficiary." This leaves the window open for the beneficiary to demand a large amount for housing. If you wanted a little more restriction, you could have instructed your successor trustee to distribute a reasonable amount to the beneficiary for housing costs. There is still room to argue about the magic word *reasonable,* but it adds some restrictions on what the successor trustee can distribute for housing, and therefore limits what the beneficiary can demand.

**FACT**

If your instructions are specific, and the successor trustee fails to make the required distribution, the beneficiary is entitled to petition the local probate court to force the successor trustee to make the distribution defined in the trust.

# The Power to Sell Your Property

A trust document should always include a section defining the powers of the trustee. While you are serving as trustee, you typically want the document to give you the power to change the trust document, revoke the trust document, and to manage the property in the same fashion in which you could have managed the property when it was in your individual name. However, you need to decide what powers you are going to give your successor trustee when you are gone.

## Defining the Trustee's Power

Typically, you do not want the successor trustee to be able to change the core decisions about your plan. Therefore, you should define what powers she will have regarding the management of the trust property. Your successor trustee is usually given all of the powers any property manager would have, such as the power to invest, reinvest, borrow, rent, or improve the property. Notice that these standard powers will give your successor trustee the power to sell your property.

## Placing Restrictions on the Selling of Property

If you do not want one or more pieces of your trust property sold, you need to include a restriction in the trust document prohibiting the successor trustee from selling that piece of property.

It is difficult to have a trust stay in existence for very long after you are gone if the successor trustee is not given the power to sell the trust property. The economy frequently changes, and the successor trustee needs to be able to manage the property effectively during economic ups or downs.

You may not want the trustee to be prevented from selling an asset forever, but merely for a period of time. This is a common restriction used when a parent wants the trustee to keep his home until his children reach a particular age.

## The Power to Sell as an Incentive

Alternatively, you may use the power to sell as an incentive to keep your beneficiaries from arguing. If your trust document directs the successor trustee to divide the trust property among your beneficiaries, you might consider including an instruction in your trust document that says if the beneficiaries do not agree on how the trust property will be divided and distributed within a certain amount of time, the trustee is instructed to sell the property and divide the proceeds. This type of instruction often serves two purposes: It motivates the beneficiaries to reach an agreement, and it prevents your beneficiaries from filing a complaint with the local probate court if they cannot agree.

# CHAPTER 13

# Choosing a Trustee

People create trusts for different reasons. Some people create a trust because the nature and extent of
their property is so complicated that they need professional management. Others create a trust because
they simply want to avoid probate and maintain pri-
vacy. Your motivation for creating a trust is going to
have a significant impact on your choice of trustee.

# Sequence of Trustees

There is a sequence of three trustees in most trust documents. The initial trustee serves while you are living; typically this is yourself. Then you need to name a successor trustee to serve after you are gone. Finally, you should name a second successor trustee to serve in the event that the first successor is not available or willing to do so.

## The Initial Trustee

Although most people name themselves as the initial trustee, this isn't always the case. You might name someone else to serve as the initial trustee because you are nervous about managing your own property. This could be because your health is failing, or your property is sufficiently complicated that you feel someone else could manage it better. If the latter applies to you, you should consider naming a professional trustee.

**FACT**

You usually name yourself as the initial trustee because you want to maintain 100 percent control of your property, and you feel you are competent to manage it. But there is no rule that says you have to.

There are numerous options for you to choose from if you want a professional trustee. The best place to look is your local bank. Most banks maintain a trust department. The nice thing about this choice is that your local bank controls your accounts, and that makes it easier for them to be of service to you.

If you don't want to use your bank, there are trust companies whose sole function is to manage trust assets and act as trustees. Most brokerage companies can also serve as trustee for you. The advantage of naming a professional trustee is that your assets are professionally managed. Just be sure to ask for a fee schedule before turning over management of your trust.

## Successor Trustee

The second in the sequence of trustees is called a successor trustee. This is the person or entity that will serve as successor trustee when the initial trustee is not available to serve. When you serve as your own initial trustee, there must be a successor trustee who can serve after you are gone.

Banks and trust companies frequently charge hefty fees for managing a trust. Check with your bank first, before naming it in your trust, to determine the management fees and the minimum annual charge for overseeing your trust. Also ask whether there is a minimum trust amount that it will manage.

Deciding who will be your successor trustee is not easy. However, this chapter will guide you through the duties and responsibilities of a trustee, which should help you decide who would serve your plan best.

## Second Successor Trustee

The third in the sequence of trustees is still called a successor trustee, but it is the second successor trustee. This is the person or entity that will serve as trustee if your first successor trustee is not available.

If you name a professional trustee such as a bank, a trust company, or a brokerage firm to serve as your initial trustee, you don't usually need to name a successor trustee because the professional trustee won't die or become unavailable to serve. As has occurred in recent months, however, institutions sometimes fail or go out of business. Your trust should include language reserving the right to change trustees as well as allowing another institution to take over as trustee in the event of a failure.

## Duties of the Trustee

Your trustee has two duties. She must manage the trust property and distribute the trust property to the beneficiaries. When you create your trust you put two sets of instructions in your trust document. The first set of instructions deals with how to manage the trust property, and the second set deals with what the trustee is supposed to do with the trust property for the benefit of the beneficiaries.

## Management of the Trust Property

There are two duties your trustee has regarding the management of your trust property. The first duty of the trustee is to follow the instructions you have provided in the trust document. Typically, those instructions regarding the management of the trust property are standard directions.

Most trust documents give the trustee very broad management powers. If you don't want your trustee to be able to exercise a particular management power over the trust property, you need to restrict the trustee's power. For instance, some creators of trusts do not want to give the trustee the power to borrow against the property. Be aware, however, that if your trust is going to stay in place for a long time after you are gone, it is very difficult for your trustee to manage the trust property if you place too many restrictions on what she can do with it.

**ALERT!**

Restricting the power of your trustee to manage your property could be detrimental to your beneficiaries. Your trustee will be unable to act contrary to your instructions, even if doing so would be in the best interest of those to whom you left property.

If your trust is not going to last very long, it may be important to you that the trust property not be sold. Your goal may be to delay the distribution of the trust property until the beneficiaries are older. In that case, prohibiting the trustee from selling trust property may meet your goals. You need first to consider the purpose of your trust, and then decide how or if you want to restrict the management powers of the trustee.

## Duty Established by Law

Regardless of the specific instructions you place in your trust document, your trustee has a duty that is established by law. Your trustee must manage the trust property as a reasonably prudent person would do. There are two different standards for this. Some state laws say that the trustee must manage the trust property as a reasonably prudent person would do if he were managing his own property. Other states say that the trustee must manage the trust property as a reasonably prudent person would do if she were managing the property of another.

If the person you choose as your successor trustee is not very sophisticated in making decisions about money or investments, you could be subjecting that person to a lawsuit by the beneficiaries, even though she was doing the best job possible under the circumstances.

If the trustee is not reasonably prudent with the trust property, your beneficiaries have a right to have the trustee removed and/or to sue the trustee. If your beneficiaries sue the trustee, they can recover the losses caused to the trust property from the trustee's personal assets. However, it is difficult and expensive for your beneficiaries to win such a lawsuit.

It can be a sticky situation for your spouse if you name him as successor trustee and you have children from a previous marriage. For instance, let's say you name your second spouse as successor trustee, and you name your children from a former marriage as beneficiaries of your trust assets after your second spouse is gone. If the trust assets go down in value, your children may become angry and sue your spouse for not managing the trust assets in a reasonably prudent manner.

## Duties to the Beneficiaries

As you know, your trustee must follow the specific instructions you have put in your trust document. But if you choose to give your trustee discretion regarding what trust property to distribute or when to make the distributions, your trustee must exercise her discretionary powers in a reasonably prudent manner. The more specific your instructions are, the easier it will be for your trustee to follow those instructions.

## Important Considerations

There are several factors you should consider when choosing a trustee:

- How long will your trust remain in place after you are gone?
- How difficult will it be for your trustee to manage the trust property?
- What is the relationship between the proposed successor trustee and your beneficiaries?
- Do any of your beneficiaries have special needs?

People create trusts for different reasons. When you name an individual to serve as your trustee, you should be confident that the person you name has the skills to serve and will follow the instructions in your trust document.

If the property that will be owned by your trust is complex, you should choose a successor trustee who has the skills to manage that type of property. If you have given your trustee a great deal of discretion about when and how to make distributions to your beneficiaries, it may be more important that you name a trustee who will understand the emotional needs of your beneficiaries.

If your trustee is going to distribute the trust assets to your beneficiaries shortly after you are gone, you can choose a successor trustee who is efficient, well-organized, and able to handle the paperwork to make the distributions. But if your trust is going to exist for many years after you are gone, it becomes more challenging to choose a successor trustee.

## Relationship Considerations

You should also consider the successor trustee's relationship to the beneficiaries. If you name your spouse as successor trustee, and the spouse is not the natural parent of your children—who are also beneficiaries—there is greater possibility for conflict. If you are creating a trust in which your children are the beneficiaries, and you name one child to act as your successor trustee for the benefit of your other children, there can be hard feelings between the child you choose and your other children. This can be particularly troublesome if the child who is serving as your successor trustee is also a beneficiary of your trust.

The more careful you are about creating your plan and choosing the right trustee, the more likely it is that your plan will be successful and will accomplish the goals you want to achieve for your family.

## More than One Trustee

You can have more than one trustee. When you have more than one trustee, they are called co-trustees. Naming more than one trustee could alleviate some of the concerns you might have about trying to decide who should serve as your trustee.

For instance, if the property owned by your trust is complex, but you want the personal touch, you might consider naming a person you can rely on to make the right personal decisions for your beneficiaries as one co-trustee, and a financial professional as the second co-trustee. The co-trustees will make the decisions together, and this can provide the best of both worlds for your beneficiaries.

Naming a professional co-trustee may not be a financially realistic option for you. All professional trustees charge a fee for serving. There is typically a minimum annual fee plus a charge computed as a percentage of all of the assets owned by the trust. The percentage ranges from three-quarters of 1 percent to 2 or 3 percent, depending on the value of all of the trust assets. You may want a professional trustee, but it could be cost-prohibitive if your trust assets are not large.

There is no limit to the number of co-trustees you can name in your trust document. You could name three, four, or even more co-trustees. However, if there are too many fingers in the pie, there does come a point at which it isn't practical to expect the co-trustees to make unanimous decisions. If they can't all agree, your trust instructions may be thwarted and no one will be happy.

## The Trustee and Your Property

As stated earlier, there are two things the trustee must do with your trust property. He must manage the trust property with reasonable care, and follow the instructions you have put in the trust document. When you create your trust, you will define the management powers of your trustee.

### Selling the Property

There are several reasons you might prohibit your trustee from selling your property. For instance, it might be your goal to keep the trust property in the family, but you want to make sure the beneficiaries are old enough to properly care for that property. Therefore, you place the property in trust and instruct the trustee to distribute it to your beneficiaries at a later time. Or you may feel that it is the best choice to make sure the trust property is not sold for a period of time because you feel that the particular property will provide the best income or security for your beneficiaries.

**FACT**

You don't have to name a professional to act as your co-trustee. You may have two children whom you feel would bring different talents to the job. Therefore, you name both children to act as co-trustees. You need to make sure that the two persons you name can work together. Unless you specify differently in your trust document, the co-trustees must make all decisions together.

### Dividing Your Property

Whether or not your property is physically divided depends on the instructions you put in your trust document. Some types of property can be easily divided. If your goal is to make certain a beneficiary receives a portion of a specific piece of property, instruct the trustee not to sell the property but to physically divide the trust property among the beneficiaries.

**ALERT!**

Even after the beneficiaries and the trustee present their side of the argument to the judge, if your instructions were not clear or there were no specific instructions, the judge will often order the property sold, and the proceeds divided among the beneficiaries.

Remember those sheets of paper that describe each piece of property you own? You can make notes on the pieces of paper about whether you would like the trustee to sell that piece of property, divide the property among your beneficiaries, or distribute it to a particular beneficiary. The more thought you put into the instructions you give your trustee about your property, the less likely it is your beneficiaries will disagree after you are gone.

## If Your Family Doesn't Agree

If the beneficiaries of your trust do not agree with what the trustee is doing, they may file a lawsuit. The beneficiaries will file papers with the court explaining to the judge why the trustee is making, or is about to make, a bad decision about your trust property. Lawsuits are expensive. The beneficiary who is dissatisfied will need to hire a lawyer, the trustee will need to hire a lawyer, and often the other beneficiaries who will be affected will need to hire a lawyer. At $250 to $300 per hour, if three lawyers are involved, it could cost $750 to $900 or more per hour to resolve the dispute!

There are two solutions: You can either be very specific in your trust document about what each beneficiary will receive (though this may not be practical if your trust is going to remain in place for a long time) or you can put a provision in your trust document that says if the beneficiaries disagree about how the trust property is going to be divided and distributed, the trustee is to sell the property and divide the proceeds. This instruction gives the trustee, rather than the local courts, the authority to solve the dispute.

# *Financial Guardian for Your Minor Child*

There are two types of guardianships for a minor child: legal guardian and financial guardian. As you know, the legal guardian is the physical guardian of your child. A trust can name a financial guardian for your minor child, but it cannot name a legal guardian.

If you create a trust for your minor child, your successor trustee in essence becomes the financial guardian of that child. The successor trustee will follow the instructions you put in the trust document about how to manage and distribute your property for the benefit of the child.

When people divorce, they often overlook the fact that if they die and leave their assets to their minor child, the surviving natural parent becomes the physical guardian and also controls the assets that were left to the child.

**FACT**

You can prevent your ex-spouse from having control of your children's money and property by placing your assets in trust and naming a successor trustee who you are confident will manage and spend the money only for the benefit of your child.

Another possibility is that both parents could die in a common accident. Therefore, you may want to create a will to name a person who will be physical guardian of your minor child, but create a trust that names a successor trustee to manage the property for that child.

## CHAPTER 14

# Creating a Trust

It is now time for you to see a real trust. As you review each section of the trust document, you will see the decisions Jane made for her family, and how she incorporated her plan into her trust document. You can use this sample document as a road map to create a trust for your family.

# Identify the Parties and Describe the Property

Trust documents are broken into parts. Each part of a trust document accomplishes a purpose that is typically described by the title of the article. Besides the legalese, a trust document reads like a book. Each chapter covers a different topic. The first part identifies the parties and describes the property involved.

> ### JANE ADAMS DOE
> ### REVOCABLE TRUST AGREEMENT
>
> I, JANE ADAMS DOE, a resident of Sarasota, Florida, do hereby enter into the JANE ADAMS DOE REVOCABLE TRUST between myself as Settlor and myself as Trustee.

Jane has identified herself as the one entering into the trust (the creator or settlor), and she has identified herself as the initial trustee.

> ### ARTICLE I
> ### ESTABLISHMENT OF TRUST
> 1.1 <u>Name of Trust.</u> This Trust may be referred to as the JANE ADAMS DOE REVOCABLE TRUST.

In **Article 1.1,** Jane gives her trust a name, the "JANE ADAMS DOE REVOCABLE TRUST." You can give your trust any name. For instance, Jane could have called her revocable trust the "Mickey Mouse Trust." However, if your trust is going to own your property while you are alive, and you are going to be the initial trustee, it is best not to create confusion by giving your trust an unusual name.

> 1.2 <u>Declarations.</u> I am a married woman. My husband is JOHN ALEXANDER DOE. I have two (2) children: JACK JOSEPH DOE and JAMIE ANN DOE. Except as otherwise qualified, the words "child" or "children" when used in this Agreement with reference to me shall mean all my above-named children. The words "child" or "children" when used in this Agreement with

reference to any person other than me shall mean all natural and adopted children including natural children born after the death of their parent but excluding stepchildren and foster children. The word "descendants" when used in this Agreement shall mean all of the person's lineal descendants of all generations, except those who are descendants of a living descendant, with the relationship of parent and child at each generation being determined under governing law. To be a child or descendant by virtue of adoption, the person must be adopted while a minor.

**Article 1.2** is the declaration portion of the trust. You should list all the persons who are going to be beneficiaries of your trust and define the relationship of those persons to you. If you are going to name brothers, sisters, friends, or neighbors as beneficiaries, describe the people and their relationship to you.

1.3 <u>Trust Corpus.</u> I hereby transfer and deliver the property listed on Schedule A. All trust property shall be held by the Trustee in trust as is provided in this Agreement.

**Article 1.3** declares that you are going to attach Schedule A to describe the property owned by the trust. It is very important for you to understand that listing the property as owned by the trust does not automatically make the trust the owner. You must change the ownership of the property from yourself to your trustee, even if you are serving as the initial trustee. If the trustee does not own the property, the trust will have no effect on how your property is distributed.

1.4 <u>Additional Trust Property.</u> From time to time I or any other person(s) may individually or jointly transfer additional property to this Trust or to any separate trust established hereunder. Additions of property may be made from any source by assignment, conveyance, or delivery, or by any testamentary disposition or appointment. Additions of life insurance policy proceeds or other monies payable on death may be made by designation of the Trustee as a beneficiary thereof.

**Article 1.4** gives the trustee the power to accept property from other persons or sources. For instance, perhaps your parents are doing their estate planning. You could recommend that their estate planning documents leave property to the trustee of your trust rather than directly to you. Remember, one of the goals of your trust is for your family to avoid probate after you are gone. Your property must be titled in the name of the trust to accomplish that goal.

# Assigning the Power to Control the Trust Property

This is the part of your trust document that gives you 100 percent control of the trust property. You as the creator of the trust document are keeping the power to change or revoke the trust without anyone's approval.

ARTICLE II
RESERVATIONS

2.1 <u>Amendment and Revocation.</u> I may, during my lifetime and without the consent of anyone, revoke this Agreement in whole or in part (whereupon the trust property or the part affected by such revocation shall be distributed in accordance with my instructions) or amend it from time to time in any respect.

ARTICLE III
LIFETIME MANAGEMENT

3.1 <u>Income.</u> The Trustee shall pay to me the net income, if any, in such installments and amounts as I direct. In the absence of such direction, net income not distributed shall be accumulated and become part of the principal.

3.2 <u>Invasion of Principal.</u> The Trustee shall have the discretionary power to pay me such principal as will, when combined with my other income, support and maintain me so that I might, as near as possible with due regard to my total estate and my future financial requirements for myself and my dependents known to the Trustee, continue to enjoy the standard of living to which I am accustomed. This power shall be liberally construed without regard to remaindermen's interests and shall also include amounts for the care, support, education, medical and dental care, and general welfare and well-being of persons dependent on me, premiums on life insurance on my life whether or not such policies are assigned to or payable to the Trustee, and all sums necessary to preserve and protect my property.

**Article III** directs the trustee (who is probably you) to pay you (the beneficiary while you are alive) all of the income and any principal you need or want. If you have named someone else as the initial trustee, you are instructing that trustee to distribute any income or principal you request. The trustee cannot say no.

> ARTICLE IV
> <u>CONSEQUENCES OF DEATH</u>
> 4.1 <u>Death.</u> At my death this Agreement shall be irrevocable. The Trustee shall receive and hold as part of this Trust all then remaining principal and undistributed net income as well as any proceeds of any insurance on my life and all other property received by the Trustee at my death or at any time thereafter from any source. After my death the Trustee shall administer and distribute this Trust in accordance with the provisions of Article V.

**Article IV** makes the trust irrevocable when you die. The person or entity you name as your successor trustee will automatically become the new trustee, and Article V will now control what the successor trustee may do with the trust property.

## Timing and Distribution of Assets

When you review **Article V** you will see that Jane has given her successor trustee different instructions for different beneficiaries. Your plan does not have to be the same for all of your beneficiaries. The flexibility to create different plans for each beneficiary is one feature that makes a trust a very attractive estate planning document.

## ARTICLE V
## DURATION AND DISTRIBUTION OF TRUST

5.1 <u>Trust Share and Taxes, Debts, and Expenses.</u> The Trustee may pay from the Trust all federal estate taxes, including any interest or penalties thereon, for which my estate shall be liable. The Trustee shall also pay from the Trust such of the inheritance, estate, succession, transfer, and other estate taxes, both federal and state, including any interest or penalties thereon, charged against my estate or any person or entity, which become payable by reason of my death, whether in respect to property passing under this Trust, my Will or otherwise. If there is no probate estate and therefore no Personal Representative of my estate, the Trustee shall pay such taxes and, in addition, all debts, expenses of my last illness, expenses of my funeral, burial, cemetery marker, cremation, or other disposition of my body, administration expenses and all other expenses and charges of a similar nature that the Trustee determines are a proper charge against my estate.

**Article 5.1** instructs your successor trustee to pay all of your debts, final expenses, and any taxes you or your estate may owe after you are gone, even if there is no probate. If you have done your homework and put the title to all of your property that would have been subject to probate in the name of your trust, there will be no probate. That is why your successor trustee needs authority to pay your debts and expenses.

5.2 <u>Distribution for the Benefit of My Husband, JOHN ALEXANDER DOE.</u> If my husband, JOHN ALEXANDER DOE, is living, the rest and remainder of the accumulated income and principal shall be distributed to JOHN ALEXANDER DOE, Trustee of the JOHN ALEXANDER DOE REVOCABLE TRUST.

The instructions you give your successor trustee about how to distribute the trust property after you are gone is the meat and potatoes of your trust document. Jane created a trust in which her successor trustee is instructed to distribute all of her trust property to her husband's trust when she dies. Jane must have been satisfied that John's trust included a plan for any property his trust receives from her trust. Jane and John probably calculated whether John's estate would be exposed to federal estate taxes if Jane died first and John's trust ended up owning all of the marital property. If the combined property would create a federal estate tax, the trust provisions described in Chapter 18 should be considered to reduce the federal estate tax exposure.

Jane could have created her trust differently. Jane's trust could have instructed the trustee to distribute income only to John, instructed the trustee to distribute a stated amount of cash annually to John, given her successor trustee the power to evaluate and distribute what John needed, or included a provision in her trust that John receives distributions only as long as he does not remarry.

5.3 <u>Distribution If My Husband, JOHN ALEXANDER DOE, Is Not Living.</u> If my husband, JOHN ALEXANDER DOE, is not living, the accumulated income and principal shall be distributed as follows:

5.3(a) <u>Trust for the Benefit of My Son, JACK JOSEPH DOE.</u> One-half (½) of the accumulated income and principal shall be held in trust for the benefit of my son, JACK JOSEPH DOE. The Trustee shall distribute the accumulated income and principal equally over a ten-year period. The Trustee shall also distribute such amounts of income and principal as the Trustee feels my son needs for his health, education, maintenance, and welfare. Except, when Jack reaches the age of forty-five years old, the Trustee shall distribute the remaining accumulated income and principal to my son, JACK JOSEPH DOE. If JACK JOSEPH DOE is deceased before he receives his complete distribution, the undistributed income and principal shall be held in trust for the benefit of his children. The Trustee shall distribute such amounts of income and principal for the benefit of the children of JACK as the Trustee feels the children need for their health, education, maintenance, and welfare. The Trustee does not need to make distributions in equal amounts for the benefit of the children of JACK, but shall use his or her discretion to determine how much income or principal each child needs. When the youngest child of my deceased child reaches the age of twenty-five, the Trustee shall then divide and distribute the remaining accumulated income and principal equally between the surviving children of JACK JOSEPH DOE. If JACK is not living and has no surviving children, the remaining accumulated income and principal shall be distributed according to the provisions of Article 5.3(b) for the benefit of his sister.

Jane made certain decisions while she was living about what Jack should receive if John, her husband, was not living. She instructed her successor trustee to divide the trust into two equal parts, one for the benefit of Jack and one for Jamie; distribute Jack's trust equally over a ten-year period; in addition to the one-tenth distribution annually, evaluate and distribute any additional amount he determines Jack needs for his health, education, maintenance, and welfare; and when Jack reaches age forty-five, distribute all of Jack's remaining trust property to him.

Jane obviously felt that it would be best for Jack to receive distributions equally over a ten-year period. Notice, if Jack is forty-one years old when Jane and John are both gone, Jack will receive one-tenth of his share of the trust per year for four years, and when he turns forty-five, he will receive the balance of his trust. If Jack is forty-six when Jane and John are both gone, Jack will receive all of his trust immediately because the triggering event, turning forty-five, has already occurred.

Jane also included a plan if Jack should die before he receives a complete distribution of his trust. If Jack has children, the successor trustee will keep Jack's remaining property in trust for the benefit of Jack's children and use his judgment to determine how much they need for health, education, maintenance, and welfare. The trustee does not have to treat Jack's children equally, but when Jack's youngest child turns twenty-five years old, the trustee must divide the remaining trust account into as many equal shares as Jack has living children and distribute the balance of the trust equally among them. Jack's children do not receive anything from the trust unless Jack dies before receiving his full distributions. Jane also directed the trustee to add Jack's share to Jamie's share if Jack dies without children before the trust is completely distributed.

5.3(b) <u>Trust for the Benefit of My Daughter, JAMIE ANN DOE.</u> One-half (½) of the accumulated income and principal shall be held in trust for the benefit of my daughter, JAMIE ANN DOE. The Trustee shall distribute one-half (½) of the accumulated income and principal when JAMIE ANN DOE reaches the age of thirty years old and the Trustee shall distribute the remainder of the accumulated income and principal to JAMIE ANN DOE when she reaches the age of thirty-five years old. The Trustee shall also distribute such amounts of income and principal as the Trustee feels my daughter needs for her health. However, if Jamie does not graduate from college with a four-year degree by the time she reaches the age of thirty years old, her share shall be forfeited, and shall be paid to her brother's trust according to the terms of Article 5.3(a). If JAMIE ANN DOE is deceased before she receives her complete distribution, the undistributed income and principal shall be held in trust for the benefit of her children. The Trustee shall distribute such amounts of income and principal for the benefit of the children of JAMIE as the Trustee feels the children need for their health, education, maintenance, and welfare. The Trustee does not need to make distributions in equal amounts for the benefit of the children of JAMIE, but shall use his or her discretion to determine how much income or principal each child needs. When the youngest child of my deceased child reaches the age of twenty-five, the Trustee shall then divide and distribute the remaining accumulated income and principal equally among the surviving children of JAMIE ANN DOE. If JAMIE is not living and has no surviving children, the remaining accumulated income and principal shall be distributed according to the provisions of Article 5.3(a) for the benefit of her brother.

Jane made different decisions for Jamie. The successor trustee must divide the trust into two equal parts, one for the benefit of Jack and one for Jamie; distribute one-half of Jamie's trust to her when she turns thirty years old and the remaining one-half when Jamie turns thirty-five (it is irrelevant that the successor trustee is distributing Jack's share equally over ten years); and distribute anything Jamie needs for her health, even if Jamie has not reached the triggering age of thirty or thirty-five. The successor trustee can distribute for Jack's health, education, maintenance, or welfare, whereas the successor trustee can distribute only for Jamie's health. The instructions to the successor trustee about how to distribute Jamie's trust property if she dies before receiving complete distributions are the same as the instructions for Jack's share.

Jamie's trust has a triggering event that is a penalty. If she does not earn a four-year degree by the time she is thirty years old, she forfeits her share of the trust for herself and her children. Maybe this provision was placed in the trust document because Jack already earned his degree, and Jane felt very strongly that Jamie should be motivated.

5.4 <u>Absence of Named Beneficiaries.</u> If there are no beneficiaries named as final distributees living at the termination of this Trust or any Trust created hereunder, then the property remaining in the Trust or Trusts shall be paid and distributed to my heirs at law as though I had died intestate, a resident of Florida.

You should include a provision that tells your successor trustee what to do if all of the beneficiaries you name are gone. In the unlikely event that John, Jack, Jamie, and all of the children of Jack and Jamie are gone, the trust will be distributed as if Jane died intestate. This means the successor trustee will look at the state law in Florida and distribute the trust property to the persons who would have received the property had Jane died without a will. The laws are different in each state about who receives your property when you die without a will. You don't have to have your "absence of named beneficiaries clause" direct a distribution according to the intestate laws of your state. You can include instructions to your successor trustee to distribute the trust property to other named persons or perhaps to a charity in the event your family is gone.

## Assigning a Trustee

When you are naming your successor trustees, you need to ask yourself whether the successor trustee you are considering will be capable, or even alive, to serve. You might want to revisit Chapter 13 to review the information about choosing a trustee.

ARTICLE VI

<u>TRUSTEE</u>

6.1 <u>Trustee While JANE ADAMS DOE Is Living.</u> I hereby appoint myself, JANE ADAMS DOE, as Trustee.

**Article 6.1** names Jane as her own trustee. You will probably name yourself as initial trustee as well.

6.2 <u>Trustee If JANE ADAMS DOE Is Not Living.</u>

6.2(a) <u>Trustee If My Spouse, JOHN ALEXANDER DOE, Is Living</u>. If JANE ADAMS DOE is not living or is not capable of serving, I hereby appoint my husband, JOHN ALEXANDER DOE, to serve as trustee.

**Article 6.2(a)** names the successor trustee after Jane is gone or not capable of serving. Jane named her husband, John, as the first successor trustee. If Jane is dead, John will pay all of the debts and any taxes, and then he will distribute the remaining property to his trust.

6.2(b) <u>Trustee If JANE ADAMS DOE and JOHN ALEXANDER DOE Are Not Living.</u> If JANE ADAMS DOE and JOHN ALEXANDER DOE are not living, I hereby appoint ABC BANK to serve as Trustee of any trusts created for the benefit of my children, JACK JOSEPH DOE, JAMIE ANN DOE, or the children of JACK JOSEPH or JAMIE ANN DOE.

**Article 6.2(b)** names a successor trustee to serve if both Jane and John are gone or not capable of serving. Jane named a bank as successor trustee when John is gone or not available to serve. She might have chosen a bank because she knew the trust was going to be in place for a long time and didn't want to worry about who would serve as successor trustee for Jack and Jamie or for their children if either of them died before receiving his or her full trust distribution.

If this were your trust, you might have named Jamie as successor trustee for Jack's trust and Jack as successor trustee for Jamie's trust. You might feel uncomfortable about a bank making decisions for your children or grandchildren. Again, the choices you make depend on what you think is best for your family.

6.3 <u>Fees.</u> The Trustee shall be compensated a reasonable fee for serving as Trustee. The Trustee shall also be reimbursed for all expenses and charges incurred in the performance of its duties or by reason of its office as Trustee.

6.4 <u>Disabled Trustee.</u> A Trustee is "disabled" (and while disabled shall not serve as Trustee) if the next successor trustee receives written certification that the examined trustee is physically or mentally incapable of managing the affairs of the trust, whether or not there is an adjudication of the trustee's incompetence.

6.4(a) <u>Certification of Disability.</u> This certification shall be valid only if it is signed by at least two (2) physicians, each of whom has personally examined the trustee and at least one (1) of whom is board-certified in the specialty most closely associated with the alleged disability. This certification need not indicate any cause for the trustee's disability. A certification of disability shall be rescinded when a serving trustee receives a certification that the former trustee is capable of managing the trust's affairs. This certification, too, shall be valid only if it is signed by at least two (2) physicians, each of whom has personally examined the trustee and at least one (1) of whom is board-certified in the specialty most closely associated with the former disability.

6.4(b) <u>Reliance on Certification.</u> No person is liable to anyone for actions taken in reliance on the certification under this paragraph, or for dealing with a Trustee other than the one removed for disability based on these certifications.

**Article 6.4** puts a plan in the document in the event that any trustee becomes incapacitated. This is an important provision because without a way to certify a trustee's disability, if Jane became disabled, John would have to have Jane declared judicially incompetent in order to serve as successor trustee. This is a very expensive and cumbersome process that can be avoided by including a process in the trust document to have a trustee removed in the event that she becomes disabled and unable to serve.

## Miscellaneous Trust Provisions

The remainder of a trust document can be described in a summary manner. The provisions are important to include in your trust document but do not represent the substance of your plan. Several of the more important miscellaneous trust provisions are described here, but the full text of the remaining trust provisions can be found in Appendix D.

## Diversification

You may want your successor trustee to be able to keep the property the trust owned while you were alive even though the trust property might not be the property a reasonably prudent trustee should keep. Therefore, you need to include a clause that does not require the successor trustee to diversify the property owned by the trust after you are gone. See **Article 7.2** in Appendix D.

## Creditors Clause and Spendthrift Provision

You can include a clause in your trust document that prevents your beneficiary from selling or transferring her interest prior to the date of distribution you have specified. It wouldn't do much good to put a detailed plan into place about how the successor trustee should distribute the trust property after you are gone if the beneficiary could sell or transfer his interest to get money early. A sample trust provision to accomplish these goals is included at **Article 7.4** in Appendix D.

The trust can also include a provision that prevents a creditor of your beneficiary from attaching your beneficiary's trust interest before a distribution is made.

One of the reasons for having a trust payout over a period of years is to prevent creditors of one of your beneficiaries from taking the whole inheritance. This clause will prevent creditors from attaching the trust principal, but they can still go after any current income your beneficiary might receive.

## *Accountings*

It is important for your trust document to give your successor trustee instructions regarding how and when the beneficiaries must be provided with accountings. If your successor trustee is not required to give your beneficiaries accountings, the beneficiaries would have no way of knowing what the trustee is doing. If your trustee is not doing her job, your beneficiaries can take the accountings and file a lawsuit to have her removed. See **Article VIII** in Appendix D for the full text of a typical accounting provision.

## *Signature, Witnesses, and a Notary*

Just as you do for a will, you should sign your trust document in the presence of two witnesses and a notary. Some states do not require you to sign in the presence of two witnesses, and other states don't require a notary. However, your trust is an important legal document. Don't risk that your trust will be found invalid because it lacked a witness or your signature was not notarized.

# CHAPTER 15

# The Lowdown on Life Insurance

While life insurance traditionally pays a death benefit so that your family has enough money to pay the bills, it has also become an investment and a retirement vehicle. This chapter will talk about the types of products available and will guide you through the rules on how life insurance should be owned and paid to maximize the value of the insurance for your family.

# Three Parties to a Policy

In order to evaluate how your life insurance policy should be owned and paid, it is important for you to understand the legal relationship of the parties to a life insurance policy. There are three parties to a life insurance policy: the insured, the owner of the policy, and the beneficiary of the policy.

The insured is you. When you die, the policy pays a death benefit. The owner of the policy is the one who makes all of the decisions about the policy. For instance, the owner owns all of the insurance policy benefits, such as the cash value, if there is any, and can change the beneficiary or make elections about how the policy proceeds will be paid to the beneficiary. Then there is the beneficiary. This is the person or entity that the owner of the policy names to receive the death benefits. Unless you have done some sophisticated planning, you are usually both the owner and the insured of your life insurance policies.

# Types of Life Insurance

There are two types of life insurance: term insurance, and life insurance policies that have cash values. There are hundreds, maybe thousands, of different varieties of insurance policies within these two types.

**ALERT!**

Depending on your age and your health, the newer life insurance products may provide you with more benefits for the same money. You should contact your life insurance agent to find out whether you would be better off converting your existing policy to one that gives you more bang for your buck.

## Term Insurance

Term insurance is life insurance that has no benefit associated with the policy other than a death benefit. You pay a premium for the term and, if you die while the term insurance is in effect, the insurance company pays a death benefit to the person or persons you named as your beneficiaries. If you don't die while the term insurance is in effect, you have nothing left at the end of the term other than the peace of mind of knowing that if you had died, a death benefit would have been paid to your beneficiary.

## Life Insurance with Cash Value

A life insurance policy with cash value has two components. It has a death benefit and cash value. In the old days, the insurance company guaranteed a minimum rate of return on the cash component of the policy. If you decided to terminate the policy, you could withdraw at least the guaranteed cash value. If the insurance company earned more than it expected, your cash value could be larger. The variety of insurance products that have a cash value component has increased dramatically over the years.

**FACT**

Trying to direct insurance proceeds through your will or trust will not work. The insurance company is bound by the contract to pay the proceeds in accordance with the beneficiary form you have signed.

There is more emphasis on the cash value of life insurance products than there was in the past. You should shop around. Contact several agents. You will be surprised to learn how many different products are available.

The insurance companies have become very creative with the options you have regarding the cash value component. For instance, the cash value of some policies is being invested and the growth is being used to pay future premiums. Other policies are using the growth on the cash value to provide a larger death benefit. The goal of yet another type of policy is to maximize the investment yield on the cash value by investing the cash value in mutual funds that own stock to create a larger cash value for you to withdraw.

## Choice of Beneficiary Is Contractual

As you have read previously, there are several ways to direct funds to a beneficiary: will, trust, joint property, and pay-on-death accounts. When you designate a beneficiary of your life insurance policy, you have entered into a contract with the life insurance company. In return for your premium payments, the life insurance company promises to pay the proceeds of the policy to the person or entity you designate.

The only way to change the beneficiaries of your life insurance policy is to complete a new designation form with the company. You can make changes at any time by requesting and completing a new designation form.

## Life Insurance and the Probate Process

Life insurance proceeds can avoid probate if you have selected the right beneficiary. If your life insurance policy is payable to a person and is not paid to your estate, the life insurance death benefit will not be subject to probate. This means that as soon as the named beneficiary files a claim with the insurance company, and the claim is approved, the insurance company will make a direct payment to the named beneficiary.

**ALERT!**

When you are organizing the information about your property, you should locate your life insurance policies. Contact the insurance companies and ask them to send you a copy of your beneficiary election. You may be surprised to recall who you named as a beneficiary or beneficiaries when you purchased the policy.

If you have more than one beneficiary, the insurance company will pay the death benefit to the beneficiaries in the proportion you designated when you applied for and purchased the insurance or according to any changes of beneficiary you have made since then.

### Payable to the Estate

If you name your estate as the beneficiary of your life insurance, the death benefit will be paid to the executor of your estate when you die and will become subject to probate. You might name your estate as the beneficiary of your life insurance if you aren't sure who you want to name. However, you usually buy life insurance because you want to make sure the person you name as the beneficiary has enough money when you are gone. It would be unusual not to have a specific beneficiary in mind when buying insurance.

If you have group life insurance through your employment, you should ask the administrator to provide you with a copy of any beneficiary elections you made. If you have named your estate, you should consider changing the election to a person or persons. Some employers may establish life insurance as a benefit to its retirees. Check with the administrator to learn whether this is a benefit offered by your employer, how much it is worth, and who is named as beneficiary.

Then again, some people may have named their estate as the beneficiary because they didn't realize it would make any difference. You might think that naming your estate as beneficiary is the same as naming a person, because you know that your estate will belong to your family. Your life insurance proceeds may end up going to your family but, when you name the estate, you are unnecessarily subjecting the insurance death benefits to the cost and delay associated with probate.

### Circumstances to Consider

There are other circumstances in which you might have named your estate as beneficiary. It is not uncommon when you are employed that your employer provides employee benefits. One of the benefits that might be offered to you is what is called *group life insurance*. Group life insurance is typically term insurance. It is in force only as long as you are employed and the premiums are paid by you or your employer. There is rarely a cash value associated with it. Group life insurance does not mean that a death benefit is paid to a group of people; it means that because you are a member of the employer's group, you are entitled to a stated amount of insurance benefits paid to the beneficiary or beneficiaries you name.

**QUESTION?**

**What happens to my life insurance policy if I divorce and my ex-spouse is still listed as my beneficiary?**
If you die before changing your beneficiary designation, the court will more than likely treat the ex-spouse beneficiary as deceased, and the insurance proceeds would go to your estate. You should promptly change your beneficiary designation form if you are divorced.

When you were filling out all of the paperwork before you started your job, you may not have given much thought to who you wanted to name as the beneficiary of the group life insurance benefit. You may have checked the box on the paperwork that said "pay the death benefit to my estate." In the back of your mind you might have thought that it didn't matter if the beneficiary was a person or your estate; the death benefit would ultimately go to your heirs. However, as you've learned, it does make a difference.

## Tax Consequences

Many people believe that you do not owe any taxes on the life insurance death benefits. There is some truth to this belief, but it depends upon the value of your entire estate.

### Income Tax

Most of the time, your beneficiary will not have to report a death benefit on his income tax return. The beneficiary you name does not owe income taxes on the death benefit because the law contains an exemption for death benefits received from a life insurance policy, regardless of whether the beneficiary is a person or estate. There are some exceptions to this rule that probably do not apply to your policies. But if an exception does apply, your beneficiaries will have to report the death benefit on their income tax returns and pay taxes.

### Estate Taxes

The fact that life insurance death benefits are not subject to *income* taxes is what leads most people to conclude that there are no taxes owing on these benefits at all. This is not always true. Most people are both the insured and owner of their life insurance policies. When you die, the insurance proceeds are paid to the beneficiary or beneficiaries you name in the policy. Even though the death benefit is paid to a beneficiary, it is added to your other property and becomes part of your taxable base, subject to federal estate taxes. Don't panic! Read Chapter 17 to estimate whether you'll owe federal estate taxes.

## If Your Estate Exceeds the Exclusion

If you discover that your life insurance will cause your estate to owe estate taxes, it's not too late to change that situation. It is absolutely unnecessary for your family to pay federal estate taxes on the life insurance death benefits they receive.

**FACT**

When your estate owes federal estate taxes, the starting tax rate for $10,000 over the unified credit exclusion is 18 percent as of 2009. That rate jumps to 34 percent for an excess of $250,000 to $500,000, and increases to 45 percent for a taxable estate of $2 million or more. This makes income taxes look cheap!

If your estate is subject to federal estate taxes, you should strongly consider forming an irrevocable life insurance trust or engage in other planning to remove the life insurance from your taxable estate. See Chapter 18 for further discussion on creating this form of trust.

# A Simpler Solution for Life Insurance

There is an easier way to remove your life insurance from your taxable base: You can give the policy to your beneficiary. By doing this, you will still be the insured person, but now your beneficiary will be both the owner and the beneficiary. If your beneficiary also owns your life insurance policy, the policy proceeds payable at your death will not be subject to federal estate taxes.

Be aware that if you make your beneficiaries the owner of your life insurance policy, you have given them all the rights you had, including the right to withdraw the cash value from the policy. In addition, you are making a gift that must be valued and, if over the annual exclusion of $13,000, must be reported as a taxable gift.

Remember, you need only be concerned about your life insurance if your taxable base, as described in Chapter 17, is more than the unified credit amount in the year of your death. When the cost of making a mistake is paying the federal government a rate from 18 to 45 cents on the dollar, it's well worth the time to get some help.

If you decide to take the simple path and give your insurance policy to your beneficiaries, you will still need the assistance of a professional to help you compute the value of the gift you might be making.

# CHAPTER 16

# Reviewing Retirement Accounts and Annuities

If you are considering a retirement plan, an annuity, or already have one of these investment options in place, it is important to know what happens to those assets when you are gone and how they will be taxed when you or your heirs make withdrawals.

# Retirement Accounts, Annuities, and the Probate Process

All retirement accounts and annuities are alike, whether they are IRAs or employer-provided plans, as far as whether they will be subject to probate. The only way these assets can be subject to probate is if you named your estate as the beneficiary or if the beneficiaries you named are dead.

If your employer established a retirement account for you, the administrator of the retirement account gave you an application to complete. On that application, you named one or more beneficiaries to whom your retirement benefits would be paid after your death. You may have completed that paperwork years ago.

If you have a retirement account established by your employer, you need to contact your employer's plan administrator to learn the rules about who you can name as beneficiary and how the retirement account proceeds will be taxed. You should also ask your employer's plan administrator for a copy of your beneficiary election.

You may also have multiple IRA accounts with different brokerage firms or banks. You should contact the administrator of each of your IRA accounts or annuities to request a copy of your beneficiary election form.

It is important, also, to keep all of your IRA and annuity administrators up-to-date on your current address. If your address changes after your last contact with these administrators, and the forwarding order expires, it may be difficult for correspondence from the administrators to reach you.

As you are now well aware, the beneficiaries of your retirement benefits or annuities are governed entirely by your beneficiary designation form on file with the administrator. Unless you have named your estate as the beneficiary, whatever you put in your will or trust will be completely disregarded.

## Naming Your Beneficiary

In the old days, choosing a beneficiary of your retirement accounts or annuities was a simple matter. The husband named the wife as beneficiary, and the wife named the husband as beneficiary. The children were typically named as successor beneficiaries who received the retirement benefits if both spouses were gone. This was the typical pattern because it met the needs of the traditional family. It would be fair to say that there are more families today that are nontraditional.

Because divorces and remarriages are common today, choosing a beneficiary of your retirement or annuity plans may require balancing the security you want to provide your current spouse with the needs of your children from a former marriage. Don't feel pressured to name your spouse as the beneficiary, especially if you have children from a former marriage. Remember, this is your decision to make.

For instance, you may decide to name your children from a former marriage as beneficiaries of your retirement plan and provide for your current spouse with other property. In order to decide what is best for your family, you need to understand the rules about naming your spouse as the beneficiary of your retirement plan as opposed to naming someone else, such as your children.

## Naming Your Spouse as Beneficiary

When you name your spouse as the beneficiary of your IRA, your spouse has two options: She can transfer the balance of your IRA into a new IRA or into her existing IRA, or she can assume your IRA; that is, take over as owner of the IRA under the same rules established when you were living.

If your spouse transfers your IRA either into a new IRA or into her existing IRA, she will be able to change the successor beneficiaries. For example, suppose that you name your spouse as your primary beneficiary, and your children from a former marriage as your successor beneficiaries so that they will receive the IRA after your spouse is gone. Upon your death, your spouse could change the successor beneficiaries to someone you did not choose. Your children from a former marriage might discover after the death of your spouse that they will not receive the remaining retirement benefits you worked so hard to accumulate and had intended for them.

The second election your spouse can make is to assume your existing IRA. If this happens, your spouse's age in the year after your death will determine how rapidly she must withdraw from your IRA. The advantage of having your spouse assume your IRA is that the persons you name as successor beneficiaries will receive the remaining balance after your spouse is gone.

ALERT!

Understanding the elections your spouse has is easier today than it was a few years ago, but it is still tricky. You may want to consult with a financial professional to decide the best choice for you and your family. As you can see, there are several options for transferring IRAs, and many decisions that your spouse must make after your death.

Of course, it is much easier when you have been married to only one person and any children you may have are from that marriage. Then, you almost always name your spouse as the beneficiary and your children as the successor beneficiaries.

## Naming Nonspouse Beneficiaries

If you have children and no spouse, you probably will name your children as the beneficiaries of your IRAs and annuities. Even if you have a spouse, you may still decide to name your children as the primary beneficiaries. You might make this choice either because this is a second marriage, or you and your spouse or partner have evaluated all of your property and determined that your family unit can save taxes this way.

If you have no spouse or children, you will need to choose someone or some entity such as a charity as the beneficiary. There are no limits on who you can name. However, your choice of beneficiary may affect the way your IRA or annuity will be taxed.

Unmarried partners are more common today and it is important for you, if you are in this situation, to look carefully at your assets, how they are titled, and how they are directed. If you want your partner to be the beneficiary of your retirement funds, be sure your beneficiary designation form clearly names her.

## Penalty for Early Withdrawal from Tax-Deferred Accounts

The IRS has allowed you to set aside funds for your retirement in tax-deferred accounts. You are not allowed to defer taxes forever, however, which is why the IRS requires you to begin taxable withdrawals under its minimum distribution rules. The IRS has been waiting for you to start withdrawals so that taxes will finally be paid on the tax-deferred accounts. At the same time, it does not want you to use the retirement funds simply as a tax-deferred savings account. You must wait to begin withdrawals until a reasonable retirement age, which IRS determines is over 59½. If you choose to withdraw money from your IRA or annuity before you turn age 59½, in addition to the income tax due on the funds you receive, there will be an additional 10 percent penalty tax on the withdrawal.

There are five exceptions to the penalty for taking a distribution before you reach age 59½. You will not have to pay the 10 percent penalty if:

1. The distribution is due to your death.
2. The distribution is made because you are disabled.
3. The distribution is made for certain qualified medical expenses.

4. The distribution is $10,000 or less and is used to purchase your first home.
5. The distribution is for educational expenses following high school.

Keep in mind that you may be shortchanging your own retirement or reducing the assets for your heirs if you take early withdrawals from your IRA or annuity.

## Income Tax Consequences

There are many types of retirement accounts that could have been established by your employer. Your employer might have made all of the contributions to the retirement account on your behalf, or you might have made some of the contributions. The way withdrawals by you or by your beneficiaries will be taxed depends on when the plan was set up, who made the contributions, and how the contributions were characterized when they were made. It is impossible to make a blanket statement about how the withdrawals from an employer-provided plan will be taxed. You need to contact your plan administrator and ask.

**FACT**

Usually an employer-provided retirement plan can be transferred to your traditional IRA after you retire. Again, you'll need to contact the plan administrator to determine your options. You may find more flexibility in your planning to transfer any employer-provided retirement plan into your individual IRA.

IRAs and annuities, on the other hand, are all governed by the same IRS rules. It doesn't matter who you have chosen as administrator to hold your IRA or annuity accounts. There is one set of rules for taxing withdrawals during your lifetime, and a second set of rules about the way withdrawals will be taxed to your beneficiaries after you are gone.

## Income Taxes When You Withdraw

If you are over 59½ when you begin your withdrawals, those withdrawals from your traditional IRA or annuities must be reported on your income tax return, at your current tax rate, in the year you withdraw the money. There are no special income tax rates available for your withdrawals.

## Taxation of Traditional IRAs

You must begin taking withdrawals from your traditional IRAs no later than the year you turn 70½. The amount you must withdraw each year is established by an applicable divisor schedule that has been established by the IRS. For instance, when you are seventy-two years old, that divisor is 25.6. You must total the value of all your IRAs with all administrators and divide that value by the divisor. For example, if your IRAs are worth $100,000, you must withdraw $3,906.25 ($100,000 divided by 25.6). The following year, when you are seventy-three years old, the divisor becomes 24.7 and you repeat the process. Each year thereafter, the divisor will decline. This annual reduction in divisor is to help stretch out the IRAs to last over your lifetime, but leave nothing remaining at your death.

If you are still under 70½, in order to allow the tax-deferred accounts to continue to grow, try taking withdrawals from an asset that does not give a step-up in cost basis, such as annuities. If you find you don't need the required distribution in the current year, you can reinvest that sum or add it to your taxable portfolio. By continuing to invest in your retirement years, you will provide security for yourself and possible additional assets for your heirs.

If you are uncertain about the math, each IRA administrator can make the calculation for your required minimum distribution from the holdings it administers for you. Each account is valued as of December 31 of the prior year.

If you are married and your spouse is more than ten years younger than you, you may elect to have your IRA paid over the joint life expectancy of you and your spouse. This election will result in a lower or smaller annual distribution. With a smaller annual withdrawal, you may be able to spread out your IRA benefits to last for the rest of your life and your spouse's life.

If you would like more information about how to make the calculations and determine how much you must withdraw each year, check the required minimum distribution section of IRS Publication 590. The required minimum distribution rules for tax-deferred accounts are complicated. IRS Publication 590 is dedicated to Individual Retirement Arrangements (IRAs) and retirement plans. You should request and review this publication carefully. Check out which circumstances apply to you and your beneficiaries before taking any withdrawals.

## Taxation of Roth IRAs

If you have been purchasing Roth IRAs in addition to or instead of traditional IRAs, there will be no income tax when you begin withdrawals. Roth IRAs are established from funds on which you have already paid income tax, and they do not fit in the tax-deferred category.

**FACT**

If you have more than one IRA or annuity, it is not necessary to take a proportionate share of the required minimum distribution from each of your accounts. You can total all your tax-deferred accounts, but take the full required minimum distribution from just one account.

Because there is no income tax upon withdrawal, Roth IRAs are ideal for passing assets to your family. If you are eligible to create a Roth, it is worth considering establishment of a Roth account no matter what your age. Although there is no income tax due when withdrawing funds from a Roth, the value of your Roth is included in your taxable estate.

## Taxation of Annuity Payments

An annuity is similar to an individual retirement account, but it has some quirks that make it an uncertain estate planning tool. While you are living, the earnings from the annuity are not subject to income taxes. But as soon as you withdraw funds or receive an annual payment, you will pay income taxes on the earnings.

One advantage to the annuity is that the initial amount you paid for the annuity is not taxed because you already paid tax on those funds. If there are annuity funds remaining in your estate at death, you might think that your heirs would be getting some benefit by having to report only the earnings. There is a drawback, however; see the section on Estate Tax Consequences later in this chapter.

## Income Taxes for Your Beneficiaries

Withdrawals your beneficiaries make from your traditional IRA or annuity after you are gone are taxed in the same manner as withdrawals you might have made while you were alive. Thus, when your beneficiary makes a withdrawal from a traditional IRA, he will report that withdrawal on his income tax return at his income tax rate.

The rationale for making you take distributions from your IRA when you reach age 70½ is to try to force you to spend all of your IRA before you die—and to pay IRS the taxes. This is why the required minimum distributions are calculated based on your life expectancy.

IRAs can be divided into separate shares for each of your named beneficiaries. The life expectancy of the youngest beneficiary is used to calculate how quickly all of the beneficiaries must take their distributions. Check the IRS life expectancy tables in IRS Publication 590 to determine how rapidly your beneficiaries must withdraw from the IRA after you are gone.

The beneficiaries will need to withdraw a stated percentage each year. However, because the stated percentage is based on the life expectancy of the youngest beneficiary, the length of time over which the beneficiaries must withdraw is extended dramatically. Check the IRS brochures listed in Appendix B for further details on calculating the annual required distribution.

There is one major difference in income taxation between IRAs and annuities: The beneficiaries of your annuities pay income taxes only on the growth or gain on the annuities. With a traditional IRA (but not a Roth), your beneficiaries pay income taxes on 100 percent of the IRA distributions they receive after you are gone.

## *Estate Tax Consequences*

The full value of your traditional and Roth IRAs and annuities as of the date of your death will be included in your federal estate tax base. Chapter 17 shows you the federal estate tax exposure and the changes in place for 2009, 2010, and 2011.

**FACT**

The combined estate tax and income taxes on your IRAs and annuities can go as high as 80 percent of the value of your IRA. If your federal estate tax rate is 45 percent, and the income tax rate your beneficiaries pay is 35 percent, then 80 percent of the value of your IRA will be paid in taxes.

You may have thought that because your IRAs and annuities avoid probate and are payable directly to a named beneficiary, they are not subject to federal estate taxes. Unfortunately, this isn't true. When you die, both your traditional and Roth IRAs will be included in your taxable estate and, if over the exemption amount for that year, will be taxable.

## Annuities and Cost Basis

One reason some advisers think annuities are not a good investment is the result at your death. Think back to the discussion about cost basis. When you buy a piece of property, the amount you pay for the property is your cost basis. On many assets, your heirs receive a step-up in cost basis to the date-of-death value. Annuities are different. There is no step-up in basis for an annuity, which is a major disadvantage to your heirs.

## Planning Ahead

You should consider spending your annuities or IRAs while you are living, and let your other property grow in value. As you have now learned, most of the other property you own, such as a home, stocks, and art, will receive a new cost basis equal to the value of property when you die. There will be no income taxes owing on those properties when your heirs receive your property as there is with a traditional IRA or annuity.

**ALERT!**

Keep in mind that Congress may well change the laws regarding estate taxes or tax rates at any time. Although the rates for 2009–2011 are currently known, be aware that the unified credit and tax rates could be changed by the time of your death.

If you follow the recommendation about how to analyze the property you own, you will be determining whether your estate has a federal estate tax exposure. You will also be thinking about which properties will create the least tax for your beneficiaries or heirs. Remember, you don't have a crystal ball. If you knew when you and your spouse were going to die, you would know exactly how much to withdraw from each asset to minimize the taxes owing by you or your heirs. You can only make an educated guess. This is why it is important that you review your plan at least every year to see if it still meets your needs.

# CHAPTER 17

# Death and Taxes

You've heard people say that only two things in life are certain: death and taxes. You work your whole life to accumulate property only to discover that when you die, the federal government becomes your heir. When you understand the rules about federal estate taxes, it is much easier to reduce the federal government's share and to increase your family's inheritance.

## What Is the Federal Estate Tax?

The tax your estate might owe when you die is technically a transfer tax. You pay tax on the right to transfer your assets to another person or institution. Taxable gifts made during your lifetime are added to the transfers you make when you die to determine a taxable base. The taxes your estate owes at your death are a percentage of your taxable base if your taxable base exceeds the unified credit amount. Confused? Don't worry, keep reading.

### Unified Transfer Tax

The federal estate tax is not a stand-alone tax. In 2001, Congress made changes to the way federal estate taxes are computed. It divided the taxable transfers into two pieces—one for gifts and one for estates. The first piece covers taxable gifts you make during your lifetime. The second piece includes taxable transfers you make at your death. The IRS requires you to add gifts and transfers at death together. The total of the two transfers are subject to what the IRS calls a "unified transfer tax or unified credit."

**FACT**

You are required to file gift tax forms for gifts exceeding the annual exclusion, currently $13,000, or the lifetime exclusion (other than gifts to your spouse), currently $1 million. You must keep track of all the taxable gifts you make during your lifetime. At death, the records you've kept will assist your executor in determining how much of the unified credit remains.

The easiest way to understand the unified transfer tax is to think of it as a savings account. The federal government grants you a savings account of a dollar amount that is exempt from taxation. The dollar amount on which no taxes are due includes two *exclusions*. There is a gift tax exclusion amount and a unified credit exclusion amount. These amounts are not the same, and the gift exclusion is a subset of the unified credit amount. You can use the gift tax exclusion to shelter gifts or transfers while you are living, and you can use the unified credit exclusion to shelter transfers you make at death. Continue reading for further details.

## Savings Account or Unified Credit Amount

Congress has changed the savings account amount over the last fifteen years. In May 2001, Congress increased the exclusion from $675,000 per person to $1 million per person for both gifts and estate transfers. For example, suppose that your savings account in 2002 was $1 million. If you made a taxable gift of $300,000 while you were living, you had $700,000 of savings or exclusion remaining at your death.

However, Congress then changed the exclusions for several subsequent years and separated the gift and estate transfer amounts. In 2009, the gift tax portion will be $1 million, but the unified credit for both gifts and transfers at death will be $3.5 million per person. Let's take an example of a gift in 2009.

You give your son $513,000 and your daughter $513,000. As you have just read, you are allowed to give $13,000 annually without tax, but any gift exceeding $13,000 is a taxable gift. Therefore, in this example, you subtract $13,000 from your gifts to each child. The balance of $500,000 to each child is taxable. You have made taxable gifts of $1 million ($513,000 plus $513,000 minus $26,000). Later in 2009 you die. Your executor calculates your taxable base of all other assets as $2 million.

If you have made prior gifts to your children, in excess of the annual exclusion of $13,000, those gifts will be included as part of your taxable gifts. If you have made gifts during your lifetime to your children exceeding $1 million, the amount in excess of $1 million will be taxed even if your total estate is less than $3.5 million.

Because the total exclusion in 2009 is $3.5 million, you first subtract your taxable gift of $1 million leaving a savings account or unified credit of $2.5 million. Because your gifts did not exceed the $1 million gift tax exclusion, there is no tax owed on your gifts to your son and daughter. And, because your estate, which the executor calculates at $2 million, is less than your remaining unified credit total of $2.5 million your estate will not owe any taxes.

In the year 2010, according to the present schedule, there will be no estate tax, but there will continue to be a gift tax. The highest tax rate on gifts in 2010 will drop from the 2009 rate of 45 percent to 35 percent. If you die that year, you will be able to transfer your estate property at death and pay no transfer taxes.

To complicate things even further for you and your family in your planning, in 2011 the savings account or unified credit amount is scheduled to revert to a unified exclusion of $1 million, which was the figure in place for many years prior to the 2001 Tax Act. The highest tax rate will jump back up to the former 55 percent rate.

Congress frequently changes the tax rates and rules when they figure out that the tax breaks they provided cost the government too much in lost revenue. Pay attention to future changes to the rates and unified credit, as changes could well affect your well-thought-out plan.

What follows in 2011 or beyond is still uncertain. Congress makes estate planning difficult by periodically changing the rules! You or your heirs can plan only on the unified credit in effect in the year of your gift or of your death.

## Property That Is Subject to Federal Estate Taxes

The property that is taxed when you die, along with the taxable gifts you made while living, is referred to as your taxable base. Almost everyone understands that property you own when you die might be subject to federal estate taxes or transfer taxes. What most people don't understand is that the taxable base is much broader than merely property you own when you die. By the time you finish reading this chapter you may find yourself adding pieces of paper to your notebook to describe property you never dreamed would be taxed.

## Property You Own When You Die

The first category of property included in your taxable base is all of the property you own in your individual name. You may have organized this information in your notebook or when you completed the Asset Inventory Worksheet found in Appendix C. If you own property in joint name with your spouse or someone else, do not include that property on your list yet. There is a section in this chapter that will teach you how to calculate the amount of property that must be included in your taxable base attributable to joint property. The first step to computing your taxable base is to add up the value of all of the property that is titled in your individual name.

## Life Insurance

The amount of life insurance proceeds that will be paid to anyone when you die is the second category of property subject to transfer taxes at your death. You probably don't consider life insurance as property you own. As a matter of fact, you may have thought that because your life insurance is paid directly to the beneficiary named in the policy, there are no taxes. While life insurance benefits are not subject to income taxes or probate, the proceeds are included in the calculation of your taxable base.

Imagine how shocked your family will be if they find out that the $500,000 life insurance policy you paid for all of your life pushes your taxable base over your exclusion amount. If you were to die in 2009, your estate could owe anywhere from 18 percent to 45 percent in taxes, depending on how much your estate exceeds the exclusion.

You should return to your notebook and prepare a separate piece of paper for each life insurance policy you have. Before you list the necessary information about your life insurance policies, you may want to reread Chapter 15. That chapter describes the difference between the owner, the insured, and the beneficiary of the life insurance policy. Chapter 18 will discuss a method of removing the life insurance proceeds from your taxable base.

## Retirement Accounts

You may think that because your retirement accounts are paid directly to a named beneficiary, they are not subject to transfer taxes at death. This is simply not true. The full value of most retirement accounts is included in your taxable base. As you learned in Chapter 16, there are some special rules for certain employer-provided retirement accounts, so you should always check the rules with your plan administrator. In order for you to calculate your transfer tax exposure when you die, you need to add up the value of all of your retirement accounts.

Keep in mind that in addition to transfer taxes that might be owed because of your death, the beneficiaries of your retirement accounts will also pay income taxes on distributions they receive after you are gone. Chapter 18 gives you valuable tips on how you can structure your retirement account beneficiary choices to reduce income taxes for your heirs.

## Annuities

When you prepared your pieces of paper describing each piece of property you own, you should have also completed one piece of paper for each annuity. Chapter 16 taught you how annuities are taxed and how you might plan now to minimize those taxes. The value of any annuities received by anyone because of your death is included in your taxable base. This may confuse you.

You were probably told that one of the terrific things about annuities is that they grow in value tax-free. This is not totally accurate. While you do not pay income taxes on the growth of your annuity while you are alive, the value of the annuity on the date of your death is included in your taxable base. If your taxable base exceeds the exclusion amount in effect in the year of your death, you will owe estate tax on the excess over the unified credit amount.

## Joint Property

A portion or all of your joint property is included in your taxable base even though the property passes automatically to the surviving joint tenant. The amount that is included in your taxable base is different if the joint tenant is your spouse as opposed to a joint tenant who is not your spouse. If your joint tenant is your spouse, you include 50 percent of the date-of-death value of the joint property in your taxable base. It does not matter which spouse paid for the property. The other 50 percent is credited to the surviving spouse.

If you own property with a joint tenant who is not your spouse, the percentage you contributed toward the purchase price of the property will be included in your taxable base. For instance, if you paid for 100 percent of the cost of the joint property, 100 percent of the value of the joint property will be included in your taxable base. If you paid for 80 percent of the cost, and the other joint tenant paid for 20 percent, you will include 80 percent of the value of the property in your taxable base.

## Property in Your Power

If you make any transfer of property while you are living but you keep the power to alter, amend, or revoke the transfer, the full value of the property you transferred will be included in your taxable base. The value of the property at the date of your death will be what is counted, not the value the property had when you made the transfer.

The most common example of property you might transfer where you hold a power to revoke is a revocable trust. The property in the revocable trust will avoid probate but, because you hold a power to revoke the trust, you are considered to be the owner of that asset. Thus, the value of the trust assets will be included in your taxable base.

If you transfer property but are still using or enjoying the property when you die, it is still included in your federal taxable base. This is a tricky one for the person who tries to do his own planning. The classic example is when you deed a piece of property to someone else. For instance, you deed your home to your child. Your child owns the property, but you continue to live in the home, rent-free. Because you enjoyed the use of the property until you died and did not pay rent, the value of the property is included in your taxable base.

## General Powers of Appointment

If you hold a general power of appointment over property, the full value of that property will be included in your federal taxable base. If you think you hold a general power of appointment over property, you might want to read about powers of attorney in Chapter 20.

It is a tedious process to calculate your federal estate tax exposure. But this is what your family is going to have to do after you are gone. It is so much better if you are alive to list all the property that will be included in your taxable base. Although Congress may change the rates in the future, having a list of taxable property will make your family aware of property to be included in your taxable base. Trying to pull this information together after you are gone could be very difficult.

## Taxable Gifts

Because you need to add taxable gifts you made during your life to your taxable base when you die, you need to understand the definition of a taxable gift. It would be unrealistic to expect you to keep records of every single gift you make. Therefore the law defines a taxable gift as a gift above a certain amount per year made to any person. The amount you can give each year without owing gift taxes is called the annual exclusion. Gifts to any individual above that exclusion amount, other than to a spouse, are taxable gifts.

**FACT**

Recipients of your gifts do not pay taxes on your gift. If you make a gift that exceeds the exclusion, you as the giver are obligated to file the gift tax form and pay the gift tax.

For many years the gift tax exclusion was $10,000 per year per person. As part of the tax reform passed by Congress, the annual gift tax exclusion amount will be increased periodically to adjust for inflation. Beginning in 2009, the gift tax exclusion went to $13,000. Currently, any annual gift to an individual that exceeds that amount is a taxable gift. In addition, any gifts that exceed your annual exclusion and also exceed $1 million over your lifetime are taxable.

## *Gifts That Are Not Taxable*

Because the annual exclusion is available for as many persons as you would like to give to, you can reduce your taxable base substantially by making annual gifts at an amount less than the annual exclusion to each person. Making annual gifts is a core building block in many estate plans. You may want to include this in your estate plan as well, especially if you suspect that your taxable base will exceed the savings account amount.

It is important to understand that the gift tax exclusion is a per-person exclusion. If you have four children and six grandchildren, you could give $130,000 per year, or $13,000 to each person, without making a taxable gift that would affect your savings account.

You and your spouse can each give $13,000 per person to an unlimited number of people without making a taxable gift. Jointly, you and your spouse can give $26,000 to as many individuals as you wish. This exclusion will rise in increments of $1,000 depending on inflation. In future years you may be able to make even larger annual gifts.

## *Deductions Against Your Taxable Base*

The information you gathered in your notebook will help you determine the deductions you can take against your taxable base. There are four categories of items that can be deducted against your taxable base:

1. Funeral and administration expenses, claims against your estate, unpaid bills, and debts and taxes
2. Casualty and theft losses
3. Charitable gifts you make at your death
4. Most property you leave to your spouse

Because your executor will need to gather this information before filing final estate tax returns, it will be helpful for your family to keep a file or notebook listing all their expenses for the funeral and noting any other costs of administering the estate within those four categories that they know about.

## Debts and Funeral Expenses

If you prepared the notebook described in Chapter 2, you have already listed the debt owing against each piece of property you own. Or, if you completed the Asset Inventory Worksheet in Appendix C, you listed and summarized the debts you owe. All debts you owe at the time of your death are deductible against your taxable base.

Funeral expenses such as funeral home costs, a reception or luncheon following a service, flowers, and burial arrangements are all deductible against your taxable base.

## Charitable Gifts

Any contributions to a qualified charity are deductible from your taxable base. If your will or trust contributes cash to a charity, the amount of cash you contribute will be deductible from your taxable base. If your estate leaves property to a charity, the value of the property on the date of the gift is deducted from your taxable base. See Chapter 19 for several opportunities to make charitable gifts to reduce your taxes.

You usually don't need to worry about whether a charity is qualified. Churches, schools, hospitals, and most national and state associations that benefit a purpose are qualified charities.

The reason there are limitations on donating to a nonqualified charity is that the government does not want you to try to transfer property to your family, friends, and neighbors and to characterize the transfer as a charitable gift.

## *Property Left to Your Spouse*

When you compute your taxable base, you are allowed to subtract the value of all property transferred to your surviving spouse, as long as you are leaving your spouse a qualified interest. This is called the *marital deduction*. If you leave property to your spouse with no strings attached, this is a qualified interest. "No strings attached" means your spouse can do whatever she wants with the property after you are gone. Chapter 18 covers the restrictions you can place on a transfer to your spouse and still qualify for the marital deduction. Before you learn what types of restrictions you can place on a transfer to your spouse at death, you need to fully understand why you may or may not want to use the marital deduction.

A marital deduction operates like this: If you die with a $500,000 taxable base and you leave all of your property to your spouse, your estate will subtract the $500,000 transfer to your spouse, and the estate's taxable base will be zero. Remember, your taxable base includes all of the items described in this chapter. When your taxable base is zero, your estate is not taking advantage of any of your savings account or unified credit.

**FACT**

If the combined taxable bases for you and your spouse exceed $1 million, you should consider not leaving all of your property outright to your spouse. However, if the combined taxable base of both spouses is under $1 million, there is no adverse estate tax consequence to leaving all of your property to your spouse.

When your spouse dies, he will have all of the property that would have been included in his own taxable base, plus the $500,000 he received from you. If, because of the size of your gift to him, he then has an estate that exceeds his savings account or unified credit amount, his estate will owe federal estate taxes.

## Should You Leave All of Your Property to Your Spouse?

The answer depends on the total value of the marital taxable base. The marital taxable base is the sum of the husband's taxable base and the wife's taxable base. Again, for the purpose of simplicity, the unified credit exclusion is referred to as your savings account amount.

For instance, using the anticipated $1 million exclusion for 2011 as the example, assume the husband has a taxable base of $750,000. Assume the wife has a taxable base of $500,000. If the husband leaves all of his property to the wife, his estate will have a zero taxable base because his estate subtracts the $750,000 left to his wife. The husband did not use any of his exclusion. Now his wife dies. If she does not reduce her assets while living, her taxable base is $1.25 million ($750,000 received from her husband plus her own $500,000 taxable base). Her estate exceeds the exclusion amount by $250,000, which will be subject to taxes at the estate tax rate in her year of death (rates up to 55 percent in 2011 unless Congress makes another change!).

Each individual has a savings account, but it is a "use it or lose it" benefit. If you do not use your savings account when you die, it is gone; you can't transfer your exclusion amount to your spouse.

Again, using $1 million as the exclusion amount, assume the husband left $500,000 to his wife outright, and $500,000 of property in a way that his wife could have the benefit of the property but did not own it outright. Then, when his wife died, her taxable base would be $1 million ($500,000 received outright from her husband and her own $500,000 taxable base).

Chapter 18 will show you how the extra $500,000 in this example can be directed for the benefit of the surviving spouse, but not be included in her taxable base.

In the preceding example, the surviving spouse at her death would use her own $1 million savings account to offset any transfer taxes owed. Assuming the exemption is still $1 million in the year of her death, her estate would owe no taxes.

## *Figuring Your Federal Estate Taxes*

It's time to figure out your taxable base and whether or not you would owe federal estate tax if you were to die in the next couple of years. First take out your notebook and add up all property that is taxed when you die. Keep a separate list of taxable gifts you made while living. This gives you your taxable base. Next add up all deductions you might take as described in this chapter. Then subtract the deductions from the taxable base. This number will provide an estimate of your taxable base when you die.

However, because the estate tax rates and the unified credit amount will probably change after 2010, you will not be able to determine the actual tax rate just yet. You can, however, use $1 million as a guide for the minimum unified credit to calculate what you might owe if the exclusion rate remains unchanged.

If your taxable base, after all other deductions, is more than the current unified credit amount, carefully read Chapters 18 and 19. Several methods to reduce the transfer taxes are covered, including charitable giving and charitable trusts. If any of the tax planning suggestions described in those chapters appeal to you, you have more homework to do before you make your final decision. Developing a plan to pay no gift or estate taxes is part of your own puzzle. There are many ways to fill in the pieces!

**CHAPTER 18**

# How to Reduce Taxes

It is very gratifying to create an estate plan that reduces or eliminates taxes. The federal estate tax is very expensive, and it is not the only tax your family might owe. You may also be subject to state taxes and generation-skipping taxes if you are leaving assets to grandchildren. The top rate for federal transfer taxes in 2009 is expected to be 45 percent. You will discover that, with some planning, most families can substantially reduce or eliminate this tax.

# Credit Shelter Trusts (or Bypass Trusts)

Credit shelter trusts or bypass trusts are used only between spouses when needed. The credit shelter trust is really a layman's term for a method of being sure both spouses take advantage of the estate tax unified credit amount.

When federal transfer taxes are computed on your estate, your estate is actually granted a tax credit equal to the savings account discussed in Chapter 17. When you create a credit shelter trust or a bypass trust, you are creating a trust that uses the tax credit associated with the savings account amount, thus sheltering or protecting your assets from taxes. That is why it is called a credit shelter trust. Don't worry; as you continue reading, these concepts will become understandable.

If you add your taxable base to the taxable base of your spouse, and the total exceeds one savings account amount or unified credit exclusion, you should definitely consider using credit shelter trusts.

A credit shelter trust is not a separate trust, but is created within a revocable trust. While you are alive, you are your own trustee and have full control over the trust property. When you die, the successor trustee takes over and begins following the instructions you put in your trust document. The credit shelter trust comes into being when you die if the combined taxable bases of you and your spouse exceed one savings account amount. This savings account is based on the allowable exclusion for the year in which you die. In 2009 the exclusion is $3.5 million each, but that will change in 2010, 2011, and possibly in later years.

If your taxable base plus the taxable base of your spouse is less than one savings account amount, your successor trustee will probably be instructed to transfer the entire balance of your trust to your spouse's trust or to your spouse outright since you don't need a credit shelter trust to reduce your estate taxes. It is only when your surviving spouse would have a taxable base larger than the exclusion amount that you need to create a credit shelter or bypass trust for estate tax planning.

When you die, your revocable trust becomes irrevocable. If you have created a credit shelter trust, the terms of that trust will include instructions in the trust document. Those instructions will tell your successor trustee to look at your surviving spouse's potential taxable base. There are two possible sets of instructions that could be given, depending on the combined taxable base of you and your spouse.

## The First Set of Instructions

The first set of instructions would cover the situation in which the combined taxable base of your estate plus your spouse's estate in 2011 (and possibly beyond) is between $1 million and $2 million. If this occurs, the first thing your successor trustee will do is calculate what your surviving spouse's taxable base would be if she died.

Perhaps there are reasons other than tax savings for not giving your spouse access to all your property. In that case, you may instruct your successor trustee to keep your property in trust to be managed for the benefit of your spouse or your other beneficiaries after you are gone.

Remember, upon your death your spouse might receive property from sources other than your trust. If your spouse receives insurance proceeds, annuities, or retirement accounts because of your death, those amounts should be included in her taxable base. The successor trustee will then be instructed to transfer enough property from your trust to your surviving spouse or her revocable trust to leave her with a taxable base equal to the tax exclusion figure in the year of your death.

Suppose in 2011 the combined taxable base of you and your spouse is $1.5 million, and you die in that year. Your trustee should direct to your credit shelter trust the amount that would exceed $1 million of your surviving spouse's base. This is a good way to take advantage of your unified credit or savings account.

For example, assume your surviving spouse has a $700,000 taxable base. This taxable base already includes insurance, annuities, or retirement plans your spouse received because of your death. Assume your taxable base is $800,000. If the exclusion is still $1 million, your trustee would transfer $300,000 of your trust property to your spouse. This would give your spouse a taxable base of $1 million (your $300,000 plus her $700,000) and no tax due. Your credit shelter trust now has $500,000 remaining (your taxable base of $800,000 minus the $300,000 transferred to your spouse's trust). The credit shelter trust provides income to your spouse but is not part of her taxable base.

## *The Second Set of Instructions*

The second set of instructions tells your successor trustee what to do if the combined taxable base of you and your spouse is over $2 million. If your combined taxable bases exceed $2 million at your death, your successor trustee will be instructed to transfer all of your trust property over $1 million to your spouse's trust.

Don't move everything in your estate to the surviving spouse's trust. You could be limiting your spouse's outright access to funds he might want or need.

As another example, let's assume your taxable base is $1.2 million and your spouse's taxable base is $1.1 million when you die. Your successor trustee would keep $1 million in your credit shelter trust and transfer $200,000 to your spouse or her revocable trust. The $200,000 is deducted from your taxable base because you can deduct property you give to your spouse. This would leave your estate with a taxable base of $1 million. Your estate would pay no taxes because the taxable base equals the unified credit exclusion.

If your surviving spouse is left with a taxable base of more than $1 million she should then be able to do some planning to reduce her taxable base below $1 million.

These examples assume that neither you nor your spouse made any taxable gifts during your lives that would reduce the available gift exclusion when you die. Of course, property can increase or decrease in value after being transferred to your spouse or her trust. You may want to give your spouse the opportunity to spend down the estate or to make more annual gifts.

## Power over the Trust Property

In the first example, you had $500,000 left in the credit shelter trust. In the second example, there is $1 million the maximum exclusion amount, in the credit shelter trust. The credit shelter trust is irrevocable after you are gone. Your successor trustee will manage the money or property in the trust for the benefit of your family according to the instructions you put in the document.

You cannot name your spouse as successor trustee of your credit shelter trust. If you do, the credit shelter trust will be included in your spouse's taxable base when he dies, and you will have wasted your time creating it. Your spouse should not have full control over the credit shelter trust property, but the trustee can usually provide funds as needed in line with your instructions.

You can give your trustee any of the powers that are described in Chapters 11 and 12 over the trust property. As you may recall, you can be very specific about how, when, and why your successor trustee distributes the credit shelter trust money and property for your spouse, your children, or other beneficiaries you might name. But, frankly, what most people want is to provide the surviving spouse with as much access to the property in the credit shelter trust as possible.

You can give your spouse the absolute right to all of the income from the property. In addition, you can give your trustee the power to distribute as much money or property from the credit shelter trust as your spouse needs for her health, education, maintenance, or welfare. And you can give your surviving spouse the right to demand the greater of $5,000 per year or 5 percent of the value of all of the credit shelter trust assets. This power to demand is in addition to the other rights and powers.

# Make Gifts of Your Assets

Giving property to your family while you are living is an excellent estate planning device. It is simple and does not involve expensive legal fees to accomplish. You can reduce the size of your taxable estate very quickly by making annual gifts that do not exceed the annual exclusion and, thus, are not taxable and do not consume your savings account. Reread Chapter 17 for information about gifts that are not taxable.

## Gifts of Property

You do not have to give cash to use the annual gift exclusion. You can give real or personal property as well. And you don't have to give all of one piece of property in only one year. For example, assume you have four children, and you own a piece of real estate that is worth $300,000. You and your spouse could give 34.66 percent of the real estate to your children this year ($104,000), 34.66 percent next year ($104,000), and the remaining 30.66 percent ($92,000) in the third year. You can do this without using any of your savings account because you and your spouse jointly gave each child $26,000 for the first two years and $23,000 in the third year, all within the annual gift exclusion amount.

**FACT**

You may also reduce your estate by paying school tuition or medical bills for others by making payments directly to a school or medical facility instead of to an individual. For example, you can make a payment of $15,000 directly to a university for your child's tuition; that is not considered a taxable gift even though it exceeds the annual exclusion.

If you exceed the annual gift exclusion amount for any person during the year, you begin to consume your savings account. If you own property that you think is going to increase in value very rapidly, it might make sense to use up your exclusion with taxable gifts. If you give away a $1 million-piece of property, using all of your lifetime gift exclusion, and the property becomes worth $3 million by the time you are gone, the $2 million of growth is not in your estate.

Wealthy individuals frequently use annual gifts to decrease their taxable estates. When you analyze the property you own, the cost basis of each piece of property, and your family's exposure to federal estate taxes, you will be able to decide whether you want to make current gifts to reduce your taxable base.

Keep in mind that property is valued at the time of the gift. If you use the gift exclusion to give your property to your children, they will not get a step-up in cost basis upon your death because they already own the property.

## Charitable Bequests and Gifts

Another way to reduce your estate tax is to make current gifts to charity or to leave a gift to charity through a bequest or other method. Charitable giving methods will be covered in more detail in Chapter 19.

# More Sophisticated Methods for Reducing Taxes

There are other methods to reduce taxes, all of which will require the assistance of a lawyer. Three methods for your consideration are covered briefly in this chapter. If you think your estate might exceed the gift or unified credit amount, or that your family might otherwise benefit from any of these options, make a note of your questions about each and discuss them with an experienced estate planning lawyer.

## Irrevocable Life Insurance Trust

An irrevocable life insurance trust is a tool to change ownership of a life insurance policy. It removes the policy from your control and places it in an insurance trust. Once out of your name and control, the policy will no longer be counted as part of your taxable base. An irrevocable trust is like the trusts you have already learned about.

Although it is simpler to give your life insurance policy directly to your beneficiaries, they would then be able to do what they want with it. You would no longer have the control you would have if you transferred ownership of your policy to an irrevocable trust. When you create an irrevocable insurance trust, you name a trustee who must follow the instructions you put in the document. These instructions can both protect the current cash value of your policy and put a plan in place for managing and distributing the death benefit after you are gone.

If you have a $100,000 life insurance policy that would have triggered a sizable federal estate tax bill, it is well worth your time and money to create an irrevocable insurance trust! Your heirs then receive the full value of the policy, not just what's left after taxes.

To create a life insurance trust, you transfer ownership of the life insurance policy to your chosen trustee. You will still be the insured on the policy, but you will no longer be the owner. In addition, the beneficiary of the policy will be changed to name the trustee of your life insurance trust. The trust will now be owner and beneficiary.

There are three major factors in an irrevocable life insurance trust that differ from your revocable trust. First, of course, the trust is irrevocable. Second, you should not serve as the trustee of the irrevocable life insurance trust. Third, there may be a gift tax consequence for transferring your life insurance policy to the trustee of the irrevocable insurance trust. Determining the value of the gift of the policy to the trust is difficult and has a particular name—the interpolated reserve value. You should contact your insurance agent and ask her for that figure so you will know the size of gift you are making and whether it exceeds the annual exclusion.

## Qualified Personal Residence Trust

Many of the more complicated estate tax reduction tools use the concept of giving away property today at a discounted value. A qualified personal residence trust is one of those estate tax reduction techniques. A qualified personal residence trust is referred to as a QPRT. A QPRT is a way to transfer your personal residence to the next generation at a fraction of the transfer tax cost. The amount of savings your family will enjoy will depend on two factors: the length of time for which you establish your QPRT and your age when you create the QPRT.

### Understanding QPRT

The best way for you to understand a QPRT is to imagine that the title to your home is represented by a piece of paper. If you take that piece of paper and cut it into two pieces, you have divided the title to the property into two pieces. This is really what you do when you create a QPRT. You cut the title to your property into two pieces. One piece represents the use of your home for a specified number of years, called the term of years. The second piece of the paper represents the title to your home after the term of years, called the remainder interest.

When you create a QPRT, you decide how long or how many years you want the term of years to last. You will keep the first piece of the title for that number of years, meaning you continue to live in your home the way you did before you created the QPRT. Then you give the other piece of the paper, representing the remainder interest in your home, to someone else, typically your children. After the end of the term of years, your children own your home.

The goal is to give property to your family at the lowest possible value in order to consume the least amount of your savings account.

### There's a Catch

There is a trick to the QPRT. In order to have the QPRT respected when you die, you have to outlive the number of years you choose for your QPRT. For example, if you create a five-year QPRT and die anytime during the five-year period, it's as though you didn't do anything. The house will be included in your estate and the gift you made when you created the QPRT will be ignored. It is important if you are going to create a QPRT to pick a number of years that you realistically think you will outlive. The further you go into the future, the more tax advantage you gain from creating a QPRT, but you have to live the specified number of years.

### Disadvantages to a QPRT

You, the owner of the property, suffer the main disadvantage associated with a QPRT. At the end of the QPRT period, you have to either move out of your house or rent it back from the recipients of the QPRT. You don't own your home any more. If you stay in the home, you must pay rent. And the rent needs to be the same amount of rent a stranger would pay if he rented the home. Paying rent can be a good thing because it is another way for you to reduce the size of your taxable estate. A QPRT is a sophisticated estate planning device that is typically used by wealthy families as part of their estate plan to reduce taxes. Wealthy families usually use a combination of tax-saving devices. But a QPRT is not just for rich people. It is a technique available for any family that needs to reduce its federal estate tax bill.

## *Grantor Retained Annuity Trusts*

A grantor retained annuity trust, referred to as a GRAT, is another tax-planning device that allows you to make a gift at a discounted value. The theory of a GRAT is very similar to a QPRT.

A GRAT is a trust wherein you transfer property into the name of a trustee who holds and administers that property for your benefit and then, after a stated number of years, conveys the property to the persons you designate as your beneficiaries. The number of years you choose for a GRAT will affect the amount of discount you receive on the transfer. The amount of discount you receive from a GRAT is identical to the amount of discount you receive when you create a QPRT.

The GRAT is also like a QPRT because you must live for at least the number of years for which you establish your GRAT. If you create a GRAT for five years, and you die after four years, the property in the GRAT trust will be included in your estate. If you own property that you think will appreciate in value very rapidly and might push your estate over the unified credit amount, a GRAT is an excellent estate planning tool. However, it is not a device that you can create without the help of a qualified lawyer. The calculations involved in computing the value of the gift and filing the necessary gift tax returns necessitate the advice of a very competent professional. Knowing how a GRAT operates will help you decide whether this is an appropriate part of your estate plan.

## CHAPTER 19

# Charitable Gifts Can Reduce Taxes

One of the easiest ways to reduce taxes, both current income tax and future estate taxes, is to make charitable gifts to qualified charities. Charitable gifts provide support for your favorite institutions—religious, educational, medical, or other nonprofit. The gifts are deductible on your income tax return when you are living and on your estate tax return upon your death.

## *Gifts During Lifetime*

If you are looking to reduce the size of your estate or your current income taxes, or you simply wish to support a charity while you are living, there are many methods of making gifts. Outright cash is always welcome by charities, and most charities have annual campaigns requesting such support. You can simply write a check each year, or you can make a pledge for a certain sum over a period of years to have a greater impact.

**FACT**

If you give appreciated assets to charity, you are eligible for a deduction for the full fair-market value on the date of gift. You avoid payment of capital gains tax that would result if you were to sell the assets yourself. In addition, you remove that asset from your taxable base.

You could also give tangible gifts such as your books, your art, or your office equipment to a charity. If you give a charity tangible property for its related purpose, you are usually eligible for a charitable deduction based on the current, appraised value of the gift. Thus you reduce your estate, and you also receive a current income tax deduction for your gift.

If you have assets such as stocks or bonds that have appreciated over the years but that you think might decline in value in the future, consider giving those assets to a charity.

If you decide to retain the assets until your death, your heirs will receive a step-up in basis, but the value could do what you anticipated—decline over time. And they will remain in your estate.

There are limits or reductions in charitable deductions if you are in a particularly high income bracket. Check the IRS booklet, Publication 526, on charitable contributions to see whether you're affected.

### Real Estate

If your family is not interested in your primary residence, a second home, or a business property you own, you might consider a gift of that property during your lifetime. Again, the property would be valued as of the date of gift, and you will have removed a major asset from your taxable base.

### Life Insurance Gifts

If you find you have a life insurance policy that you no longer need for your family's support, you can donate that policy to your favorite charity by making the charity both owner and beneficiary of the policy. You remove the value of the policy from your estate, and you receive a charitable deduction in the year of the gift.

You may name a charity as beneficiary of a policy but, at the same time, you should turn over ownership. If you do not also transfer ownership of the policy to the charity, you have not relinquished control. Thus you will not be eligible for a charitable deduction, and the value will remain in your estate as part of your taxable base.

Examples of policies you may no longer need include a policy you bought to cover your mortgage payments or educational expenses for your children. If the house is now paid for and your children have graduated, you might consider giving this policy away.

Another way to support your charity through life insurance is to give it a paid-up policy. It can be a policy that no longer has premiums due or it can be a new policy requiring a single premium.

By naming a charity both owner and beneficiary of a policy, you give up control of the asset. You are then able to remove that asset from your taxable base. Such a gift could also provide you with a charitable income tax deduction in the year of the gift, which might be useful for your financial picture.

# Planned Gifts During Lifetime

Many charitable organizations today have planned giving offices as part of their fund-raising departments. They offer expertise on creative methods of giving that can be beneficial to you as well as to the charity.

**QUESTION?**

**What is "planned giving"?**
Planned giving has been described as a way of giving that requires expert assistance. It is usually associated with bequests or with life income gifts, but it is much broader than that. It is a method, simply, of planning your gifts as part of your overall financial or estate planning.

A planned gift can be a single outright gift that fits your financial plans, a series of annual gifts you commit to, or some other giving plan. It is any thoughtful gift arrangement that involves planning ahead and not just writing a $25 check out of your checkbook.

## Life Income Gifts

There are three main categories of life income gifts that usually come under the heading of planned giving. These options combine a gift to a qualified charity and lifetime income for you. If you wish, they can also provide income for another beneficiary such as a spouse, partner, child, or friend.

## Charitable Gift Annuities

The charitable gift annuity (CGA) is the easiest and most popular life income gift. It is created as a contract between you and the charity you wish to support. For example, you make a gift of $10,000 (a frequent minimum gift annuity amount). In return for your gift, the institution promises to pay you a specified payout rate for your lifetime based on your age.

When you and the charity discuss setting up the annuity, you will decide the frequency of payments you will receive. The usual choice is quarterly, but monthly, semiannually, or annually also are options.

At your death, payments will start going to a second beneficiary if there was one (or, if the annuity is a joint contract with your spouse, will simply continue for the surviving spouse) until her death. When both beneficiaries are gone, the value remaining in the gift annuity will go to the charity for the purpose you indicated at the time you made the gift.

## Taxation of Annuities

The taxation of annuity payments to you comprises three parts. The first piece is a tax-free portion that, like regular annuities, is considered a return of your own already-taxed funds. The second piece is capital gains tax if you used appreciated securities to fund the gift. The third piece is taxable as ordinary income in the year the payments are received. The charitable deduction for a life income gift is based on the age of the beneficiary, using the IRS life expectancy table, and the established payout rate for the gift.

**ALERT!**

Life income gifts may not be available from every charitable institution. Be sure that the organization you choose to support through a life income gift has a firm financial base. The contract with the institution requires it to make payments to you for your lifetime, and you want to be sure it's capable of making those payments for that length of time.

Although the income from a charitable annuity is less than a commercial annuity, the tax benefits make it a very popular way to make a gift and to retain lifetime income. The amount you used for the gift is no longer in your estate.

## Deferred Charitable Gift Annuity

You may create a deferred gift annuity (DGA) when you don't need immediate income. You can indicate you wish to have payments start at a later date. For example, you tell the charity that you want the income to start when you reach age seventy or seventy-five, or whatever age you choose. That payment date will become part of your contract. By delaying payments for a year or more, your payout rate usually increases, as does your charitable deduction.

The contract will include the exact payment you will receive when payments begin as well as the breakdown of the taxable portions.

Deferred gift annuities are considered an excellent retirement tool for several reasons. You remove funds from your estate, you are eligible for a charitable deduction in the year of the gift, and you will have guaranteed income starting at a date of your choosing.

**FACT**

You cannot add to annuities, but you can create as many new ones as you wish at the minimum gift amount. Some individuals create deferred charitable gift annuities in successive years, reducing their estate further, and building up the income that will begin sometime in the future.

For example, you can create a charitable gift annuity in 2010 for $10,000, with income to begin in 2020. In 2011, you create another annuity for $10,000 with income to begin in 2020. You can create annuities each year with the same start date for payments. By the time payments begin, you will have assured yourself of a nice, guaranteed income in addition to the annual gift to your favorite charity.

To avoid owing any estate tax, you and your spouse could set up separate individual annuities that end when each of you die. Because the annuity contract ends at death, it would no longer be part of either estate.

## Pooled Income Funds

Another form of life income gift is a gift to a pooled income fund (PIF). A PIF is much like a mutual fund in that many donors make gifts to a single fund. Your gift is added to the fund and your share is prorated within the fund into units.

The minimum gift is often $10,000, but you should check with your charity to determine its requirements. You can usually make smaller additions to the fund later on, which will increase your prorated share of units.

Payments to you are determined by the actual earnings of the fund, the same as a mutual fund. There are management fees, which are deducted first. You will receive a pro rata share of those net earnings, usually quarterly.

Payments can go up or down depending on the market, and payments are fully taxable as ordinary income.

**ALERT!**

Many charities have more than one PIF, each with different investment goals. You should check with your charitable organization to learn what the annual investment goal is as well as its historical performance before making a gift.

The value of a PIF rises and falls with the market, and there is no guaranteed return on your gift. At your death, your units are valued and removed from the fund. Those funds are then directed to the program of your choosing or for general operating funds of the charity.

## Charitable Remainder Trusts

In prior chapters you read in detail about personal trusts. A charitable remainder trust (CRT) is similar in structure except that the trustee is frequently the charitable organization itself or a bank that oversees the charity's trusts. You make an irrevocable gift of your assets to the trustee when you establish a CRT. Like the charitable gift annuity and PIF, a CRT is a life income gift to a charitable organization with income to you.

**FACT**

Because trusts are more complex than cash gifts, annuities, or pooled income fund gifts, they require active management by a trustee. As a result, minimum gifts can be as much as $100,000 or higher. There is also an annual management fee involved with CRTs, just as with PIFs.

You may set up a trust for your life or for a term of years up to twenty years. The IRS requires at least a 5 percent annual payout based on either the value at the time of the gift or its value at a set time each year. You select which type of payout you prefer when you set up the gift. As with other life income gifts, the remainder in the trust at your death is directed to the program you specified when you signed the agreement.

## *Charitable Gifts from Your Will or Trust*

An easy way to make a gift to your religious organization, health organization, your alma mater, or other qualified charity is to include a bequest in your will or trust. You can give a specific sum, a percentage of your gross estate, or a specific sum or percentage of your residuary estate.

You can direct a gift of cash, tangible property such as art works, books and collections, real estate, intangibles such as stocks or bonds, or almost any asset you own. Bequests to charity through a will or trust are the most common kinds of planned gifts.

You may decide that you have enough assets to leave to your family and still make a charitable gift. You might want to discuss your plans ahead of time, however, to be sure the family does not have objections. At the same time, if you are going to owe estate taxes unless you reduce your taxable base, you may decide a charitable gift is best for your overall plan.

Many lawyers don't think to ask clients whether they have any charitable intent. Don't wait for the lawyer to ask; be prepared with your charitable wishes.

Before making a charitable gift through your will, think about the amount you'd like to leave, the purpose of your gift, and whether you want any restrictions. For example, you might want to specify that a bequest to your religious organization be used to create or add to an endowment fund for a specific purpose. Or, you might want to create a named scholarship fund at your educational institution. These gifts are part of your legacy, and you should be prepared to discuss charitable gifts with a lawyer for inclusion in your will or trust.

## Gifts of Other Property Through Your Will or Trust

Just as you can during your lifetime, you can make a gift through a will or trust of your special collection of history books to your school's library, medical equipment to the dental or medical school, or inventory from your business as long as the gift is related to the charity's purpose.

You can also leave your primary residence, second home, or business property to an institution that it can either use or sell for its charitable purposes. If you don't have heirs who need or want your real estate, giving it away through your estate can save your executor time in trying to sell the property. Some institutions, however, may request that the executor sell the property and send the proceeds—they don't want to be in the business of selling real estate, either!

## Individual Retirement Arrangements (IRAs)

You can direct a percentage or the entire amount of any IRA you own to a charity. By making a gift of an IRA to charity, you remove the tax liability on the IRA. Although individuals must pay income tax on the income received each year from an IRA, charities do not. The value of the IRA is also deducted from your taxable base. Thus, you maximize the benefit of your IRA assets because there is no reduction in value for payment of either income or estate taxes.

**FACT**

Remember that the way to transfer an IRA is to complete a beneficiary designation form. If you wish to make a gift to a charity, you must contact your IRA administrator and complete a form stating the percentage to be directed to the charity.

If you have more than one IRA, you might choose to specify 100 percent of one IRA to charity and 100 percent of other IRAs to your family. Separating your IRAs makes it is easier for your executor to distribute an entire IRA account instead of having to determine percentages.

If you have assets that will receive a step-up in basis at death, and you have traditional IRAs that will require payment of income taxes, consider giving your IRA to charity and your other property to family members. Your family will receive the property with a step-up in value and will not owe any income taxes on those assets, as they would if you left them an IRA.

### Life Income Gifts Through Your Will or Trust

When you are preparing the details for a will or trust, you should think about the potential benefits of creating a life income gift for your heirs. If you wish to support your heirs and also provide a gift for your favorite charity, any of the life income options discussed in this chapter might fit into your estate planning puzzle.

You can set up a CGA, PIF, or CRT through your will or trust to benefit your heirs when you are gone. You reduce your taxable base by a portion of the gift (the portion IRS says will remain for the charity), and you also assure your heirs of annual income. Your estate would be entitled to a charitable deduction based on the age(s) of the beneficiaries when the life income gift is created. At the death of the beneficiaries, the balance or remainder would go to your charity. If you think your heirs might not handle their inherited assets carefully, a planned gift provides income they can count on, but cannot be frittered away.

## Advantages and Disadvantages of Charitable Gifts

The most immediate advantage to you for making a charitable gift during your lifetime is the reduction of your taxable base. In addition, you are able to control where the assets are going and how they will be used. You are creating your legacy by supporting an organization you care about. As a bonus, you are entitled to a charitable deduction on your income tax return in the year you make the gift (depending on your income level). If you make a charitable gift through your estate, your estate is eligible for the charitable deduction, thus reducing your taxable base.

## *Disadvantages of Charitable Gifts*

One of the cited advantages of life income gifts—removal from your estate—could be a disadvantage if you later need funds for medical care or some other emergency. If you become ill and need cash for your health care, you cannot retrieve these funds. If your estate assets decline in value and there is less than you anticipated for your family, you cannot take back the gift you made to the charity.

Once a life income gift is created, it is irrevocable and IRS will not allow it to be undone. With people living much longer than in years past and possibly needing nursing care in later life, it is important for you to be sure you won't need these gift funds in the future.

If you are insurable, you could buy additional insurance for your heirs to replace the charitable gifts you intend to make. You will need to keep the value of the policy under your exclusion amount or think about using an irrevocable life insurance trust, which was explained in Chapter 18.

Your family might also be annoyed with you for not leaving them a greater inheritance. If you are able, during your lifetime, to explain what you plan and how charitable gifts fit into the plan, your heirs may be less disappointed. And, if the inheritance would be going to taxes anyway, your plan should make sense to them.

There are many reasons for making charitable gifts, either during your lifetime or through your will or trust. Sometimes individuals seek tax benefits, to reduce both their annual income tax and the potential estate tax. Many individuals, however, wish to support their favorite charities in some way, and the tax benefits are secondary. For whatever reason you might consider a charitable gift—either now or through your estate planning—be sure that the gift does what you want it to do for the charity and that it does not hurt your family.

## CHAPTER 20

# Powers of Attorney

A power of attorney is a legal document that gives someone else, referred to as the holder of the power of attorney, the right to do something for you. Powers of attorney are used to give the holder the power to make legal or financial decisions for you and to sign the necessary papers to accomplish the task. In addition, a medical power of attorney gives a designated person the right to make decisions about your health care.

20

## Types of Power of Attorney

Your power of attorney can be very broad or it can be very narrow. A broad power of attorney allows the holder of the power of attorney to speak or act on your behalf or to sign almost any documents you could have signed.

Your family may never need to have a power of attorney because, you hope, you will never be incapacitated. But when tragedy strikes, your family has so many issues to deal with, it is an act of love for you to be prepared.

A limited power of attorney, on the other hand, allows the holder of the power of attorney to perform only the specific acts you include in the document. You can give the holder of your power of attorney the ability to use his powers at any time, or you can create a triggering event that allows the holder of your power of attorney to exercise his powers once the triggering event occurs.

If you think you have been given a power of appointment or a power of attorney, but aren't certain which it is, ask for a copy of the document. You should definitely have a copy of a durable power of attorney in the event you need to act on someone's behalf in the future. You will need the document to prove you have the right to act.

## Broad Power of Attorney

A very broad power of attorney typically gives these powers to the person you designate:

- Power to do any act, thing, or personal or business transaction that you can do
- Power to sue in your name and collect money owed to you from any source
- Power to establish any financial accounts in your name
- Power to terminate any financial accounts in your name

- Power to buy or sell any type of property owned in your name
- Power to improve, maintain, rent, or lease any of your property
- Power to sign any contract in your name
- Power to sign your name to any tax returns

There are only a few situations in which you cannot give authority to the holder of a power of attorney to act on your behalf. Typically you cannot grant someone the power to fulfill a contract that requires your personal services. For example, if you are the quarterback for your area's NFL team, you cannot give someone else the power to throw the football at next Sunday's game. You can't grant a power for someone else to complete a legal affidavit that requires your personal knowledge. You can't give someone the power to vote in an election for you. And you cannot give someone else the power to make a will for you.

## Limited Power of Attorney

By creating a limited power of attorney, you can either limit what the person who holds a power of attorney can do or specify a triggering event that must happen before the holder of the power can exercise it. It is very common to give someone a limited power of attorney to get something done for you when you are not available.

**QUESTION?**

**What is the difference between a power of appointment and a power of attorney?**
A power of appointment is a right given to a specified person within a will or trust to distribute your property. A power of attorney is a legal document granting a specified person the right to act on your behalf during your lifetime.

For example, you can give someone limited power of attorney to buy or sell property in your name. The described property could be a car, a house, or a boat. You name it, and you can give someone the power of attorney to buy or sell that piece of property on your behalf. Alternatively, your power of attorney might include a triggering event that must happen before the power of attorney is valid. The most common triggering event is your becoming disabled or incapacitated.

## Reasons for Having a Power of Attorney

You should have a power of attorney that gives the holder of the power the authority to sign necessary documents in the event that you become disabled or incapacitated. Most young people don't think about what would happen if they become incapacitated, because it seems so unlikely that it will happen. Many older persons don't like to admit that incapacity is a probability; therefore, they ignore what might happen. The bottom line is, if you are incapacitated, no one can sign your name on anything that is in your individual name without a power of attorney.

> You may want to review your documentation to determine what property is titled in your individual name. If your family would need to access any of that property in the event that you become incapacitated, you need a power of attorney.

Consider the following example. You and your wife are both forty years old. You are driving down the street when your car is hit head-on. You are unconscious and transported to the hospital, where you remain in a coma for several months. It is expected that you are going to recover; it's just going to take time. Luckily, your employer provided disability insurance benefits. But the insurance company must issue the benefit check in your name. If your wife does not have a power of attorney, she can't sign your name. Further, assume that the savings account where you keep most of your money is also in your name. Again, your wife can't withdraw money. Her only recourse is to file a petition in court to have you declared incompetent, so that she can access the savings account and your disability checks.

A power of attorney that continues beyond your incapacity is called a *durable power of attorney*. Years ago, a power of attorney would become invalid if the person giving the power of attorney became incompetent. Courts have recognized that a durable power of attorney is exactly what would be needed upon someone's incapacity. Be sure that any power of attorney you sign is a durable power of attorney.

You might think that if your property is in joint name with your spouse, you don't need a power of attorney. Consider the example about the car accident. If both you and your spouse were incapacitated, there would be no one who could access any of your funds. If you have minor children, someone would have to petition the court to have a guardian named. If your money is not available, it would be very difficult to pay a lawyer to help.

## Sample Durable Power of Attorney

A power of attorney is very easy to prepare and can be such an important document for your family. The following is a sample durable power of attorney. As you will see, this is a very broad power of attorney. When creating your own, you will need to decide what powers to give to the holder of the power of attorney.

DURABLE POWER OF ATTORNEY

KNOW ALL MEN BY THESE PRESENTS, that I am hereby creating a Durable Power of Attorney.

That I **[insert your name]**, of **[insert city]**, **[insert state]**, do hereby appoint **[name the person you would like to appoint]** as my attorney-in-fact for me and in my name, place and stead, and for my use and benefit to exercise all of the powers enumerated below, should I be incapacitated. If **[person you named]** is not reasonably available or is unable to act, then I appoint **[name a successor person]** as substitute or successor attorney-in-fact to serve with the same powers, in the event I am incapacitated.

## I. POWERS

**SECTION 1**: To exercise, do, or perform any act, right, power, duty, or obligation whatsoever that I may have or may acquire the legal right, power, capacity to exercise, do, or perform in connection with, arising out of, or relating to any personal item, thing, transaction, business, business property, personal property, or real property (including my homestead), or matter whatsoever.

**SECTION 2**: To ask, demand, sue for, collect, and hold all sums of money, debts, bonds, notes, checks, drafts, accounts, legacies, interest, dividends, stock certificates, certificates of deposit, annuities, pension retirement benefits, insurance benefits and proceeds, and documents of title as I now have or shall hereafter become due, owing, payable, owned, or belonging to me or in which I have or may acquire any interest.

**SECTION 3**: To establish, utilize, and terminate accounts (including margin accounts) with security brokers; to establish, utilize, and terminate managing agency accounts with corporate fiduciaries.

**SECTION 4**: To establish accounts of all kinds, including checking and savings, for me with financial institutions of any kind, including but not limited to banks and thrift institutions, to modify, terminate, make deposits to and write checks on or make withdrawals from and grant security interests in all accounts in my name or with respect to which I am an authorized signatory (except accounts held by me in a fiduciary capacity), whether or not any such account was established by me or for me by my attorney-in-fact, to negotiate, endorse, or transfer any checks or other instruments with respect to any such accounts; to contract for any services rendered by any bank or financial institution.

**SECTION 5**: To purchase, lease, invest, exchange, assign, and acquire, and to bargain, contract, sell, agree to lease, purchase, and exchange, and take, receive, and possess any real or personal property, intangible or mixed, wherever located, including without being limited to commodities, contracts of all kinds, securities of all kinds, bonds, debentures, notes (secured or unsecured), stocks of corporations, regardless of class, interest in limited partnerships, real estate or any interest in real estate, including but not limited to my homestead, whether or not productive at the time of investment, interest in trusts, investment trusts, whether of the open and/ or closed funds types, and participation in common, collective, or pooled trust funds or annuity contracts, without being limited by any statute or rule of law concerning investments by fiduciaries, whatsoever upon such terms and conditions as my said attorney-in-fact shall deem proper and to execute any leases, deeds, conveyances, bills of sale, or other instruments of conveyance in connection with either the purchase or sale of any said property, real or personal; to make gifts to my family but not to exceed $13,000.00 to any one person per year, and to any charitable organization described in Section 170(c) and 2522(a) of the Internal Revenue Code of 1986.

SECTION 6: To improve, repair, maintain, manage, insure, rent, lease, sell, release, convey, mortgage, and hypothecate and in any way and manner deal with all or any part of any personal or real property (including my homestead), business, business property, or any other property, which I now own or may hereafter acquire.

SECTION 7: To sign, endorse, execute, acknowledge and deliver, receive and possess such contracts, agreements, options, deeds, conveyances, mortgages, security agreements, bills of sale, leases, insurance policies, documents of title, checks, drafts, certificates of deposit, notes, satisfactions of mortgages, and such other instruments in writing of whatever kind and nature as may be necessary or proper to the exercise of the rights and powers herein granted.

SECTION 8: To prepare, execute, and file any income, gift, or other tax return or claim, federal, state, or municipal, or agency thereof, specifically including Federal Income Tax Return Form 1040 for the years 2007 through 2035, for which I am responsible or to which my property is subject, and to do all things reasonably necessary with respect thereto; to pay any taxes, duties, or assessments, and collect any claims arising therefrom; to negotiate with the appropriate tax authorities, and to litigate or compromise any differences that may arise, with respect to any tax obligations.

SECTION 9: To create a Qualified Income Trust within the meaning of the Medicaid Act, or rules promulgated thereunder, and/or the Omnibus Budget Reconciliation Act as they now exist or may hereafter be amended.

SECTION 10: I grant to my said attorney-in-fact full power and authority to do and perform all and every act and thing whatsoever requisite, necessary, and proper to be done and exercise any of the rights and powers herein granted, as fully to all intents and purposes as I might or could do if personally present.

## II. LIMITATION OF POWERS

Notwithstanding the powers contained in this Durable Power of Attorney, my attorney-in-fact may not:

1. Perform duties under a contract that requires the exercise of my personal services;
2. Make any affidavit as to my personal knowledge;
3. Vote in any public election on my behalf;
4. Execute or revoke any will or codicil on my behalf;
5. Create, amend, modify or revoke any documents or other disposition effective at my death or transfer assets to an existing trust created by me unless expressly authorized by this Power of Attorney; or
6. Exercise powers and authority granted to me as trustee or as a court-appointed fiduciary.

## III. STANDARD OF CARE

Except as otherwise provided herein, any attorney-in-fact named herein is a fiduciary who must observe the standards of care applicable to trustees. My attorney-in-fact is not liable to third parties for any act pursuant to this Durable Power of Attorney if the act was authorized at the time. If the exercise of power is improper, my attorney-in-fact is liable to interested persons for damage or loss resulting from a breach of fiduciary duty by my attorney-in-fact to the same extent as the trustee of an express trust. If my attorney-in-fact has accepted appointment either expressly in writing or by acting under this Power, my attorney-in-fact is not excused from liability for failure either to participate in the administration of assets subject to this Power or for failure to attempt to prevent a breach of fiduciary obligations hereunder.

### IV. STANDARD OF CARE LIMITATION

My attorney-in-fact shall not be liable for any acts or decisions made by him in good faith and under the terms of this Durable Power of Attorney.

### V. THIRD PARTY RELIANCE

1. Any third party may rely upon the authority granted in my Durable Power of Attorney until the third party has received notice as provided herein.

2. Until a third party has received notice of revocation pursuant to the terms contained herein, partial or complete termination of this Durable Power of Attorney by adjudication of incapacity, suspension by initiation of proceedings to determine incapacity, my death, or the occurrence of an event referenced in this Durable Power of Attorney, the third party may act in reliance upon the authority granted in this Durable Power of Attorney.

3. A third party that has not received written notice hereunder may, but need not, require that my attorney-in-fact execute an affidavit stating that there has been no revocation, partial or complete termination, or suspension of this Durable Power of Attorney at the time the Power of Attorney is exercised. A written affidavit executed by my attorney-in-fact under this paragraph may, but need not, be in the form prescribed by F.S. §709.08, as amended.

4. Third parties who act in reliance upon the authority granted to my attorney-in-fact hereunder and in accordance with the instructions of the attorney-in-fact will be held harmless by me from any loss suffered or liability incurred as a result of actions taken prior to receipt of written notice of revocation, suspension, notice of a petition to determine

incapacity, partial or complete termination, or my death. A person who acts in good faith upon any representation, direction, decision, or act of my attorney-in-fact is not liable to me or to my estate, beneficiaries, or joint owners for those acts.

### VI. NOTICE

1. A notice, including, but not limited to, a notice of revocation, partial or complete termination, suspension, or otherwise, is not effective until written notice is served upon my attorney-in-fact or any third party relying upon this Durable Power of Attorney.

2. Notice must be in writing and served on the person or entity to be bound by such notice.

### VII. DAMAGES AND COSTS

If any third party unreasonably refuses to allow my attorney-in-fact to act pursuant to this Durable Power of Attorney or challenges the proper exercise of authority of my attorney-in-fact, the prevailing party in any judicial action under the applicable section will be entitled to damages, including reasonable attorney's fees.

### VIII. REVOCATION OF PRIOR INSTRUMENTS

By this instrument I hereby revoke any power of attorney, durable or otherwise, that I may have executed prior to the date of this Durable Power of Attorney.

I hereby confirm all acts of my attorney-in-fact pursuant to this Power.

Any act that is done under this Power between the revocation of this instrument and notice of that revocation to my attorney-in-fact shall be valid unless the person claiming the benefit of the act had notice of the revocation.

## IX. VALIDITY AND DURATION

This Durable Power of Attorney shall not be affected by my subsequent incapacity and shall be exercisable from the date in which I have executed this Power of Attorney, notwithstanding my later disability or incapacity. All acts done by my attorney-in-fact pursuant to the powers conferred herein during any period of my disability or incapacity shall have the same effect, and inure to the benefit of and bind the principal or his or her heirs, devisees, and personal representatives as if the principal were competent and not disabled. The powers, rights, and duties conferred by this Power of Attorney upon my attorney-in-fact shall begin on the date set forth below and shall continue until my death or until it shall be revoked by me in writing.

This Durable Power of Attorney shall be nondelegable, except as to the authority to execute stock powers or similar documents on my behalf and delegate to a transfer agent or similar person the authority to register any stocks, bonds, or other securities either into or out of mine or a nominee's name, and shall be valid until such time as I shall die, revoke the Power, or shall be adjudged totally or partially incapacitated by a court of competent jurisdiction.

I may revoke this Power only by providing written notice to my attorney-in-fact. All acts of my attorney-in-fact taken or done without actual knowledge of (1) my death or (2) my revocation, are valid and effective, and are hereby ratified and confirmed.

This instrument has been executed in multiple counterpart originals. All such counterpart originals shall have equal force and effect.

IN WITNESS WHEREOF, I have set my hand and seal this _____date.

Signed, sealed, and delivered in the presence of:

_____          _____
Witness Number One                    YOUR NAME

---

Witness Number Two
STATE OF
COUNTY OF

I HEREBY CERTIFY that on this day before me, an officer duly qualified to take acknowledgments, personally appeared **[YOUR NAME]**, who is (Notary choose one) [_____] personally known to me, or [_____] who has produced _____ as identification, and to me known to be the person described in and who executed the foregoing instrument and acknowledged before me that he executed the same.

WITNESS my hand and official seal in the state and county aforesaid this **[insert date].**

_____
Notary Public
My Commission Expires: _____

## Decisions to Make

The decisions you need to make depend on how much power you are going to give to the person who will hold a power of attorney for you. The more powers you are going to give, the more careful you need to be about the selection of the person you will name.

The decisions you need to make to create a power of attorney are:

1. What powers are you going to give?
2. When can the holder exercise his powers?
3. Who do you want to name?

Review the powers described in the sample durable power of attorney. This sample is a very broad power of attorney. However, you can go through and strike any power you don't want the holder to have.

Once you have carefully reviewed the list of powers, it will help you decide who should hold your power of attorney. You should name a person to act as the primary holder of your power of attorney and you should also name a substitute or successor who can serve if the first person you named is not available.

## *Naming More than One Person*

Naming more than one person is often a way to increase your comfort level. You may feel that you want two people to approve any decisions. Then, instead of naming just one person to hold your power of attorney, you will name two. Both signatures will be required to exercise any of the listed powers. It is typical for spouses to name each other as the primary and sole holder of the power of attorney. But in case both spouses should become incapacitated, they name two or more of their children as substitute or successor holders of the power of attorney.

**FACT**

Family dynamics are often a consideration in deciding who you want to name as your power of attorney. For instance, if it is a second marriage for you, you might not want your spouse to have sole authority over your property if you become incapacitated.

You could name three, four, five, or more persons to act. Sometimes parents name all of their children as substitute or successor holders of the power of attorney because they don't want to hurt one or more child's feelings over being excluded from the decisional process. But there does come a point at which you name too many people. It is unrealistic to expect the multiple power holders to agree, and it's difficult even to manage the logistics of obtaining everyone's signature.

## Creating a Power of Attorney

You can typically buy a power of attorney form at an office supply store and fill in the blanks. There are also numerous inexpensive computer software programs that will generate a power of attorney document. These programs allow you to insert your name, the name of the person or persons who will serve as your primary holder of the power of attorney, and the name of the person or persons who will hold the power of attorney if the first person is not available. Then the programs typically generate a list of powers you can give to the holder of your power of attorney. You should always sign your power of attorney in the presence of two witnesses and a notary. Even if your state law does not require witnesses or a notary, it is a good idea to sign the document with the formalities that would meet the laws of any state.

Although you can use do-it-yourself forms, you can see that a durable power of attorney is complex and may best be prepared by a lawyer. You want to be absolutely certain the document complies with your state law.

Be certain that the power of attorney you create meets the requirements under your state law and that you understand the powers you are giving to the holder of your power of attorney.

You can make an appointment with a lawyer to prepare your power of attorney. Interview attorneys and ask how much it will cost to have the document prepared. Make sure to tell the lawyers that you are prepared with the names, addresses, and telephone numbers of the person or persons who will hold your power of attorney. Sometimes the lawyer will want everyone's Social Security number as well. You should also tell the lawyer that you have reviewed the powers, and you are prepared to let him know which powers you want included.

# Reasons for Having a Medical Power of Attorney

Unlike the durable power of attorney that covers primarily financial or contractual powers, the medical power of attorney or medical directive, sometimes called an advance health care directive or living will, is concerned solely with decisions about your health and medical care.

You have probably read about the many cases in which family members argue over the presumed wishes of an injured or severely ill patient. You don't want to put your family in that predicament or force them to go to court for decisions about your medical care.

What happens if you and your partner are not married? If you and your partner wish to give each other the right to make medical decisions, you need to prepare a medical directive in accordance with the law of your state authorizing your partner to make decisions for you in the event of an accident or illness. Families of unmarried couples sometimes frown on the relationship and may object to your estate planning to benefit your partner or to your appointment of your partner as medical agent. Be sure your wishes are clearly spelled out in a legal document. Even then, there are no guarantees that blood relatives won't try to block your wishes.

Having a durable power of attorney in place does not cover your health care decisions in the event of your incapacity. You need a medical directive and must appoint a medical agent who can speak on your behalf if you are not physically or mentally able.

You should never keep your original medical directive or living will in your safe-deposit box. If these documents are not available because either the bank or credit union is not open or your family is having difficulty gaining access to your safe-deposit box, the wrong decisions might be made about your medical care.

Be sure to give your medical agent a copy of your medical directives, the HIPAA form, and any information that will guide her in making decisions about your health care. Also be sure that your medical directive meets the laws of your state. You should also keep extra copies to take to hospitals, doctors, or other individuals who need to know your wishes.

Some lawyers include a durable power of attorney, a health care directive (or living will), and the HIPAA form as part of an estate planning package that meets your state's requirements. Ask your lawyer whether he can do that for you.

A sample health care directive is included in Appendix E. It includes your directions for your own health care, appointment of your agent to speak for you, and an optional section on organ donations if you wish to be an organ donor. Ask your lawyer about the HIPAA form if he doesn't mention it or include it in your package.

## CHAPTER 21

# Guidance for Your Family

The most important thing you can do for your family is to be prepared. By planning ahead and making as many decisions as you are able, you can ease the burden of your loved ones after you pass on. However, your plan can only be implemented if your family knows a plan exists and where to locate the paperwork to carry out your plan.

## What Instructions to Provide Your Family

It is important to leave instructions for your family so they know what needs to be done when something happens to you. It is equally important that these instructions be clear and easy to find. The first thing you need to do is to put the pieces of your puzzle in one place.

Chapter 2 provided you with step-by-step guidance on what information you need to gather about each piece of property you own. Throughout the rest of the book, you have made decisions regarding what type of plan to create and what information and instructions to include within the plan. By now your studies have resulted in the creation of a plan, and you have drafted documents that meet your wants and the needs of your loved ones.

It's not enough just to have a plan; you need to make sure that your family *knows* you have a plan. You don't have to tell your family exactly what your plan is, but they need to know that it exists. And, of course, your family needs to know where to find your documents and paperwork.

## Where to Keep Your Documents

If your family can't find your will, trust, or your important paperwork, your property may not be distributed in the way you planned. Your family's first job after you are gone is to find your paperwork. This may not be as easy as it sounds. As discussed in Chapter 9, there are numerous places where you might keep your paperwork: in your home, with your lawyer, filed with your local probate court, or in your safe-deposit box.

There is no one right answer as to where you should keep your original documents and your important papers. But after you have weighed the advantages and disadvantages of each option, make a decision and be sure to inform your family.

### At Home

If you keep your original documents in your home, you need to make sure that your family knows where to find them. You may think your desk or home office is very organized, but everybody has a different filing system. What makes sense to you may not be what your family expected.

The notebook is a highly recommended method of staying organized. Your original documents can be neatly placed in your notebook, along with your other important papers. If something happens, your family will know exactly where to look.

If you keep your original documents at home, you do run the risk that if something happens to your home, your documents will be destroyed. This isn't very likely, but it could happen. Or perhaps you think that because your spouse knows how to find your documents, you are prepared. However, if something happens to both you and your spouse, the rest of the family might not know where to look.

## With the Lawyer

You could leave your original documents with your lawyer. Your lawyer will be happy to keep your original will or trust. It is unlikely, however, that the lawyer will want to become the custodian of your other important documents, such as your life insurance policies, retirement plans, annuities, information about your financial accounts, or investments. Also, when you leave your original documents with your lawyer, your family typically feels obliged to hire that lawyer to handle your affairs after you are gone.

## Filed with the Probate Court

If you have a will, you can place the original on deposit with your local probate court. This prevents anyone from tampering with your will, and your family will have easy access to the document after you are gone. You need to be sure your family knows that's where the will is stored. Again, however, your local probate court will not become the custodian of any of your other important papers.

# Safe-Deposit Boxes

There are many practical issues regarding a safe-deposit box that you might not have considered. Although the purpose of a safe-deposit box is to have a place that is secure to keep important papers or valuable items, a safe-deposit box can be difficult to access if you are incapacitated or gone.

## Giving Out Keys

The first issue involves who has keys to your safe-deposit box. Even if you have filled out the proper forms at your bank or the location of your safe-deposit box to give someone else access to your box, the person you authorize can't get into the safe-deposit box without being charged unless they have a key or know where to locate your key.

Obviously, you need to let your family know where you keep the keys. If your family can't find your keys, the person authorized to enter your safe-deposit box can access the box, but the cost of opening a safe-deposit box without a key can be $150 or more. You can save your family this frustration and expense by being prepared.

## Authorizing Access

As already stated, you can authorize someone to have access to your safe-deposit box. However, you should carefully consider this decision. If you and your spouse are the only ones authorized to open the box and you both are gone, it will be very difficult for your family to gain access to your important documents.

It is a good idea to list another person besides your spouse to have access to your safe-deposit box. If you are worried and don't want anyone besides your spouse to have access, you will just have to run the risk that it will be more difficult and costly if you become incapacitated or die.

If a person you authorized to open your safe-deposit box is no longer living, your family will have to get a court order to gain access. Your local probate court judge typically enters the order. The person who needs to obtain the court order is the executor you named in your will. However, before your executor can get a court order to open your safe-deposit box, he has to have your original will. He will then need to open your estate, have himself appointed as executor, and seek a probate court order directing the bank to allow him access to your safe-deposit box. This process can take a while.

If your executor cannot locate your will, but believes that you have a will in your safe-deposit box and that he is appointed as executor, he will need to file a request with your local probate court to obtain an order for the limited purpose of opening your safe-deposit box to look for your will. If the will is not found, he will need to petition to open a probate proceeding following the procedures for a person who died without a will. Then, after this person is appointed as your executor, he will file a petition to have full access to your safe-deposit box.

You might want to keep a list at home of your safe-deposit contents so that the family and the executor will know whether or not your will or other estate planning documents have been stored there.

As you can see, if you have not provided the bank or credit union with the proper authorization to give someone access, it is very difficult, time-consuming, and expensive to gain access to your safe-deposit box.

## Documents to Keep in a Safe-Deposit Box

If you have organized all of your important information in one three-ring binder or notebook, as recommended in Chapter 2, you can put that into your safe-deposit box. Your notebook will contain:

- The original deed to your real estate
- Title to your vehicles or boats
- Original stock certificates
- Bonds
- Certificate of deposit
- Life insurance policies
- Annuity contracts
- Business ownership

If you don't like the concept of using a notebook, you could put these documents in one or more envelopes and put the envelopes in your safe-deposit box. When you keep original documents in your safe-deposit box, you don't have to worry about the documents being lost or destroyed. You just need to make sure someone you trust has access to the box after you are gone.

# Funeral or Cremation Instructions

You can ease the emotional burden on your loved ones by making decisions and leaving instructions regarding your wishes for funeral or cremation arrangements. While this is probably the last thing you want to think about, your family will never know what you truly wanted if you don't tell them. At the very least, you should let them know whether you would prefer a funeral and burial or cremation. If you want to be more specific than that, there are plenty of other decisions to be made.

If you are active in a religious organization and are likely to have a funeral in the religious facility, you might want to consider giving a copy of your funeral wishes to that organization. It can keep your preferences on file and be ready to provide the kind of service you've requested.

## Funeral and Burial

If you want a funeral and burial when you die, the major decisions should be made first. For instance, you might first decide if the burial will be inground or aboveground entombment. Next is where the burial will take place. It's likely that you will know of a cemetery in which you would like a plot. Perhaps you have family and friends who have already passed away and you want to have the same final resting place. Then you will probably want to decide on a funeral home. You could even shop around to find which funeral home would provide the best services for the best price.

Other decisions you may want to make include:

- Who you wish to be pallbearers
- What type of casket you prefer
- Whether you want an open or closed casket
- Whether you would prefer to have a funeral service in a location other than the funeral home
- Name of the clergy you want to preside over the service
- What you want to be buried in (clothing, jewelry, and so on)
- What music you want to be played at the service
- Specific religious passages or literature you want read
- Who you want to do the readings
- Instructions regarding flower arrangements

Of course, there are other instructions that can be left for your loved ones. How detailed you want to be is entirely up to you but, remember, the more decisions you make for your family, the easier it will be on all involved.

## *Cremation*

Though cremation is becoming more common, many families still do not accept it as a proper process. If you want to be cremated, it's best to discuss it with your family in addition to leaving instructions. If you do not discuss it and make your reasons known, some family members may raise objections when you die, causing discord at a difficult time.

The decisions you make regarding cremation are very similar to those made for a funeral and burial. However, one major decision that may be considered is what you want done with your remains. You can have them all placed into one urn, you can request that they be scattered in a specific location, or you can even have them divided up among certain people. You will likely want to include this topic in your discussion with the family.

Most cremations include a memorial service of some type. You can be as specific as you want regarding the service, if you want one. Some services allow the family members to view the body before it is cremated;

others simply have pictures and belongings on display. Take a look at the list of considerations regarding the funeral service and see if any apply to the service you have in mind for cremation.

## Prepayment Plans

You can make all of the selections about your final arrangements and prepay for the funeral and burial or cremation. Frequently, making your arrangements with a prepayment plan can be cheaper than waiting until your death.

If you decide to prepay for your funeral expenses, you will be able to make all of the decisions and not leave your family guessing or wondering about what you wanted. You may be surprised to find how many choices there are about funeral arrangements. Your family won't know if you wanted a $2,000 funeral or a $20,000 funeral unless you tell them.

You can also select a funeral home and provide that company all the details of your wishes without making any payment. If that firm goes out of business, you will still have a copy of the instructions you had given to the funeral home. If you pay for your arrangements in advance, however, you need to put the paperwork confirming the payment in a place where your family can find it.

**FACT**

The average funeral can range in cost from $3,000 to $12,000. Families often feel guilty wondering how much their loved one wanted them to spend. Help out. Give your family some direction.

Although it may seem more expensive to pay at the time of your death, you will know that your funds won't be lost to a company that is bankrupt or has closed. If you don't want to pay for your funeral arrangements before you are gone, you should at least make sure that you have left clear instructions about what you want. The more specific you can be, the better.

Your instructions are not typically included in your will or trust. Therefore, your instructions should be handwritten or typed and left with your other important documents. If you are keeping a notebook as an organizational system, that would be the perfect place to store your instructions.

## Organ Donations

If you would like to donate any of your organs, you should leave your family instructions regarding your intentions. There is a uniform donor card you can complete at *www.organdonor.gov/donor/index.htm*. There is also general information about organ donation and issues to consider, including notifying your family about your wishes to donate your organs. Of course, you don't have to use forms to let your family know your wishes.

Many states include your intentions about organ donations on your driver's license. It is very likely that you would have your driver's license with you if it were necessary to make a decision about an organ transplant. Some medical directives may include this optional information. See the sample health care directive in Appendix E.

You can also prepare a paper that states your name and lists the organs you would like donated, and sign the paper in the presence of two witnesses. Although many states do not require a notary, it's a good idea to sign in the presence of two witnesses and a notary. Then, make sure you have informed your family about what you want done. Many times, if the desired organ is not preserved shortly after your death, your intentions will not be met because it will not be medically possible to preserve the organ while your family looks for your organ transplant instructions.

## Keeping Your Plans Up-to-Date

Once you have completed all your plans, don't simply tuck them away and assume you're finished. You should mark your calendar for a specific time every year—January, April after taxes, your birthday—to review your assets and determine whether you need to make any noteworthy additions or deletions. Are all the people you have included in your plans still living? Do you wish to keep the same individuals in your plan? Has there been a marriage, divorce, birth, or death that would affect your plans?

If you do an annual review, you can make adjustments, if needed, and be reassured that everything is in place for your family.

## Estate Planning Checklist

Now that you've prepared a notebook or other record of your plan, use the following checklist to be sure you've covered everything:

- You've listed your property and the persons to support.
- You have a will and/or codicils and a memorandum covering your plans.
- You've considered and possibly established a revocable or testamentary trust.
- You've named a guardian for your minor children.
- You've made arrangements for any pets you may have.
- You've executed a durable power of attorney in the event of your incompetence.
- You've executed a living will or health care directive, have selected an agent to make medical decisions for you, have completed a HIPAA document and have given a copy of your directives to your agent.
- Your funeral plans are in place.
- Your family knows where to find your documents.

Other things you might want to include in your notebook:

- Physical location of keys—to home, car, safe-deposit box, storage
- List of safe-deposit box contents
- Location of bank statements, tax records, brokerage or retirement accounts, and contact numbers
- Any prenuptial agreements; note location of original
- List of credit card companies, numbers, location of cards

- List of any automatic payments being made to credit cards or bank accounts
- Copy of home insurance, auto insurance, vacation home insurance
- Any military papers and contacts in event of benefits
- List of doctors and any medicines in the event of your incompetence
- List of any debts owed to you

These suggestions are just that, and are not all-inclusive. The idea is to anticipate anything your family may need to deal with when you are gone, and to take steps to provide the necessary information to smooth their way in the days following your death.

**FACT**

There is no one right plan. Learning the rules will help you choose the best legal documents and types of property ownership that will meet your goals for your family, the charities you want to support, and your own legacy.

The death of a loved one who has not left a plan can create untold hours of work and anguish for heirs. By creating your own plan, you are making sure your family won't suffer additional stress by having to figure out what you wanted. Congratulations to you for taking the time to prepare your plan—you have made a generous gift to your family!

# Glossary

**annuitant**
The person, usually the owner of the annuity, who receives the annuity payouts.

**annuity**
A contract or agreement between you and the issuing company. You give the issuing company a certain amount of money and, in turn, it promises to invest your money and repay you according to the option or payment method that you choose.

**articles**
The parts of a will. Each article is designed to accomplish a purpose.

**beneficiary**
The person for whose benefit a trust is created. The person named to receive your life insurance, annuity, or retirement plan.

**charitable gift annuity**
A charitable gift in the form of an annuity contract with a qualified charity. You make a gift, and the charity promises to pay one or two beneficiaries a fixed income for life. Balance at death of beneficiary goes to the charity.

**charitable remainder trust**
An irrevocable trust that pays a fixed or variable income annually to you or someone you name for a term of years or a lifetime. Remainder goes to charity at death of beneficiary.

**codicil**
An amendment to a will.

**cost basis**
The amount you subtract from the sale price of a property to compute your gain or loss when you sell a piece of property.

**creditor**
Any person or entity to whom you owe money.

**credit shelter trust**
A trust; usually created within a revocable trust that typically places the estate tax exclusion amount into a trust for the benefit of the surviving spouse.

**deferred charitable gift annuity**
A contract with a charity that pays lifetime income, deferred more than a year after the gift, to named beneficiary. Balance at death of beneficiary goes to charity.

**devise**
A transfer of property after your death by your will.

**devisee**
The person or organization to whom you transfer property in your will.

**durable power of attorney**
A power of attorney that continues beyond the incapacity of the person who granted the power.

**estate tax**
The tax your estate might owe when you die, sometimes called a "death tax."

**executor**
The person you name to carry out the instructions in your will. In some states the executor is called a personal representative.

**exemption equivalent**
The government grants a tax credit, which shelters a specified amount in an estate.

**gift**
A voluntary transfer of property without receiving payment.

**gift tax exclusion**
The amount of money or property you can give each year without tax, or the amount you can give over your lifetime.

**grantor**
The person who creates a trust; also known as settlor or creator.

**grantor retained annuity trust**
A sophisticated tax-planning device that allows you to make a gift at a discounted value; often referred to as GRAT.

**group life insurance**
Typically term insurance offered through your place of employment. As a member of the employer's group, you are entitled to a stated amount of insurance benefits paid to the beneficiary or beneficiaries you name.

**guardian**
The person you name in your will who has the power and duty to care for your minor child or children after you die.

**HIPAA**
Health Insurance Portability and Accountability Act of 1996 which limits access to medical records except to those specifically named by you in writing.

**heir**
Any person who inherits from your will or who would receive your property if you died without a will.

**holographic will**
A will that an individual writes entirely by hand.

**intangible property**

Property you cannot feel or touch. Intangible property represents evidence of ownership such as bank accounts, stocks, bonds, promissory notes, or property of a similar nature.

**interpolated reserve value**

A technical term for the value of a life insurance policy for gift or estate purposes.

**intestate**

When a person dies without making a will or without leaving instructions as to wishes with respect to the disposal of her property after death.

**intestate laws**

Laws each state has on how property will be distributed when someone dies without a will.

**IRA**

Individual Retirement Arrangement; a retirement account that allows you to take advantage of tax-deferred contributions and/or growth or tax-free growth.

**irrevocable trust**

A trust that cannot be revoked or made void, canceled, rescinded, or reversed by anyone.

**life insurance trust**

A trust to which ownership of your life insurance policy is transferred and held by a trustee for benefit of heirs.

**living will**

A medical directive that indicates the level of health care you want, or don't want, in the event of incapacity.

**marital deduction**

The right to subtract the value of property transferred to your surviving spouse, as long as you are leaving your spouse a qualified interest.

**marital taxable base**

The sum of the husband's taxable base and the wife's taxable base.

**memorandum**

A document allowed by some states in which you list tangible property you wish to be directed to heirs.

**payable-on-death accounts**

Bank or brokerage accounts that can be established naming a beneficiary who will become owner of the account upon death of the creator of the account.

**per capita**

A method of dividing property in equal shares among a number of persons. If a named person is not alive, his share is divided equally among the other named persons who are living.

**per stirpes**

A method of dividing property whereby if the person to whom you have left property is not living, that person's share is divided in equal shares among her descendants.

**personal property**
All property other than real estate.

**pooled income fund (PIF)**
A form of irrevocable trust in which donors make a gift to a pooled fund held by a charity. Donor or beneficiaries receive a proportionate share of actual income earned each year. Balance at death of beneficiaries goes to the charity.

**power of appointment**
A person named in your trust document or will who has the power, upon your death, to alter the distribution of shares to the beneficiaries and/or to change the beneficiaries named in the document. There are two types of power of appointment: limited and general.

**power of attorney**
A legal document that gives the holder of the power of attorney the right to act on your behalf.

**probate**
The legal process to prove the validity of your will. Probate has become the word used to describe the entire legal process that occurs when a person dies with or without a will.

**qualified personal residence trust**
A sophisticated tax-reduction technique that allows you to transfer your personal residence to the next generation at a fraction of the transfer tax cost; often referred to as QPRT.

**real property**
Real estate including buildings, lots, and vacant land.

**residuary devise**
When you leave the rest and remainder of your property, this is a residuary devise. A residuary devise is made in the residual clause of your will.

**retainer**
An amount of money the lawyer requires be placed on deposit before he starts a job.

**revocable trust**
A trust wherein you or someone you name is given the power to change or revoke the document.

**Roth IRA**
An individual retirement account that you can create with after-tax income, depending on your income level. Withdrawals may be made tax-free after a Roth IRA has been in place for five years.

**settlor**
The person who creates a trust. The settlor is often referred to as a grantor.

**specific devise**
When you leave specifically described property to a person or organization, you have made a specific devise.

**successor beneficiaries**
In a trust document, the persons you name who will enjoy the benefits of the property when you are gone.

**successor trustee**
A person or an entity you name to serve as trustee when you are gone.

**tangible property**
Property you can feel and touch.

**taxable base**
The property that can be taxed when you die, along with the taxable gifts you made while living.

**taxable gift**
A gift made to any person that exceeds the gift tax exclusion amount per year or the lifetime exclusion.

**testamentary trust**
A trust that is contained inside of a will.

**testate**
When a person dies with a will.

**trust**
A legal document that transfers title of a property to an individual or entity for the benefit of another person or entity.

**trust corpus**
The property that you transfer into the name of a trust. Trust corpus is often called the trust principal.

**trustee**
The person or entity named to carry out the instructions contained in the trust document. The trustee also holds legal title to the trust property.

**unified credit**
The federal tax credit that is applied to both the gift tax and estate tax; sometimes called the gift tax exclusion and the estate tax exclusion amount.

**unlimited marital deduction**
The right to give your spouse an unlimited amount of property without gift taxes.

**will**
The document that directs and instructs your executor or personal representative to distribute your property after you are gone.

# Resources

## *Online Resources*

*www.abanet.org*
This is the Internet site of the American Bar Association, which provides a lawyer locator. Check the Public Resources section, then "Get Legal Help."

*www.bestcase.com/statebar.htm*
This site will guide you to the state bar association that regulates lawyers in your state. Each bar association site has different features, though most will guide you to a lawyer referral service regulated by the bar association.

*www.agingwithdignity.org*
This site includes the Five Wishes program and guidance for medical directives or living wills.

*www.funeralswithlove.com/funeralcosts.htm*
On this site you can find a listing of funeral expenses and average costs, as well as choices for funerals or services.

*www.irs.gov*
The IRS website includes federal income, gift, and estate tax forms and publications that you can read and/or download. Most commonly used for income tax is Publication 17. See Publications 526 for Charitable Contributions, 559 for Survivors, Executors and Administrators, 590 for details about Individual Retirement Arrangements (IRAs), and 950 for an Introduction to Estate and Gift Taxes.

*www.legacywriter.com*
This is an Internet site that allows you to complete an easy-to-understand questionnaire that creates a will according to your answers. The cost for a last will and testament is $19.95. The site also provides a complete estate planning package for $39.95.

*www.organdonor.gov/donor/index.htm*
This site provides information on organ donations and how to register in your state. It also has a printable card you can download and complete to keep in your wallet or with your estate plans.

*www.savingforcollege.com*
This site describes 529 plans for education, how to calculate college costs, and how to select a plan.

*www.collegeanswer.com/paying/content/529_plan_statebystate.jsp*
This site compares 529 plans in each state and allows you to examine possibilities within your own state.

## *Publications*

*Kiplinger's Personal Finance* magazine is rich with articles on every conceivable estate planning topic. The best way to access the archive of Kiplinger publications is via the website at *www.kiplinger.com/magazine.*

An outstanding resource of estate planning, investing, and budgeting articles can be found online at *http://money.cnn.com/magazines/moneymag/money101/lesson21.* Categories include saving for college, planning for retirement, insurance, taxes, and several other financial topics.

*The American Bar Association Guide to Wills & Estates* (New York: Random House, 1995).

Joan M. Burda, *Estate Planning for Same-Sex Couples* (Chicago: ABA General Practice, Solo & Small Firm Section, 2004).

Check your local library for additional estate planning reference materials.

# Asset Inventory Worksheet

## FAMILY INFORMATION

Your legal name: _____
Social Security number:_____Date of birth: _____

Your spouse's name: _____
Social Security number:_____Date of birth: _____
Date of marriage: _____

State of residency: _____U.S. citizen? Yes _____No _____

Former spouse(s): _____
Date of divorce(s): _____
Terms of divorce or separation (if any of the terms of the divorce or separation are applicable to your current estate): _____
Parents (if living): _____

*Information about your children and grandchildren*
Child 1: _____ Social Security Number: _____
Dependent? _____Date of Birth: _____Married: _____
Address: _____
Does your child have any children?
Names of grandchildren: _____

Child 2: _____ Social Security Number: _____
Dependent? _____Date of Birth: _____Married: _____
Address: _____
Does your child have any children?
Names of grandchildren: _____

*Insert a page including the information about additional children.*

## ADVISERS

List the name, address, and telephone number for each.

Attorney: _____

Accountant: _____

Banker: _____

Insurance agent: _____

Investment adviser: _____

Stockbroker: _____

Trust officer: _____

Others: _____

## ASSET INFORMATION
### REAL ESTATE
### Property I

Please place a copy of all deeds in your estate planning organizer.

Address: _____

Personal residence? (Primary or secondary, and period of occupancy and ownership):

_____

Owned in name of: _____

Form of ownership: _____

Date of purchase: _____

How acquired (gift, purchase, etc.): _____

Cost: _____

Current market value: _____

Debt on property: _____

Name of debt holder: _____

Amount of remaining debt: _____

Monthly payments (principal and interest): _____

Annual taxes: _____

*Insert an additional page for each piece of real estate.*

## CASH

| | Bank Name | Husband's | Wife's | Joint |
|---|---|---|---|---|
| Checking account | _____ | _____ | _____ | _____ |
| Balance | _____ | _____ | _____ | _____ |
| Savings account | _____ | _____ | _____ | _____ |
| Balance | _____ | _____ | _____ | _____ |
| Certificates of deposit | _____ | _____ | _____ | _____ |
| Balance | _____ | _____ | _____ | _____ |
| **TOTAL** | _____ | $_____ | $_____ | $_____ |

## STOCKS

| Description | Ownership | # of Shares | Cost Basis | Acquisition Date | December 31, 20__ Value | Current Value | Annual Dividend |
|---|---|---|---|---|---|---|---|
| _____ | _____ | _____ | _____ | _____ | _____ | _____ | _____ |
| _____ | _____ | _____ | _____ | _____ | _____ | _____ | _____ |
| _____ | _____ | _____ | _____ | _____ | _____ | _____ | _____ |
| _____ | _____ | _____ | _____ | _____ | _____ | _____ | _____ |
| _____ | _____ | _____ | _____ | _____ | _____ | _____ | _____ |
| _____ | _____ | _____ | _____ | _____ | _____ | _____ | _____ |
| _____ | _____ | _____ | _____ | _____ | _____ | _____ | _____ |
| _____ | _____ | _____ | _____ | _____ | _____ | Totals $_____ | $_____ |

*Insert additional pages as needed.*

## BONDS

| Description | Ownership | # of Shares | Cost Basis | Acquisition Date | December 31, 20__ Value | Current Value | Annual Dividend |
|---|---|---|---|---|---|---|---|
| _____ | _____ | _____ | _____ | _____ | _____ | _____ | _____ |
| _____ | _____ | _____ | _____ | _____ | _____ | _____ | _____ |
| _____ | _____ | _____ | _____ | _____ | _____ | _____ | _____ |
| _____ | _____ | _____ | _____ | _____ | _____ | _____ | _____ |
| _____ | _____ | _____ | _____ | _____ | _____ | _____ | _____ |
| _____ | _____ | _____ | _____ | _____ | _____ | _____ | _____ |
| _____ | _____ | _____ | _____ | _____ | _____ | _____ | _____ |
| _____ | _____ | _____ | _____ | _____ | | | |

Totals  $_____    $_____

*Insert additional pages as needed.*

## MUTUAL FUNDS

Name of fund: _____

Value of fund: _____

Cost basis of fund: _____


Name of fund: _____

Value of fund: _____

Cost basis of fund: _____

*Insert an additional page for each fund owned.*

## LIFE INSURANCE

Company: _____ Policy number: _____

Address: _____

Type of policy: _____ Face amount: _____

Ownership rights: _____

Beneficiary designation: _____

Cash value: _____ Cash value at retirement: _____

Annual premiums: _____ Paid by: _____

Settlement options: _____

Where is your original policy located? _____

*Insert an additional page for each life insurance policy owned.*

## EMPLOYEE BENEFITS

Employer: _____

Address: _____

Type of plan: _____

Value of current plan: _____

Retirement benefits: _____

Death benefits: _____

How to contact the plan administrator: _____ Telephone number: _____

Where is the information about your plan located? _____

_____

_____

_____

## INDIVIDUAL RETIREMENT ACCOUNTS

### Your IRA

Location of benefits (bank or custodial name): _____

Value of current plan: _____

Retirement benefits: _____

Death benefits: _____

Where is the information about your IRA located? _____


### Your Spouse's IRA

Location of benefits (bank or custodial name): _____

Value of current plan: _____

Retirement benefits: _____

Death benefits: _____

Where is the information about this IRA located? _____


*If you and your spouse have multiple IRAs, provide the requested information about each IRA.*

## SOCIAL SECURITY

Estimated basic Social Security benefit for:

Husband: _____

Wife: _____


Do you receive any other retirement or death benefits?

Private: _____

Employer: _____

Credit card death benefits: _____

## MISCELLANEOUS ASSETS

Please enter a dollar amount in the following table for each item that applies to your family.

| Item | Husband's | Wife's | Joint |
|------|-----------|--------|-------|
| Furniture | $_____ | $_____ | $_____ |
| Automobiles | _____ | _____ | _____ |
| Jewelry | _____ | _____ | _____ |
| Artwork | _____ | _____ | _____ |
| Boats | _____ | _____ | _____ |
| Other: _____ | _____ | _____ | _____ |
| Other: _____ | _____ | _____ | _____ |
| Other: _____ | _____ | _____ | _____ |

## LIABILITIES
## OTHER THAN LIABILITIES ON REAL ESTATE

Name of creditor: _____Due date: _____Balance owing: _____
Address: _____
Account number: _____

Name of creditor: _____Due date: _____Balance owing: _____
Address: _____
Account number: _____

Name of creditor: _____Due date: _____Balance owing: _____
Address: _____
Account number: _____

Name of creditor: _____Due date: _____Balance owing: _____
Address: _____
Account number: _____

## SUMMARY OF ASSETS AND LIABILITIES
### ASSETS

Enter a dollar amount for each asset in the following table.

| Asset | Husband | Wife | Joint |
|---|---|---|---|
| Cash | $_____ | $_____ | $_____ |
| Stock | _____ | _____ | _____ |
| Bonds | _____ | _____ | _____ |
| Mutual funds | _____ | _____ | _____ |
| Real estate | _____ | _____ | _____ |
| Personal residence | _____ | _____ | _____ |
| Life insurance | _____ | _____ | _____ |
| Employee benefits | _____ | _____ | _____ |
| Miscellaneous assets | _____ | _____ | _____ |

### LIABILITIES

Enter a dollar amount for each liability in the following table.

| Liability | Husband | Wife | Joint |
|---|---|---|---|
| Real estate | $_____ | $_____ | $_____ |
| Other bank debt | _____ | _____ | _____ |
| Credit cards | _____ | _____ | _____ |
| Taxes | _____ | _____ | _____ |
| Other debt | _____ | _____ | _____ |

# Sample Trust

Articles I–VI are reproduced and described in Chapter 14. The remaining portion of the trust document contains provisions that are standard to most trust documents.

## ARTICLE VII
### POWERS OF TRUSTEE AND OTHER PROVISIONS

7.1 <u>Powers of Trustee.</u> In the administration of this Trust, the Trustee shall have the following powers, in addition to and not in limitation of the Trustee's common law powers and statutory powers, provided (1) that such common law and statutory powers shall only be exercised to the extent they are not in conflict with the provisions of this Article and (2) that such common law and statutory powers shall be exercised in a fiduciary capacity in accordance with the general standards of trust administration imposed upon trustees.

(a) To receive and retain the initial Trust corpus and all other property which I may transfer to the Trustee either during my lifetime, by Will or other testamentary disposition, or which any other person may hereafter transfer to the Trustee. The Trustee shall receive all such property as part of the Trust even though it may not be a legal investment for the Trustee and even though such property by reason of its character may not be an appropriate trust investment apart from this provision. The Trustee is authorized to retain its own stock or other securities or stock or securities of any affiliate or holding company that owns the Trustee.

(b) To sell, exchange, give options upon, partition, or otherwise dispose of any property that the Trustee may hold from time to time, at public or private sale, or otherwise, for cash or other consideration or on credit, and upon such terms and for such consideration as the Trustee deems advisable; and to transfer and convey such property free of all trust.

(c) To invest and reinvest in any property, real or personal, including (without limiting the generality of the foregoing language) securities of domestic and foreign corporations and investment trusts, bonds, preferred stocks, common stocks, option contracts, "short sales," mortgages and mortgage participations, even though such investment by reason of its character, amount, proportion to the total trust estate, or otherwise would not be considered appropriate for a fiduciary apart from this provision, and even though such investment causes a greater proportion of the total trust to be invested in investments of one type or of one company than would be considered appropriate for a fiduciary apart from this provision. Such investment may be on a cash or margin basis, and the Trustee, for such purpose, may maintain and operate cash or margin accounts with brokers, and may deliver and pledge securities held or purchased by the Trustee with such brokers both as security for loans and advances made to the Trustee and to ensure the ability of the Trustee to deliver stock against short options. In addition, the Trustee may purchase life insurance even though it is non-income-producing. The Trustee is authorized to invest in any common fund, legal or discretionary, which may be operated by and/or under the control of a corporate Trustee.

(d) To make loans, secured or unsecured, in such amounts, upon such terms, at such rates of interest, and to such persons, trusts, corporations, or other parties as the Trustee deems advisable.

(e) To improve real estate, including the power to demolish buildings in whole or in part and to erect new buildings; to lease (including leasing for oil, gas, and minerals) real estate on such terms as the Trustee deems advisable, including the power to give leases for periods that extend beyond the duration of any trust; to foreclose, extend, assign, partially release, and discharge mortgages.

(f) To collect, pay, contest, compromise, or abandon, upon such terms and evidence as the Trustee deems advisable, any claims, including taxes, either in favor of or against trust property or the Trustee; to abandon or surrender any property.

(g) To employ brokers, banks, custodians, investment counsel, attorneys, accountants, and other agents, and to delegate to them such duties, rights, and powers of the Trustee (including the right to vote shares of stock held by the Trustee) for such periods as the Trustee deems advisable.

(h) To hold and register securities in the name of a nominee with or without the addition of words indicating such securities are held in a fiduciary capacity; to hold and register securities in a securities depository or in any other form convenient for the Trustee.

(i) To participate in any voting trust, merger, reorganization, consolidation, or liquidation affecting trust property and, in connection therewith, to deposit any trust property with or under the direction of any protective committee and to exchange any trust property for other property.

(j) To exercise any stock or other kind of option.

(k) To keep trust property in **[Florida]** or elsewhere, or with a depository or custodian.

(l) To determine (reasonably and in accordance with sound trust account-ing principles) as to all sums of money or other things of value received by the Trustee, whether and to what extent the same shall be deemed to be principal or to be income, and as to all charges or expenses paid by the Trustee, whether and to what extent the same shall be charged against principal or against income, includ-ing the power to apportion any receipt or expense between principal and income and to determine what part, if any, of the actual income received upon any wast-ing investment or upon any security purchased or acquired at a premium shall be retained and added to principal to prevent a diminution of principal upon exhaus-tion or maturity thereof. The Trustee may also establish reserves for depreciation and anticipated expenses and fund such reserves for depreciation and anticipated expenses with appropriate charges against income. All determinations made pur-suant to this subparagraph by the Trustee shall be made fairly to balance the inter-est of the income beneficiary and the remaindermen. The Trustee shall resolve all doubtful questions in favor of the income beneficiary. If an income beneficiary also serves as one of the Trustees of the Trust, then the income beneficiary–Trustee shall not exercise any of the powers granted by this subparagraph and all such powers shall be exercised by the other Trustee(s) only.

(m) To distribute the trust estate in cash or in kind, or partly in cash and partly in kind, as the Trustee deems advisable, and for purposes of distribution, to value the assets reasonably and in good faith as of the date of distribution. Such valuation shall be conclusive on all beneficiaries. The Trustee shall not be required to distribute a proportionate amount of each asset to each beneficiary but may instead make nonpro rata distributions. In making distribution, the Trustee may, but shall not be required to, take account of the income tax basis in relation to market value of assets distributed. Distribution may be made directly to the beneficiary, to a legally appointed Guardian or Conservator or, where permitted by law, to a custodian under any Uniform Gifts to Minors Act, including a custodian selected by the Trustee.

(n) To deposit monies to be paid to a beneficiary who is a minor in any demand, savings bank, or savings and loan account maintained in the sole name of the minor and to accept the deposit receipt as a full acquittance.

(o) To accept the receipt of a minor as a full acquittance.

(p) To borrow from anyone (including the Trustee or any affiliate) in the name of the Trust, to execute promissory notes therefore and to secure obligations by mortgage or pledge of trust property, provided the Trustee shall not be personally liable and that any such loan shall be payable out of trust assets only.

(q) To hold, manage, invest, and account for any separate trust in one or more consolidated funds, in whole or in part, as the Trustee deems advisable. As to each consolidated fund, the division into the various shares comprising such a fund needs to be made only on the Trustee's books of account, in which each separate trust shall be allocated its proportionate share of principal and income of the fund and charged with its proportionate share of the expenses. No such holding shall defer any distribution.

(r) To carry, at the expense of the Trust, insurance of such kinds and in such amounts as the Trustee deems advisable to protect the trust estate and the Trustee personally against any hazard or liability.

(s) To exercise all of these powers without application to any court.

7.2 Diversification. The Trustee shall not be required to diversify assets and is authorized to receive and retain in the Trust any one or more securities or other property, whether or not such security or other property shall constitute a larger share of the Trust than would be appropriate for a fiduciary to receive and retain apart from this provision.

7.3 <u>Receipt.</u> No purchaser or other person dealing with the Trustee shall be responsible for the application of any money or other thing of value paid or delivered to the Trustee, and no purchaser or other person dealing with the Trustee and no issuer, transfer agent, or other agent dealing with the Trustee shall be under any obligation to ascertain or inquire into the power of the Trustee to purchase, sell, exchange, transfer, mortgage, pledge, distribute, or otherwise in any manner dispose of or deal with any property held by the Trustee. The Certificate of the Trustee that the Trustee is acting in conformance with the terms of this Agreement shall protect all persons dealing with the Trustee.

7.4 <u>Creditors Clause and Spendthrift Provision.</u> With respect to all payments and distributions to be made pursuant to the trusts established hereunder, no beneficiary shall have any right to or interest in the income or principal therefrom until the same has been paid to him or her. Both principal and income of such trusts shall be free from the interference and control of the creditors of any beneficiary and neither the principal nor income of such trusts shall be subject to assignment or other anticipation by any beneficiary unless the Trustee determines that such assignment or anticipation is clearly and unequivocally in the best interest of such beneficiary. Both principal and income of such trusts shall be free from seizure under any legal, equitable, or other process whatsoever. If the Trustee believes the foregoing may be violated or if the Trustee believes the protection of any beneficiary requires it, the Trustee may withhold any part or all of the income and principal payments to which a beneficiary may be entitled and use and pay directly such portion thereof as the Trustee deems advisable.

7.5 <u>Corporate Merger.</u> If the Trustee merges or consolidates, the corporation formed by such merger or consolidation shall act as Trustee and shall possess and exercise all powers and authority herein provided.

7.6 <u>Exculpatory.</u> No successor Trustee shall be liable for any act or failure to act of any predecessor Trustee. With the approval of the person making the appointment of the Trustee, the successor Trustee shall not be required to review the accounts, acts, or omissions of predecessor Trustees or to take action against predecessor Trustees for breaches of trust and may accept whatever assets are turned over without further inquiry.

7.7 <u>Construction.</u> This Agreement, all trusts established hereunder, all powers of appointment, and all other matters shall be constructed under and regulated by **[Florida]** law. The validity of this Agreement and all trusts established hereunder shall be determined by **[Florida]** law.

7.8 <u>Notices.</u> All notices required or permitted hereunder shall be in writing and sent by ordinary mail to the recipient at such address as may be specified from time to time. If any person receiving notice shall be a minor or under other legal disability, a living parent, guardian, or other person having physical custody of such person may act for such person in receiving notice. Nothing contained in this paragraph shall be deemed to give such person acting in conjunction with the Trustee the power or right to enlarge, shift, or restrict the beneficial interest of any beneficiary of any Trust.

7.9 <u>Reduction or Release of Powers.</u> I give to the Trustee the power to release or renounce any power, privilege, or right (including this power) or the power to reduce the scope and extent of any power, privilege, or right (including this power). If there is more than one Trustee of this Trust, this power may be exercised by any one Trustee individually or by all of the Trustees collectively.

7.10 <u>Tax Elections.</u> The Trustee shall have the power to select tax years and make, or refrain from making, all other decisions and elections permitted under any applicable income, estate, or inheritance tax law, including the imposition of a lien on Family Trust assets to secure tax payments, without regard to the effect thereof, if any, on any beneficiary of this Trust and, if any such decision or election shall be made, to apportion or refrain from apportioning the consequences thereof among the respective interests of the beneficiaries of this Trust, all in such manner as the Trustee shall deem appropriate. If the Trustee is responsible for preparing and filing a federal estate tax return in my estate, and determines there is uncertainty as to the inclusion of a particular item of property in my gross estate for federal estate tax purposes, then such property may, in the discretion of the Trustee, be excluded from my gross estate in my federal estate tax return. Similarly, if the Trustee is responsible for preparing and filing a federal estate tax return in my estate, then the decision of the Trustee as to the valuation date for federal estate tax purposes shall be conclusive on all concerned.

7.11 <u>Termination of Trusts.</u> Notwithstanding any other provision of this Agreement, no trust or interest in a trust created pursuant to this Agreement or any trust or interest established by the exercise of a power of appointment shall (1) continue to remain contingent beyond twenty-one years after the death of the last to die of any beneficiary who is living on the date on which this Trust becomes irrevocable, or (2) continue beyond the time at which their continued existence would violate the Rule Against Perpetuities. Upon the expiration of either of these periods, any trust or interest in a trust or any trust or interest established by the exercise of power of appointment shall terminate and the assets thereof shall be distributed outright in equal shares to the income beneficiaries thereof, or if any income beneficiary shall be deceased, that beneficiary's shares to his or her descendants per stirpes.

7.12 <u>Loans and Purchases.</u> The Trustee may utilize funds contained in the Family Trust, at the Trustee's discretion, to purchase assets from my estate and/or my wife's estate and/or to lend sums of money to the Personal Representative of either of same estates in order that cash may be made available to said estates. It is my intent by this provision to specifically authorize such purchases or loans even though the Personal Representative of said estates and the Trustee may be the same person(s) or corporation(s).

7.13 <u>Captions.</u> The captions in this Agreement are for convenience only and shall not be considered as part of this Agreement or in any way limiting or amplifying the terms and provisions hereof.

7.14 <u>Severability.</u> If any provision of this Agreement shall be invalid or unenforceable, the remaining provisions shall have full force and effect.

7.15 <u>Exercise of Rights.</u> All rights (such as release, disclaimer, and renunciation) exercisable by any beneficiary shall be exercised by delivery to the Trustee of a writing, signed and acknowledged by the person exercising such right. All notices, certificates, and other communications permitted or required hereunder shall be in writing.

ARTICLE VIII
<u>ACCOUNTING</u>

Except to the extent otherwise excused by governing law, the Trustee shall keep the presently vested beneficiaries of the Trust reasonably informed of the Trust and its administration. Within thirty (30) days after my death, the Trustee shall inform in writing the presently vested beneficiaries of its name and address and of their right to request and receive a copy of the terms of the Trust that describe or affect their interest, and relevant information about the assets and administration of the Trust. The Trustee shall render annually, or as soon thereafter as reasonably practicable, and send to me or my guardian during my lifetime and after my death to each presently vested beneficiary, an annual accounting statement showing all receipts, disbursements, and distributions for the preceding year, together with a statement of all of the property then in the Trustee's possession belonging to the Trust. Such annual accounting statement shall be approved and be final and binding on me and on each presently vested beneficiary (1) when the same is approved in writing by such beneficiary or (2) unless a proceeding to raise an objection to the accounting statement is commenced within six (6) months after the date of sending by ordinary mail, or the delivery, of such annual accounting statement.

Upon termination of any Trust, the Trustee shall render and send to all beneficiaries a final accounting statement showing all receipts, disbursements, and distributions since my death, together with a statement of all the property then in the Trustee's possession and belonging to the Trust. Such final accounting statement shall be approved and be final and binding on each beneficiary (1) when the same is approved in writing by such beneficiary or (2) unless a proceeding to raise an objection to the accounting statement is commenced within six (6) months after the date of sending by ordinary mail, or the delivery of, such annual accounting statement. After approval of the final accounting statement and the payment of all the obligations of the Trust and distribution of the principal and accumulated net income of the Trust to the beneficiaries entitled to the same, the Trustee shall be released and discharged from all liability for the Trustee's acts and obligations under this Agreement. If an accounting statement is objected to as provided herein, the objection shall be heard and decided by the probate court in the county where the corporate Trustee is located.

If any beneficiary shall be a minor or under other legal disability, a living parent, guardian, or other person having physical custody of such beneficiary may act for such beneficiary in approving accounts with the same effect as if such beneficiary had been of full age or without legal disability, and had for himself approved such accounts. Nothing contained in this paragraph shall be deemed to give such person acting in conjunction with the Trustee the power or right to enlarge, shift, or restrict the beneficial interest of any beneficiary of any trust.

The books and records of the Trustee relating to duties as Trustee of this Trust shall be open during business hours for inspection by me or any beneficiary of this Trust or their duly appointed attorney, accountant, agent, or other representative.

IN WITNESS WHEREOF, we have hereunto set our hands and seals as of this _____ day of _____, 20___.
Signed in the presence of:

**Witnesses:**

_____

Witness  Number One

_____

Witness  Number Two

_____

Insert your name
Settlor-Trustee

AFFIDAVIT OF EXECUTION

STATE OF _____)
                                                 ) SS.
COUNTY OF _____)

On this _____ day of _____, 20___, before me personally appeared (insert your name), who being duly sworn, says that she has read the foregoing Trust by her signed as Settlor-Trustee and knows the contents thereof.

On this _____ day of _____, 20___, before me personally appeared the two witnesses (insert name of witness number one) and (insert name of witness number two) who, in the Settlor-Trustee's presence and the presence of each other, witnessed the Settlor-Trustee execute her Revocable Trust. They believe (insert your name) to be of sound mind.

_____
Notary Public
Sarasota County, Florida
My commission expires: _____

# Sample Advance Health Care Directive

PART I: INSTRUCTIONS FOR HEALTH CARE DECISIONS
END OF LIFE INSTRUCTIONS

Choice to Prolong Life

❑ I want my life to be prolonged as long as possible within the limits of generally accepted health care standards.

**OR**

Choice Not to Prolong Life
I do not want my life to be prolonged if (check all that apply):

❑ (1) I have a terminal condition (an incurable condition from which there is no reasonable medical expectation of recovery and which will cause my death, regardless of the use of life-sustaining treatment). In this case, I give the specific directions indicated:

|  | I want used | I do not want used |
| --- | --- | --- |
| Artificial nutrition through a conduit | ❑ | ❑ |
| Hydration through a conduit | ❑ | ❑ |
| Cardiopulmonary resuscitation | ❑ | ❑ |
| Mechanical respiration | ❑ | ❑ |
| Other (explain) _____ | ❑ | ❑ |

_____

_____

❑ (2) I become permanently unconscious (a medical condition that has existed at least four (4) weeks and has been diagnosed in accordance with currently accepted medical standards and with reasonable medical certainty as total and irreversible loss of consciousness and capacity for interaction with the environment. The term includes, without limitation, a persistent vegetative state or irreversible coma) and regarding the following, I give the specific directions indicated:

|  | I want used | I do not want used |
|---|---|---|
| Artificial nutrition through a conduit | ❑ | ❑ |
| Hydration through a conduit | ❑ | ❑ |
| Cardiopulmonary resuscitation | ❑ | ❑ |
| Mechanical respiration | ❑ | ❑ |
| Other (explain) _____ | ❑ | ❑ |

_____

_____

RELIEF FROM PAIN: Whether I choose 1 or 2 above, or neither, I direct that in all cases I be given all medically appropriate care necessary to make me comfortable and alleviate pain.

OTHER MEDICAL INSTRUCTIONS: If you wish to add to the instructions you have given above, you may do so here.

_____

_____

_____

_____

_____

_____

_____

_____

_____

PART II: POWER OF ATTORNEY FOR HEALTH CARE

Your agent may make any health care decision that you could have made while you had the capacity to make health care decisions. You may appoint an alternate agent to make health care decisions for you if your first agent is not willing, able, and reasonably available to make decisions for you. Unless the persons you name as agent and alternate agent are related to you by blood, neither may own, operate, or be employed by any residential long-term care institution where you are receiving care.

If you wish to appoint an agent to make health care decisions for you under these circumstances and conditions, you must fill out the section below. You may cross out any wording you do not want.

<u>Designation of Agent:</u> I designate _____ as my agent to make health care decisions for me. If he/she is not living, willing, or able, or reasonably available, to make health care decisions for me, then I designate _____ _____ as my agent to make health care decisions for me.

Name of individual you name as agent _____
Address _____
Phone Number _____

Name of individual you choose as alternate agent _____
Address _____
Phone Number _____

<u>Agent's Authority</u>: I grant to my agent full authority to make decisions for me regarding my health care; provided that, in exercising this authority, my agent shall follow my desires as stated in this document or otherwise known to my agent. Accordingly, my agent is authorized as follows:

*To consent to, refuse, or withdraw consent to any and all types of medical care, treatment, surgical procedures, diagnostic procedures, medication, and the use of mechanical or other procedures that affect any bodily function;*

*To have access to medical records and information to the same extent that I am entitled to, including the right to disclose the contents to others;*

*To authorize my admission to or discharge from any hospital, nursing home, residential care, assisted living, or similar facility or service;*

*To contract for any health care related service or facility on my behalf, without my agent incurring personal financial liability for such contracts;*

*To hire and fire medical, social service, and other support personnel responsible for my care;*

*To authorize, or refuse to authorize, any medication or procedure intended to relieve pain, even though such use may lead to physical damage, addiction, or hasten the moment of (but not intentionally cause) my death.*

<u>When Agent's Authority Becomes Effective</u>: My agent's authority becomes effective when my attending physician determines I lack the capacity to make my own health care decisions.

<u>Agent's Obligation</u>: My agent shall make health care decisions for me in accordance with this power of attorney for health care, any instructions I give in Part I of this form, and my other wishes to the extent known to my agent. To the extent my wishes are unknown, health care decisions by my agent shall conform as closely as possible to what I would have done or intended under the circumstances. If my agent is unable to determine what I would have done or intended under the circumstances, my agent will make health care decisions for me in accordance with what my agent determines to be my best interest. In determining my best interest, my agent shall consider my personal values to the extent known to my agent.

## PART III. ANATOMICAL GIFT DECLARATION (Optional)

I hereby make the following anatomical gift(s) to take effect upon my death. The marks in the appropriate squares and words filled into the blanks below indicate my desires:

**I give:**  ❑ my body;                               ❑ any needed organs or parts;
❑ the following organs or parts _____

**to:**  ❑ the physician in attendance at my death;
❑ the hospital in which I die;
❑ the following named physician, hospital, storage bank or other medical institution _____

for the following purpose(s):

❑ any purpose authorized by law          ❑ transplantation;
❑ therapy;                               ❑ research;
❑ medical education.

Effect of Copy: A copy of this form has the same effect as the original. I understand the purpose and effect of this document.

_____        _____
date                                                    *signature*

_____
print your name

_____
address

_____        _____        _____
city                        state                        zip

STATEMENT OF WITNESSES

SIGNED AND DECLARED   by the above-named declarant as and for his/her written declaration under 16 Del.C. §§2502, 2503, in our presence, who in his/her presence, at his/her request, and in the presence of each other, have hereunto subscribed our names as witnesses, and state:

*The Declarant is mentally competent.*

*That neither of us is prohibited by §2503 of Title 16 of the Delaware Code from being a witness.*

**Neither of us:**

*Is related to the declarant by blood, marriage or adoption;*

*Is entitled to any portion of the estate of the declarant under any will of the declarant or codicil thereto then existing nor, at the time of the executing of the advance health care directive, is so entitled by operation of law then existing;*

*Has, at the time of the execution of the advance health care directive, a present or inchoate claim against any portion of the estate of the declarant.*

*Has a direct financial responsibility for the declarant's medical care;*

*Has a controlling interest in or is an operator or an employee of a health care institution in which the declarant is a patient or resident;*

*Is under eighteen years of age.*

That if the declarant is a resident of a sanitarium, rest home, nursing home, boarding home or related institution, one of the witnesses, _____,
is at the time of the execution of the advance health care directive, a patient advocate or ombudsman designated by the Division of Services for Aging and Adults with Physical Disabilities or the Public Guardian.

**Witness**

_____          _____
date                                                                                    *signature*

                                                  _____
                                                                                    print your name

                                                  _____
                                                                                    address

_____    _____    _____
city                                           state                                    zip

**Witness**

_____          _____
date                                                                                    *signature*

                                                  _____
                                                                                    print your name

                                                  _____
                                                                                    address

_____    _____    _____
city                                           state                                    zip

*Optional*

Sworn and subscribed to me this _____ day of _____.

My term expires: _____          _____
                                                                                    Notary

# Index

## A

Affidavit of Execution, 97
Annuities
    beneficiaries, 41, 58, 177–78
    charitable gift (CGA), 211–12,
        217
    cost basis of, 184
    deferred gift (DGA), 212–13
    estate tax and, 190
    nonspouse beneficiaries,
        177–78
    overriding wills, 17–18, 35,
        57–58
    penalties for early
        withdrawal, 178–79
    probate and, 41, 49, 57–58,
        175
    tax implications, 182, 184,
        190, 212
    trusts and, 130
    wills and, 17–18, 35, 57–58
Articles, of wills, 60
Asset distribution. *See also*
    Distribution disagreements;
    Heirs
    changing wills. *See* Wills,
        changing
    combination of instructions,
        82–83, 139–40
    current distributions, 133
    dead beneficiaries and, 56,
        68, 69, 156, 157–60
    decisions, 20–21, 77, 80–83
    delayed distributions, 133–34
    executor decisions, 77
    general instructions, 82, 138

to minors. *See* Children
    restrictions and penalties,
        135–36
    specific instructions, 80–81,
        137–38
    timing, 133–35, 136–40,
        156–61
    tools for, 33–34
    triggering events, 134–35
    trust example, 157–61
    who, what, and when, 18–19,
        33–34, 78–80, 100–102, 132
Assets. *See also* Joint property;
    Personal property; Property;
    Real estate
    cost basis of, 113–15, 184
    creditor protection, 9, 24–25
    inventory worksheet, 253–60
    notebook summarizing,
        18–21, 29–31, 47, 115, 128,
        239–40
    planning inventory, 32,
        253–60
    valuation of, 20, 31, 113–15

## B

Bank accounts, 111, 129
Beneficiaries. *See also* Dead
    beneficiaries
    annuity, 41, 58, 177–78
    estates as, 55–56
    IRA, 18, 41, 176–78
    life insurance, 17–18, 41, 55–
        56, 169–71
    successor beneficiaries, 54
    trust, 41, 123, 132, 157–61

    trustee duties to, 146–47,
        165
    verifying, 41, 58
Broad power of attorney,
    220–21
Business contracts, 17
Bypass (credit shelter) trusts,
    199–202

## C

Charitable gift annuity (CGA),
    211–12, 217
Charitable gifts, 194, 208–18
    advantages/disadvantages
        of, 217–18
    life income gifts, 211–15, 217
    life insurance as, 210
    during lifetime, 209–15
    limitations on, 209
    real estate as, 210
    from will or trust, 215–17
Charitable remainder trusts
    (CRTs), 214–15, 217
Children. *See also* Guardians
    defining, in wills, 62
    divorce of, 79–80, 132
    as IRA beneficiaries, 177
    maturity level
        considerations, 7–8
    minors, 7–8, 15, 28, 49, 83–86
    as multiple joint tenants, 51–
        52, 117–18
    new babies, 3
    planning for, 7–8
    protecting inheritance of, 8,
        15, 29, 85

Children—*continued*
  remarriage issues, 7, 79, 132, 176–77
  special-needs, 28
  as successor co-trustees, 121
  supporting and educating, 4
  trusts for, 15, 28, 86
  vying for executorship, 42–43
Codicils, 105, 108
College funding, 8–9, 28
Computer software, 90
Contesting wills. *See* Distribution disagreements
Continuing specific instructions, 138
Contractual arrangements, 17–18, 50
Cost basis
  annuities and, 184
  going down, 114–15
  IRAs and, 184
  joint tenancy and, 113–15
  rules of, 113–15
Co-trustees, 121
Creditors
  paying, 44, 62–64, 92, 157
  probate and, 39, 43
  protecting assets from, 9, 24–25
  rights of, 63–64
  secured debt, 63
  will directives, 62–64, 92
Credit shelter trusts, 199–202
Cremation, 241–42
Current distributions, 133

**D**

Dead beneficiaries
  contingencies, examples, 156, 157–60
  life insurance proceeds, 56
  per capita distribution and, 69
  per stirpes distribution and, 68
  trusts and, 156, 157–60
Death notice, 43, 44
Debt payments. *See also* Creditors
  taxable base and, 194
  trusts and, 157
  wills and, 62–64, 92
Declarations. *See* Will components
Deferred gift annuity (DGA), 212–13
Delayed distributions, 133–34
Devisee, defined, 64
Devises
  avoiding conflict with, 66
  defined, 64
  heir hierarchy definitions, 68
  per capita, 69
  per stirpes, 68
  residuary, 69–70, 93
  sample will, 92–93
  specific, 64–69, 92–93
  tangible property, 64–66, 92–93
Distribution disagreements
  avoiding, 66, 98, 136–40
  cost of, 102–3

probate petitions from, 39, 136
  proving will intent, 103
  selling property and, 83, 140–41, 150
  trusts and, 146, 150
Diversification, trust, 164
Divorce
  of children, 79–80, 132
  financial guardianship and, 151
  life insurance and, 171
  remarriage and, 7, 79, 132, 176–77
Document storage, 236–40
  filing with probate court, 108, 237
  at home, 107, 236–37
  with lawyer, 107–8, 237
  safe-deposit boxes, 103, 107, 237–40

**E**

Education funding, 8–9, 28
Estate planning. *See* Planning; Planning rationale and timing; Preplan preparation
Estate taxes. *See also* Taxable base; Taxes
  annuities and, 190
  avoiding/reducing, 10–11, 31
  calculating, 197
  charitable gifts deduction, 194
  credit shelter trusts and, 199–202

Estate taxes—*continued*
debt payments deduction, 194
defined, 186
funeral expenses deduction, 194
general power of appointment and, 191–92
gifting and, 203–4
gift tax exclusion, 193
GRATs and, 207
IRAs and, 183, 184, 190
joint property and, 79, 115, 190–91
life insurance and, 31, 172, 189
marital deduction, 195
as planning reason, 10–11
property subject to, 188–92
QPRTs and, 205–7
rates, 187
retirement accounts and, 183–84, 190
return preparation, 23
savings account (unified credit amount), 186, 187–88, 193, 195–96, 197, 199
spouses and, 51, 79, 195–97
taxable gifts and, 192
as transfer taxes, 186
trusts and, 16, 127
unified transfer tax, 186
Executor
asset distribution, 77
children vying to be, 42–43
considerations about, 77–78

court naming, 42–43, 44–45
defined, 38
duties, 43, 75–78
hiring probate lawyer, 44, 45–47, 76–77
locating will, 76
paying bills, 44
powers of, 71–72, 95–96
probate petition for, 42–43
restricting power of, 72
selecting/naming, 38, 42–43, 44–45, 75, 77–78, 96
tax returns (final) by, 70–71
will specifying, 96

**F**

Families. *See also* Children; Spouses
grandchildren, 8–9
instructions to. *See* Instructions
planning for, 5–9
protecting, 5–9
remarriage issues, 7, 79, 132, 176–77
young, wills for, 14
Financial guardians, 8, 15, 29, 86, 151
Funerals
burial and, 240–41
cremation and, 241–42
expenses reducing taxable base, 194
instructions, 240–42
organ donations and, 243
prepaying, 242–43

**G**

General power of appointment, 124–25, 191–92
Gifting property, 203–4. *See also* Charitable gifts
Gift taxes
joint tenancy and, 51, 52, 118
taxable gifts, 192
unlimited marital deduction, 117, 118
Gift tax exclusion, 186, 187, 192, 193, 203
Glossary, 246–50
Grandchildren, 8–9
Grantor, 53–54, 120
Grantor retained annuity trust (GRAT), 207
Group life insurance, 170–71
Guardians
choosing, 85
contesting choice of, 84–85
ensuring selection of, 14, 15
financial, 8, 15, 29, 85, 151
functions of, 29
legal (physical), 8, 15, 29, 86, 151
multiple, 29
naming, 39–40
probate and, 39–40
trusts and, 15, 86, 151
types of, 151
wills and, 14, 15

**H**

Handwritten (holographic) wills, 89–90

Health care directive sample, 271–77

Heirs
ladder (levels) of, 61–62
selecting, 18–19, 33–34, 78–80, 100–102, 132
in trusts, 123, 132, 153–54, 157–61
in wills. *See* Devises

**I**

Income taxes. *See* Taxes

Instructions. *See also* Notebook (for plan)
document storage, 236–40
for family, 236–40
filing will with probate court and, 44, 237
funeral, 240–42
home storage, 107, 236–37
lawyer keeping, 237
safe-deposit boxes for, 237–40

Inventory, planning, 32, 253–60. *See also* Notebook (for plan)

IRAs
beneficiaries, 18, 41, 176–78
estate tax and, 183, 184, 190
gifting to charities, 216–17
nonspouse beneficiaries, 177–78
overriding wills, 18, 35
penalties for early withdrawal, 178–79
planning for, 184
probate and, 41, 57, 175

Roth, taxes, 181
spending before death, 184
tax implications, 179–81, 182–83, 184, 190
traditional, taxes, 180–81
withdrawals from, 180–81

Irrevocable life insurance trust, 204–5

Irrevocable trust, 156, 200

**J**

Joint property, 16–17, 50–52, 109–18. *See also* Asset distribution; Assets; Personal property; Property; Real estate
advantages, 16, 50, 51, 110
bank accounts as, 111
caution, 16–17
considerations, 50–52
cost basis of, 113–15
disadvantages, 16–17, 24–25, 50–52, 110–12, 115
estate tax and, 79, 115, 190–91
gift tax and, 51, 52, 118
learning rules of, 28–29
losing control with, 115
multiple joint tenants, 51–52, 117–18
with non-spouse, 116–18
probate and, 41, 49, 50–52
with spouse, 112–15
tax implications, 51, 52, 79, 113–15, 118
unexpected results, 52

unmarried partners and, 117
wills and, 16–17, 67, 111–12

**L**

Ladder of heirs, 61–62

Lawyers
changing wills without, 108
cost questions for, 25–26, 46, 76–77
document storage by, 107–8, 237
free interview, 24
functions of, 22–23
minimizing cost of, 11, 20, 34
planning for, 22–23
post-death tasks, 23, 47
power of attorney and, 233
for probate, 44, 45–47, 76–77
questions to ask, 24–26
referrals for, 22
retainers for, 26
shopping for, 21–26, 47
will preparation, 90–91, 108
written estimates from, 25

Legacy
as reason for planning, 11
tools for leaving, 11

Legal (physical) guardians, 8, 15, 29, 86, 151

Life income gifts, 211–15, 217

Life insurance, 166–73
beneficiaries, 17–18, 41, 55–56, 169–71
cash value, 168

Life insurance—*continued*
  charitable gifts, 210
  considerations, 170–71
  dead beneficiaries, 56
  divorce and, 171
  estate exceeding exclusion,
    172
  estate tax and, 31, 172, 189
  evaluating, 31
  gifting policies, 173
  group policies, 170–71
  irrevocable trust, 204–5
  overriding wills, 17–18, 35
  payable to estate, 55–56, 170
  probate and, 41, 49, 55–56,
    169–71
  tax implications, 171–72
  term insurance, 167–68
  three-party policies, 167
  trusts and, 130
  types of, 167–68
  wills and, 17–18, 35, 55–56
Limited power of appointment,
  124
Limited power of attorney,
  221–22

**M**
Marital deduction, 195
Marital tax base, 196
Medical power of attorney,
  233–34
Memorandum for tangible
  property, 65–66
Multiple joint tenants, 51–52,
  117–18

**N**
Newspaper death notice, 43, 44
No contract clause, 94–95
Notary
  for trust signatures, 165
  for will signatures, 72–73, 97,
    100, 104, 105, 108
Notebook (for plan)
  after-death use of, 47, 237,
    239–40
  alternatives, 47, 240, 253–60
  asset organization, 19–20,
    29–31, 115
  contents, 18–21, 239–40
  cost-basis updates in, 115
  keeping up-to-date, 243–44
  planning checklist, 244–45
  property transfer decisions
    and, 128
  tabs/divisions of, 18–21

**O**
Online resources, 251–52
Organ donations, 243

**P**
Per capita, 69
Personal property. *See also*
  Asset distribution; Assets;
  Joint property; Property;
  Real estate
  expense payments for, 66
  probate and, 38
  specific devises, 64–69,
    92–93
  summary, 19–20

transfer methods, 13
Per stirpes, 68
Physical guardians. *See* Legal
  (physical) guardians
Planning, 27–36. *See also*
  Planning rationale and
  timing; Preplan preparation
  checklist, 244–45
  dynamic process of, 29, 34
  implementation of, 36
  keeping up-to-date, 243–44
  notebook for, 18–21, 29–31,
    47, 115, 128, 237, 239–40
  organizing assets. *See*
    Assets; Notebook (for
    plan)
  rules of, 28–29
  tools, 34–35
Planning inventory, 32, 253–60
Planning rationale and timing,
  1–11
  avoiding probate costs, 9–10
  children, 7–8
  creditor protection, 9
  empty nest time, 4
  family protection, 5–9
  grandchildren, 8–9
  leaving your legacy, 11
  new family, 3
  remarriage, 7, 79, 132, 176–77
  retirement time, 5
  spouse, 6–7
  tax reduction, 10–11
  in your twenties, 2–3
Pooled income fund (PIF),
  213–14

Powers of appointment
   general, 124–25
   limited, 124
   sample trust, 155–56, 261–70
Powers of attorney, 219–34
   broad, 220–21
   creating, 232
   decisions to make, 230–31
   lawyers and, 233
   limited, 221–22
   medical, reasons for,
      233–34
   naming multiple people, 231
   reasons for, 222–23
   sample, 223–30
   types of, 220–22
Preplan preparation, 12–26.
   *See also* Asset distribution;
   Assets; Joint property;
   Notebook (for plan)
   family instructions, 236–40
   lawyer selection. *See*
      Lawyers
   property summary, 19–20
   property transfer
      alternatives, 13
Probate, 37–47. *See also*
   Probate, avoiding
   activities during, 44–45
   annuities and, 41, 49, 57–58,
      175
   closing estate, 45–46
   cost of, 46
   creditors and, 39
   death notice and, 43, 44
   defined, 13

distribution disagreements
   and, 39, 136
executor petition, 42–43
filing petition, 42–43
filing wills with, 44, 108, 237
guardians and, 39–40
initiating, 23, 38
IRAs and, 41, 57
joint property and, 41, 49,
   50–52
lawyers for, 44, 45–47, 76–77
learning rules of, 28–29
life insurance and, 41, 49,
   55–56, 169–71
naming executor, 42–43,
   44–45
proceedings, 42–43
property not subject to,
   40–41
property requiring, 38
protections, 45
reasons for, 38–40
retirement accounts and, 41,
   57, 175
selling property and, 150
time frame, 43, 44–45
trusts and, 41, 49, 52–55, 126,
   155
value of, 45
Probate, avoiding, 9–10, 48–58
   annuities for, 57–58
   life insurance for, 55–56
   reasons for, 49–50
   retirement accounts for, 57
   titling property for, 50–52
   trusts for, 52–55, 126, 155

Property. *See also* Asset
   distribution; Assets; Joint
   property; Personal property;
   Real estate
   combination of instructions
      about, 82–83, 139–40
   controlling, 15, 115, 126–27
   describing, in trusts, 154–55
   distribution decisions, 20–21,
      33–34, 77, 80–83, 133–40
   dividing, 149–50
   general instructions about,
      82, 138
   gifting, 203–4, 210
   going down in value,
      114–15
   heir selection, 18–19, 33–34,
      78–80, 100–102, 132
   inventory of, 32, 253–60
   managing, 15, 69–70, 77,
      126–27, 145
   minors and, 7–8, 15, 28,
      85–86
   probate and, 38, 41
   selling, 83, 140–41, 149, 150
   specific instructions about,
      80–81, 137–38
   specifying heirs. *See*
      Devises
   tangible, 64–66, 92–93
   titling, 50–52
   transfer alternatives, 13
   in trusts. *See* Trust(s)
   unaffected by wills, 17–18
   in your power, 191
Publication resources, 252

**Q**

Qualified personal residence trust (QPRT), 205–7

**R**

Real estate. *See also* Asset distribution; Assets; Joint property; Personal property; Property
charitable gifts, 210
interest savings, 31
    probate and, 38
    as secured debt, 63
    summarizing holdings, 19–20
    transfer methods, 13
    trusts and, 128–29
Real property. *See* Real estate
Remarriage
    property distribution and, 79
    as reason for planning, 7
    retirement accounts and, 176–77
    trusts and, 132
Residuary devises, 69–70, 93
Resources, 251–52
Retainers, 26
Retirement, reviewing estate at, 5
Retirement accounts, 174–84. *See also* Annuities; IRAs
    beneficiaries, 18, 41, 176–78
    employer-sponsored plans, 179
    estate tax and, 183–84, 190
    nonspouse beneficiaries, 177–78

penalties for early withdrawal, 178–79
    probate and, 41, 49, 57, 175
    tax implications, 179–84, 190
    trusts and, 130
Revocable trust
    becoming irrevocable, 156, 200
    creditor protection and, 24–25
    sample clause, 155

**S**

Safe-deposit boxes, 237–40
    authorizing access, 238–39
    distributing keys, 238
    documents to keep in, 103, 107, 239–40
Sample will, 91–98
Savings account. *See* Unified credit amount (savings account)
Second successor trustee, 144
Secured debt, 63
Selling property
    probate ordering, 150
    restrictions on, 83, 141, 149
    trusts and, 140–41, 149, 150
    wills and, 83
Settlor, 53–54, 120
Software, for wills, 90
Specific devises
    considerations, 67
    defined, 64
    of other property, 67
    sample will, 92–93

of tangible property, 64–66, 92–93
Specific instructions, 137–38
Spouses. *See also* Joint property
    credit shelter trusts for, 199–202
    dying simultaneously, 50–51
    estate tax and, 51, 79, 195–97
    as IRA beneficiary, 176–77
    leaving everything to, 196–97
    marital deduction, 195
    as reason for planning, 6–7
    remarriage issues, 7, 79, 132, 176–77
Stock transfers, 129
Successor beneficiaries, 54
Successor trustee, 54, 121, 122, 126–27, 133, 134–36, 138–41, 144, 146, 147–48, 151, 160–65, 176–77, 199–202
Surviving parent, 84
Survivorship clause, 94

**T**

Tangible property, 64–66, 92–93
Taxable base, 188–92
    annuities and, 190
    charitable gifts and. *See* Charitable gifts
    credit shelter trusts and, 199–202
    debt payments and, 194
    deductions against, 193–95
    figuring out, 197

Taxable base—*continued*
 funeral expenses and, 194
 general power of
  appointment and, 191–92
 joint property and, 190–91
 life insurance and, 189
 marital deduction, 195
 marital taxable base, 196
 property in your power and,
  191
 retirement accounts and,
  190
 taxable gifts and, 192–93
Taxable gifts, 192
Taxes. *See also* Estate taxes;
 Gift taxes
 annuities and, 182, 184, 190,
  212
 cost basis and, 113–15
 credit shelter trusts and,
  199–202
 executor responsibility,
  70–71
 gifting to reduce, 203–4. *See
  also* Charitable gifts
 GRATs and, 207
 IRAs and, 179–81, 182–83
 joint tenancy and, 51, 52, 79,
  113–15, 118
 learning rules of, 28–29
 life insurance and, 171–72
 paying, 70–71, 93–94, 157
 as planning reason, 10–11
 QPRTs and, 205–7
 reducing, 10–11, 198–207. *See
  also* Charitable gifts

retirement accounts and,
 179–84
returns, final, 45, 70–71
Term life insurance, 167–68
Testamentary trusts, 69–70,
 86
Transfer tax. *See* Estate taxes
Triggering events, 134–35
Trust corpus, 154
Trust document, 152–65
 accountings clause, 165,
  268–69
 asset distribution, 156–61
 creditors/spendthrift
  provision, 164, 265–66
 dead beneficiaries and, 156,
  157–60
 debt payments, 157
 declarations, 153–54
 describing property, 154–55
 diversification clause, 164
 duration, 157
 establishment of, 153–55
 expense payments, 157
 identifying parties, 153–54
 irrevocable clause, 156
 lifetime management,
  155–56
 miscellaneous provisions,
  163–65
 parts of, 153–55
 powers of appointment, 123–
  25, 155–56, 261–68
 reservations, 155
 samples, 153–63, 261–70
 signature, 165, 269–70

tax payments, 157
trust corpus, 154
trustee assignment, 161–63
Trustee(s), 121–22, 142–51
 accountings requirement,
  165, 268–69
 assigning, example, 161–63
 changing, 123–25
 choosing, 16
 compensation/fees, 148,
  162
 considerations, 147–49
 co-trustee, 121
 credit shelter trust, 200–202
 defined, 53–54
 dividing property, 149–50
 duties, 144–47, 165
 incapacitated, 162–63
 initial, 143
 instructions to, 122, 136–40,
  146–47
 legal duty, 146
 multiple, 148–49
 powers of appointment, 123–
  25, 155–56, 261–68
 professionals as, 144
 property management, 145,
  149–50
 relationship considerations,
  147–48
 removing, 146, 165
 second successor, 144
 selling property and, 140–41,
  149, 150
 sequence of, 143–44,
  161–63

Trustee(s)—*continued*
  successor, 54, 121, 122, 126–
    27, 133, 134–36, 138–41,
    144, 146, 147–48, 151, 160–
    65, 176–77, 199–202
  suing, 146, 150, 165
  yourself as, 54–55, 121, 143
Trust(s). *See also* Revocable
    trust
  advantages, 15–16, 52–53, 54,
    126–27
  annuity transfers and, 130
  bank account transfers with,
    129
  beneficiaries, 41, 123, 132
  charitable gifts through,
    215–17
  cost of, 128
  creator of, 120
  credit shelter (bypass),
    199–202
  current distributions, 133
  defined, 120
  delayed distributions, 133–34
  disadvantages, 127–30
  distribution options, 133–34
  dividing property, 149–50
  education, 9
  estate tax and, 16, 127
  expenses payments, 157
  financial guardians in, 151
  grantor of, 53–54, 120
  history of, 53–54
  instructions for, 122, 136–40,
    146–47
  irrevocable, 156, 200

irrevocable insurance, 204–5
learning rules of, 28–29
life insurance transfers and,
    130
management plans, 15
probate and, 41, 49, 52–55,
    126, 155
property control/
    management, 15, 126–27,
    145, 155–56
protecting child inheritance,
    15, 28, 86
public policy and, 135–36
QPRTs, 205–7
real estate transfers with,
    128–29
reasons for, 125
restrictions and penalties,
    135–36
retirement accounts and, 130
selling property and, 140–41,
    149, 150
settlor of, 53–54, 120
special-needs, 28
stock transfers and, 129
tax implications, 16, 127
testamentary, 69–70, 86
time required for, 128
triggering events, 134–35
wills vs., 15

**U**

Unified credit amount (savings
    account), 186, 187–88, 193,
    195–96, 197, 199
Unified transfer tax, 186

Unlimited marital deduction,
    117, 118
Unmarried partners, 117

**W**

Will components, 59–73. *See
    also* Devises
  Affidavit of Execution, 97
  articles, 56
  debt payments, 62–64, 92
  declarations, 61–62, 91–92
  defining children, 62
  executor appointment, 38,
    42–43, 44–45, 75, 77–78, 96
  executor powers, 71–72,
    95–96
  ladder of heirs, 61–62
  no contract clause, 94–95
  overview, 60–61
  residuary devises, 69–70, 93
  sample will, 91–98
  signature, 72–73, 96–98, 104,
    105, 108
  specific devises, 64–69,
    92–93
  survivorship, 94
  tax payments, 70–71, 93–94
Wills. *See also* Asset
    distribution; Wills, changing;
    Wills, drafting
  advantages, 14
  annuities and, 17–18, 35,
    57–58
  charitable gifts through,
    215–17
  codicils, 105, 108

Wills—*continued*

contracts overriding, 17–18, 50

executor selection, 38, 42–43, 44–45, 75, 77–78, 96

fancy wording, 60–61

filing after death, 44

filing before death, 108

former, revoking/destroying, 101–2, 106

invalidating, 72

IRAs and, 18, 35, 57

joint property and, 16–17, 67, 111–12

lawyers drafting, 90–91

lawyers keeping, 107–8, 237

learning rules of, 28–29

life insurance and, 17–18, 35, 55–56

locating, 76

new babies and, 3

notary for, 72–73, 97, 100, 104, 105, 108

original, control of, 106–8

probate and. *See* Probate

property unaffected by, 17–18

proving intent, 103

in safe-deposit boxes, 103, 107, 237–40

sample, 91–98

selling property and, 83

signature section sample, 96–98

signing, 72–73, 104, 105, 108

simple estates and, 14–15

storing, 106–8, 236–40

taxes and, 70–71, 93–94

trusts vs., 15

witnesses for, 72–73, 97, 100, 104, 105

for young families, 14

in your possession, 107

in your twenties, 2–3

Wills, changing, 99–108

amendments, 104–5

former will and, 101–2

making new will, 100–102

proving intent, 103

storing new will, 106–8

striking provisions, 102

without lawyers, 108

without your knowledge, 107

written changes, 103–4

Wills, drafting, 87–98

computer software for, 90

forms for, 88–89

handwritten (holographic), 89–90

Internet forms for, 88–89

sample will, 91–98

Witnesses

for trusts, 165

for wills, 72–73, 97, 100, 104, 105

# The EVERYTHING Series!

## BUSINESS & PERSONAL FINANCE

Everything® Accounting Book
Everything® Budgeting Book, 2nd Ed.
Everything® Business Planning Book
Everything® Coaching and Mentoring Book, 2nd Ed.
Everything® Fundraising Book
Everything® Get Out of Debt Book
Everything® Grant Writing Book, 2nd Ed.
Everything® Guide to Buying Foreclosures
**Everything® Guide to Fundraising, $15.95**
Everything® Guide to Mortgages
Everything® Guide to Personal Finance for Single Mothers
Everything® Home-Based Business Book, 2nd Ed.
**Everything® Homebuying Book, 3rd Ed., $15.95**
Everything® Homeselling Book, 2nd Ed.
Everything® Human Resource Management Book
Everything® Improve Your Credit Book
Everything® Investing Book, 2nd Ed.
Everything® Landlording Book
Everything® Leadership Book, 2nd Ed.
Everything® Managing People Book, 2nd Ed.
Everything® Negotiating Book
Everything® Online Auctions Book
Everything® Online Business Book
Everything® Personal Finance Book
Everything® Personal Finance in Your 20s & 30s Book, 2nd Ed.
**Everything® Personal Finance in Your 40s & 50s Book, $15.95**
Everything® Project Management Book, 2nd Ed.
Everything® Real Estate Investing Book
Everything® Retirement Planning Book
Everything® Robert's Rules Book, $7.95
Everything® Selling Book
Everything® Start Your Own Business Book, 2nd Ed.
Everything® Wills & Estate Planning Book

## COOKING

Everything® Barbecue Cookbook
Everything® Bartender's Book, 2nd Ed., $9.95
Everything® Calorie Counting Cookbook
Everything® Cheese Book
Everything® Chinese Cookbook
Everything® Classic Recipes Book
Everything® Cocktail Parties & Drinks Book
Everything® College Cookbook
Everything® Cooking for Baby and Toddler Book
Everything® Diabetes Cookbook
Everything® Easy Gourmet Cookbook
Everything® Fondue Cookbook
**Everything® Food Allergy Cookbook, $15.95**
Everything® Fondue Party Book
Everything® Gluten-Free Cookbook
Everything® Glycemic Index Cookbook
Everything® Grilling Cookbook
**Everything® Healthy Cooking for Parties Book, $15.95**
Everything® Holiday Cookbook
Everything® Indian Cookbook
Everything® Lactose-Free Cookbook
Everything® Low-Cholesterol Cookbook

**Everything® Low-Fat High-Flavor Cookbook, 2nd Ed., $15.95**
Everything® Low-Salt Cookbook
Everything® Meals for a Month Cookbook
Everything® Meals on a Budget Cookbook
Everything® Mediterranean Cookbook
Everything® Mexican Cookbook
Everything® No Trans Fat Cookbook
**Everything® One-Pot Cookbook, 2nd Ed., $15.95**
**Everything® Organic Cooking for Baby & Toddler Book, $15.95**
Everything® Pizza Cookbook
**Everything® Quick Meals Cookbook, 2nd Ed., $15.95**
Everything® Slow Cooker Cookbook
Everything® Slow Cooking for a Crowd Cookbook
Everything® Soup Cookbook
Everything® Stir-Fry Cookbook
Everything® Sugar-Free Cookbook
Everything® Tapas and Small Plates Cookbook
Everything® Tex-Mex Cookbook
Everything® Thai Cookbook
Everything® Vegetarian Cookbook
Everything® Whole-Grain, High-Fiber Cookbook
Everything® Wild Game Cookbook
Everything® Wine Book, 2nd Ed.

## GAMES

Everything® 15-Minute Sudoku Book, $9.95
Everything® 30-Minute Sudoku Book, $9.95
Everything® Bible Crosswords Book, $9.95
Everything® Blackjack Strategy Book
Everything® Brain Strain Book, $9.95
Everything® Bridge Book
Everything® Card Games Book
Everything® Card Tricks Book, $9.95
Everything® Casino Gambling Book, 2nd Ed.
Everything® Chess Basics Book
**Everything® Christmas Crosswords Book, $9.95**
Everything® Craps Strategy Book
Everything® Crossword and Puzzle Book
**Everything® Crosswords and Puzzles for Quote Lovers Book, $9.95**
Everything® Crossword Challenge Book
Everything® Crosswords for the Beach Book, $9.95
Everything® Cryptic Crosswords Book, $9.95
Everything® Cryptograms Book, $9.95
Everything® Easy Crosswords Book
Everything® Easy Kakuro Book, $9.95
Everything® Easy Large-Print Crosswords Book
Everything® Games Book, 2nd Ed.
**Everything® Giant Book of Crosswords**
Everything® Giant Sudoku Book, $9.95
Everything® Giant Word Search Book
Everything® Kakuro Challenge Book, $9.95
Everything® Large-Print Crossword Challenge Book
Everything® Large-Print Crosswords Book
**Everything® Large-Print Travel Crosswords Book**
Everything® Lateral Thinking Puzzles Book, $9.95
Everything® Literary Crosswords Book, $9.95
Everything® Mazes Book
Everything® Memory Booster Puzzles Book, $9.95

Everything® Movie Crosswords Book, $9.95
Everything® Music Crosswords Book, $9.95
Everything® Online Poker Book
Everything® Pencil Puzzles Book, $9.95
Everything® Poker Strategy Book
Everything® Pool & Billiards Book
Everything® Puzzles for Commuters Book, $9.95
Everything® Puzzles for Dog Lovers Book, $9.95
Everything® Sports Crosswords Book, $9.95
Everything® Test Your IQ Book, $9.95
Everything® Texas Hold 'Em Book, $9.95
Everything® Travel Crosswords Book, $9.95
**Everything® Travel Mazes Book, $9.95**
**Everything® Travel Word Search Book, $9.95**
Everything® TV Crosswords Book, $9.95
Everything® Word Games Challenge Book
Everything® Word Scramble Book
Everything® Word Search Book

## HEALTH

Everything® Alzheimer's Book
Everything® Diabetes Book
Everything® First Aid Book, $9.95
**Everything® Green Living Book**
**Everything® Health Guide to Addiction and Recovery**
Everything® Health Guide to Adult Bipolar Disorder
Everything® Health Guide to Arthritis
Everything® Health Guide to Controlling Anxiety
Everything® Health Guide to Depression
**Everything® Health Guide to Diabetes, 2nd Ed.**
Everything® Health Guide to Fibromyalgia
Everything® Health Guide to Menopause, 2nd Ed.
Everything® Health Guide to Migraines
**Everything® Health Guide to Multiple Sclerosis**
Everything® Health Guide to OCD
Everything® Health Guide to PMS
Everything® Health Guide to Postpartum Care
Everything® Health Guide to Thyroid Disease
Everything® Hypnosis Book
Everything® Low Cholesterol Book
Everything® Menopause Book
Everything® Nutrition Book
Everything® Reflexology Book
Everything® Stress Management Book
**Everything® Superfoods Book, $15.95**

## HISTORY

Everything® American Government Book
Everything® American History Book, 2nd Ed.
**Everything® American Revolution Book, $15.95**
Everything® Civil War Book
Everything® Freemasons Book
Everything® Irish History & Heritage Book
Everything® World War II Book, 2nd Ed.

## HOBBIES

Everything® Candlemaking Book
Everything® Cartooning Book
Everything® Coin Collecting Book
Everything® Digital Photography Book, 2nd Ed.

Everything® Drawing Book
Everything® Family Tree Book, 2nd Ed.
**Everything® Guide to Online Genealogy, $15.95**
Everything® Knitting Book
Everything® Knots Book
Everything® Photography Book
Everything® Quilting Book
Everything® Sewing Book
Everything® Soapmaking Book, 2nd Ed.
Everything® Woodworking Book

## HOME IMPROVEMENT

Everything® Feng Shui Book
Everything® Feng Shui Decluttering Book, $9.95
Everything® Fix-It Book
Everything® Green Living Book
Everything® Home Decorating Book
Everything® Home Storage Solutions Book
Everything® Homebuilding Book
Everything® Organize Your Home Book, 2nd Ed.

## KIDS' BOOKS

All titles are $7.95
Everything® Fairy Tales Book, $14.95
Everything® Kids' Animal Puzzle & Activity Book
Everything® Kids' Astronomy Book
Everything® Kids' Baseball Book, 5th Ed.
Everything® Kids' Bible Trivia Book
Everything® Kids' Bugs Book
Everything® Kids' Cars and Trucks Puzzle and Activity Book
Everything® Kids' Christmas Puzzle & Activity Book
Everything® Kids' Connect the Dots
    Puzzle and Activity Book
**Everything® Kids' Cookbook, 2nd Ed.**
Everything® Kids' Crazy Puzzles Book
Everything® Kids' Dinosaurs Book
**Everything® Kids' Dragons Puzzle and Activity Book**
Everything® Kids' Environment Book $7.95
Everything® Kids' Fairies Puzzle and Activity Book
Everything® Kids' First Spanish Puzzle and Activity Book
Everything® Kids' Football Book
**Everything® Kids' Geography Book**
Everything® Kids' Gross Cookbook
Everything® Kids' Gross Hidden Pictures Book
Everything® Kids' Gross Jokes Book
Everything® Kids' Gross Mazes Book
Everything® Kids' Gross Puzzle & Activity Book
Everything® Kids' Halloween Puzzle & Activity Book
**Everything® Kids' Hanukkah Puzzle and Activity Book**
Everything® Kids' Hidden Pictures Book
Everything® Kids' Horses Book
Everything® Kids' Joke Book
Everything® Kids' Knock Knock Book
Everything® Kids' Learning French Book
Everything® Kids' Learning Spanish Book
Everything® Kids' Magical Science Experiments Book
Everything® Kids' Math Puzzles Book
Everything® Kids' Mazes Book
**Everything® Kids' Money Book, 2nd Ed.**
**Everything® Kids' Mummies, Pharaoh's, and Pyramids**
    **Puzzle and Activity Book**
Everything® Kids' Nature Book
Everything® Kids' Pirates Puzzle and Activity Book
Everything® Kids' Presidents Book
Everything® Kids' Princess Puzzle and Activity Book
Everything® Kids' Puzzle Book

Everything® Kids' Racecars Puzzle and Activity Book
Everything® Kids' Riddles & Brain Teasers Book
Everything® Kids' Science Experiments Book
Everything® Kids' Sharks Book
Everything® Kids' Soccer Book
**Everything® Kids' Spelling Book**
Everything® Kids' Spies Puzzle and Activity Book
Everything® Kids' States Book
Everything® Kids' Travel Activity Book
Everything® Kids' Word Search Puzzle and Activity Book

## LANGUAGE

Everything® Conversational Japanese Book with CD, $19.95
Everything® French Grammar Book
Everything® French Phrase Book, $9.95
Everything® French Verb Book, $9.95
**Everything® German Phrase Book, $9.95**
Everything® German Practice Book with CD, $19.95
Everything® Inglés Book
Everything® Intermediate Spanish Book with CD, $19.95
**Everything® Italian Phrase Book, $9.95**
Everything® Italian Practice Book with CD, $19.95
Everything® Learning Brazilian Portuguese Book with CD, $19.95
Everything® Learning French Book with CD, 2nd Ed., $19.95
Everything® Learning German Book
Everything® Learning Italian Book
Everything® Learning Latin Book
Everything® Learning Russian Book with CD, $19.95
Everything® Learning Spanish Book
Everything® Learning Spanish Book with CD, 2nd Ed., $19.95
Everything® Russian Practice Book with CD, $19.95
**Everything® Sign Language Book, $15.95**
Everything® Spanish Grammar Book
Everything® Spanish Phrase Book, $9.95
Everything® Spanish Practice Book with CD, $19.95
Everything® Spanish Verb Book, $9.95
Everything® Speaking Mandarin Chinese Book with CD, $19.95

## MUSIC

Everything® Bass Guitar Book with CD, $19.95
Everything® Drums Book with CD, $19.95
Everything® Guitar Book with CD, 2nd Ed., $19.95
Everything® Guitar Chords Book with CD, $19.95
**Everything® Guitar Scales Book with CD, $19.95**
Everything® Harmonica Book with CD, $15.95
Everything® Home Recording Book
Everything® Music Theory Book with CD, $19.95
Everything® Reading Music Book with CD, $19.95
Everything® Rock & Blues Guitar Book with CD, $19.95
Everything® Rock & Blues Piano Book with CD, $19.95
**Everything® Rock Drums Book with CD, $19.95**
**Everything® Singing Book with CD, $19.95**
Everything® Songwriting Book

## NEW AGE

Everything® Astrology Book, 2nd Ed.
Everything® Birthday Personology Book
**Everything® Celtic Wisdom Book, $15.95**
Everything® Dreams Book, 2nd Ed.
**Everything® Law of Attraction Book, $15.95**
Everything® Love Signs Book, $9.95
Everything® Love Spells Book, $9.95
Everything® Palmistry Book
Everything® Psychic Book
Everything® Reiki Book

Everything® Sex Signs Book, $9.95
Everything® Spells & Charms Book, 2nd Ed.
Everything® Tarot Book, 2nd Ed.
Everything® Toltec Wisdom Book
Everything® Wicca & Witchcraft Book, 2nd Ed.

## PARENTING

Everything® Baby Names Book, 2nd Ed.
Everything® Baby Shower Book, 2nd Ed.
Everything® Baby Sign Language Book with DVD
Everything® Baby's First Year Book
Everything® Birthing Book
Everything® Breastfeeding Book
Everything® Father-to-Be Book
Everything® Father's First Year Book
Everything® Get Ready for Baby Book, 2nd Ed.
Everything® Get Your Baby to Sleep Book, $9.95
Everything® Getting Pregnant Book
Everything® Guide to Pregnancy Over 35
Everything® Guide to Raising a One-Year-Old
Everything® Guide to Raising a Two-Year-Old
Everything® Guide to Raising Adolescent Boys
Everything® Guide to Raising Adolescent Girls
Everything® Mother's First Year Book
Everything® Parent's Guide to Childhood Illnesses
Everything® Parent's Guide to Children and Divorce
Everything® Parent's Guide to Children with ADD/ADHD
Everything® Parent's Guide to Children with Asperger's
    Syndrome
**Everything® Parent's Guide to Children with Anxiety**
Everything® Parent's Guide to Children with Asthma
Everything® Parent's Guide to Children with Autism
Everything® Parent's Guide to Children with Bipolar Disorder
Everything® Parent's Guide to Children with Depression
Everything® Parent's Guide to Children with Dyslexia
Everything® Parent's Guide to Children with Juvenile Diabetes
**Everything® Parent's Guide to Children with OCD**
Everything® Parent's Guide to Positive Discipline
Everything® Parent's Guide to Raising Boys
Everything® Parent's Guide to Raising Girls
Everything® Parent's Guide to Raising Siblings
**Everything® Parent's Guide to Raising Your**
    **Adopted Child**
Everything® Parent's Guide to Sensory Integration Disorder
Everything® Parent's Guide to Tantrums
Everything® Parent's Guide to the Strong-Willed Child
Everything® Parenting a Teenager Book
Everything® Potty Training Book, $9.95
Everything® Pregnancy Book, 3rd Ed.
Everything® Pregnancy Fitness Book
Everything® Pregnancy Nutrition Book
Everything® Pregnancy Organizer, 2nd Ed., $16.95
Everything® Toddler Activities Book
Everything® Toddler Book
Everything® Tween Book
Everything® Twins, Triplets, and More Book

## PETS

Everything® Aquarium Book
Everything® Boxer Book
Everything® Cat Book, 2nd Ed.
Everything® Chihuahua Book
Everything® Cooking for Dogs Book
Everything® Dachshund Book
Everything® Dog Book, 2nd Ed.
Everything® Dog Grooming Book